Ghosts and the Overplus

POETS ON POETRY

Derek Pollard, Series Editor
Donald Hall, Founding Editor

TITLES IN THE SERIES
Christina Pugh, *Ghosts and the Overplus*
Norman Finkelstein, *To Go Into the Words*
Major Jackson, *A Beat Beyond*, edited by Amor Kohli
Jane Miller, *From the Valley of Bronze Camels*
Tony Hoagland, *The Underground Poetry Metro Transportation System for Souls*
Philip Metres, *The Sound of Listening*
Julie Carr, *Someone Shot My Book*
Claudia Keelan, *Ecstatic Émigré*
Rigoberto Gonzalez, *Pivotal Voices, Era of Transition*
Garrett Hongo, *The Mirror Diary*
Marianne Boruch, *The Little Death of Self*
Yusef Komunyakaa, *Condition Red*
Khaled Mattawa, *How Long Have You Been With Us?*
Aaron Shurin, *The Skin of Meaning*
Kazim Ali, *Resident Alien*
Bruce Bond, *Immanent Distance*
Joyelle McSweeney, *The Necropastoral*
David Baker, *Show Me Your Environment*

ALSO AVAILABLE, BOOKS BY
Elizabeth Alexander, Meena Alexander, A. R. Ammons, John Ashbery, Robert Bly, Philip Booth, Marianne Boruch, Hayden Carruth, Amy Clampitt, Alfred Corn, Douglas Crase, Robert Creeley, Donald Davie, Thomas M. Disch, Ed Dorn, Martín Espada, Annie Finch, Tess Gallagher, Sandra M. Gilbert, Dana Gioia, Linda Gregerson, Allen Grossman, Thom Gunn, Marilyn Hacker, Rachel Hadas, John Haines, Donald Hall, Joy Harjo, Robert Hayden, Edward Hirsch, Daniel Hoffman, Jonathan Holden, John Hollander, Paul Hoover, Andrew Hudgins, T. R. Hummer, Laura (Riding) Jackson, Josephine Jacobsen, Mark Jarman, Lawrence Joseph, Galway Kinnell, Kenneth Koch, John Koethe, Yusef Komunyakaa, Marilyn Krysl, Maxine Kumin, Martin Lammon (editor), Philip Larkin, David Lehman, Philip Levine, Larry Levis, John Logan, William Logan, David Mason, William Matthews, William Meredith, Jane Miller, David Mura, Carol Muske, Alice Notley, Geoffrey O'Brien, Gregory Orr, Alicia Suskin Ostriker, Ron Padgett, Marge Piercy, Grace Schulman, Anne Sexton, Karl Shapiro, Reginald Shepherd, Charles Simic, William Stafford, Anne Stevenson, Cole Swenson, May Swenson, James Tate, Richard Tillinghast, C. K. Williams, Alan Williamson, David Wojahn, Charles Wright, James Wright, John Yau, and Stephen Yenser

For a complete list of titles, please see www.press.umich.edu

Ghosts and the Overplus

Reading Poetry in the
Twenty-First Century

CHRISTINA PUGH

University of Michigan Press
Ann Arbor

For questions or permissions, please contact um.press.perms@umich.edu

Published in the United States of America by the
University of Michigan Press
Manufactured in the United States of America
Printed on acid-free paper
First published March 2024

A CIP catalog record for this book is available from the British Library.

Library of Congress Cataloging-in-Publication data has been applied for.

ISBN 978-0-472-03960-9 (paper : alk. paper)
ISBN 978-0-472-22144-8 (e-book)

Contents

Acknowledgments ix

Introduction: The Overplus 1

I. 2003–2010: This Work Which Is Not One

No Experience Necessary 9

Instinctual Ballast: Imitation and Creative Writing 14

On Sonnet Thought 22

Humor Anxiety 34

Allusion and Context in Contemporary American Poetry 39

Ed Roberson's Inward Lyricism 46

Light in Nagasaki: Catherine McCarthy's *We Walk on Jewels* 52

"Some Chant I'm Working At" 55

An Elegy for Dancing 59

II. 2011–2015: Gravity, Images, and the Hand

On Nonconformists and Strange Gravity 73

The Emily Dickinsons 80

"A Lovely Finish I Have Seen": Voice and Variorum in
   Edgar Allan Poe & the Juke-Box 84

"Arranging, Deepening, Enchanting":
  Catherine McCarthy's *Flower Arranging*   109

A Farm, Two Spiders, and *A Book of Luminous Things*:
  Czeslaw Milosz's Affinity for the Image   113

Turning, Troping, Wresting: Michael Ryan's
  "My Dream by Henry James"   123

"Found Breath": The Contemporary "Mainstream" Lyric   127

III. 2015–2021: Voicing the Overplus

Prosopopoeia: The Throwing of a Voice   145

"Velvety Velour" and Other Sonnet Textures in
  Gwendolyn Brooks's "the children of the poor"   149

"Cinnamon. Eyeshadow. Dove": Considering Jean Valentine
  (1934–2020)   155

On Ghosts and the Overplus   172

Works Cited   181

For my teachers, throughout my life

Acknowledgments

Grateful acknowledgment is made to the publications in which some of these essays first appeared:

American Poetry Review: "'Cinnamon. Eyeshadow. Dove': Considering Jean Valentine (1934–2020)"
Hotel Amerika: "Prosopopoeia: The Throwing of a Voice"
Literary Imagination: "On Sonnet Thought"
Poetry: "On Ghosts and the Overplus"; "Humor Anxiety"; "The Emily Dickinsons"; "On Nonconformists and Strange Gravity"; "No Experience Necessary"; "'Velvety Velour' and Other Sonnet Textures in Gwendolyn Brooks's 'the children of the poor'"
Verse: "Ed Roberson's Inward Lyricism" (as *City Ecologue*, by Ed Roberson"); "'This Chant I'm Working At'" (as *The Usable Field*, by Jane Mead")
Voltagepoetry.com, edited by Michael Theune and Kim Addonizio: "Turning, Troping, Wresting: Michael Ryan's 'My Dream by Henry James'"
"On Ghosts and the Overplus" appeared on *Poetry Daily* as the featured weekly prose for the week of March 7, 2016.
"Instinctual Ballast: Imitation and Creative Writing" first appeared in *Originality, Imitation, Plagiarism*, edited by Martha Vicinus and Caroline Eisner. University of Michigan Press, 2008.
"'Found Breath': The Contemporary 'Mainstream' Lyric" first appeared in *The Cambridge Companion to Poetry since 1945*, edited by Jennifer Ashton. Cambridge University Press, 2013.
"Velvety Velour and Other Sonnet Textures in Gwendolyn Brooks's 'the children of the poor'" first appeared in *The Whiskey of Our Discontent: Essays on Gwendolyn Brooks*, edited by Quaraysh Ali Lansana and

Georgia Popoff. Haymarket Press, 2017. It was reprinted in *Poetry* (June 2017).

"An Elegy for Dancing" first appeared in *My Life at the Gym: Feminist Perspectives on Community through the Body*, edited by Jo Malin. SUNY Press, 2010.

"'Arranging, Deepening, Enchanting'" first appeared in *Catherine McCarthy: Flower Arranging* (catalog for McCarthy's show at Ellen Miller Gallery, Boston). Heaven, 2011.

"'A Lovely Finish I Have Seen': Voice and Variorum in *Edgar Allan Poe & the Juke-Box*" first appeared in *Elizabeth Bishop in the Twenty-First Century*, edited by Thomas Travisano, Angus Cleghorn, and Bethany Hicok. University of Virginia Press, 2012.

"Allusion and Context in Contemporary American Poetry" was presented at the Association of Literary Scholars and Critics conference at Princeton University on November 7, 2010.

"A Farm, Two Spiders, and *A Book of Luminous Things*: Czeslaw Milosz's Affinity for the Image" was presented at the "After Milosz" conference at the Chopin Theater, Chicago, on October 1, 2011.

My sincere thanks to the editors who offered me the opportunity to write and to publish many of these essays: Jennifer Ashton, Peter Campion, Angus Cleghorn, Caroline Eisner, Brian Henry, Bethany Hicok, Quaraysh Ali Lansana, David Lazar, Herb Leibowitz, Jo Malin, Georgia Popoff, Elizabeth Scanlon, Don Share, Michael Theune, Tom Travisano, Martha Vicinus, Alan Weller, Christian Wiman, and Susan Wolfson.

And my thanks to those who encouraged my work on this book and its publication, offering their support in various ways: Phillis Levin, David St. John, and Rosanna Warren. I also thank Lisa Petrie, Jason Roush, Jodie Hollander, and Harriet Melrose for their friendship. Special thanks to Catherine McCarthy. I am deeply grateful to my family: my mother and sister, and the memory of my father. And my unending gratitude and love to my husband, Rick DelVisco.

Finally, my great gratitude to Derek Pollard and to the University of Michigan Press.

Introduction

The Overplus

Ghosts and the Overplus is a collection of essays that wonders at—and about—the pluralities that take up residence within lyric poetry. The title of this book is taken from its last essay, which considers the death of my father and of the poet Claudia Emerson; in it, I also express my own ambivalence about supernatural phenomena. The essay explores what I believe to be the genuine uncanniness of writing and reading poems, while also negotiating the nether world of doubt. Such a combination of faith and skepticism constitutes, for me, the indeterminate world of ghosts and writing.

What, then, is the *overplus*? It's an old word, found in Robert Herrick's plea to his dead friend Ben Jonson:

My Ben!
Or come again,
Or send to us
Thy wit's great overplus. . . . (Herrick, "Ode" 823)

While it undoubtedly plays on Jonson's storied volubility, I think Herrick's overplus is also something more. It is Jonson's (and Herrick's) cup as it runneth over, or what Robert Frost called in "Birches" a cup filled "even above the brim"—in a phrase Seamus Heaney also took for the title of his own essay about Frost (Frost, *Collected Poems* 118). In short, the overplus is the extra-ordinary, supernatural (more-than-natural) life and afterlife of lyric language.

The weird reignition perceptible in the lineage I just outlined—from Psalm 23 to Jonson and Herrick, to Frost, and then to Heaney—is itself the overplus in action. It is the quicksilver of allusion, the indispensable conservation of prior lyric moments recalling Emily Dickinson's contention that "The Poets light but Lamps"—whose function is to "stimulate" subsequent ages and histories (*Poems* 397). And that overplus is, of course, inextricable from ghosts. The ghost of Ben Jonson is what renders Herrick's overplus, quasi-mathematical as the term may be, both importunate and saturated with loss.

When I wrote the title essay of this book, then, I was unable to speak of Claudia Emerson's death in the twenty-first century without invoking the "spirits" of two seventeenth-century predecessors (and the even more shadowy presences of Frost, Heaney, and the King James Bible). And in the course of collecting this larger group of essays, on work that ranged from Dickinson to Ed Roberson to Jean Valentine and occasionally stopped to consider lyrical thinking in painting and dance, I realized that every essay here is troubled or enriched by a ghost of some kind: a ghost of a particular poet or poets, the ghost of poetic form (T. S. Eliot's "ghost of meter"), the ghost of tradition, the ghost of unspoken or silenced voices, or the ghost of refrain in its many guises (Eliot, "Reflections" 187). How do we hear, bear, interact with these ghosts? What can their value be? We can discover it best, perhaps, when we commit to reading poems on the molecular level. These essays urge that we continue to do this, amid the speed and distractions replete in our twenty-first century.

In that sense, this book's subtitle also speaks to my thinking about it *as* a book. How do these essays work together? Certainly, they all want to linger amid the many voices and variabilities within lyric poems. In addition to this, however, their gathering comprises a diorama of poetry criticism published in the United States in the first decades of the twenty-first century. This diorama is backlit by the sets of expectations I perceived around the reading and reception of poems then—especially those considered "lyric" (or "mainstream"—a nomenclature that I was once asked to employ in an essay but could only bring myself to do within quotation marks) in opposition to the poetry considered "experimental." Since I was (and am) a poet who had a commitment to communicability *and* difficulty, I was ill-suited to many circumscribed or narrowly defined "schools" or clusters of poetry—not only my predecessors like the Language poets and New Formalists, but also the so-called Elliptical poets and the poets of the New Sincerity. While assuredly none of us is an island, these essays do often seek to delineate what I felt to be my difference from the prescriptions of the poetic schools that held significant sway in the world(s) and times in which I was living.

During these years, I wrote for various audiences and at the invitation of editors who had differing aesthetic and editorial concerns. For this reason, readers will surely find differences in tone and focus throughout this book. Some of the essays are more personal, and some are more discursive. Several of them were influenced by my editorial work at *Poetry* magazine (where some were also published) from 2004 to 2020. For more than fifteen years, I kept my ear to the ground reading thousands upon thousands of poems—and thinking about the various zeitgeists, influences, and excitements happening across America and other places in the world, as poetry began to enjoy a revitalization of interest that is happening to this day, always in a new key. With Adrian Matejka, its first Black editor, *Poetry* magazine itself is taking the art form toward greater inclusivity and a plurality of voices historically underrepresented in the literary conversation.

I am amazed at the difference fifteen years can make. The voices of John Ashbery, Ai, C. D. Wright, Lucie Brock-Broido, Jane Mead, Philip Levine, Mark Strand, Seamus Heaney, Claudia Emerson, James Longenbach, and Jean Valentine, who all appear in these pages at various moments, are the subject of elegy now; but they were very much alive and constitutive of the American poetic landscape when these essays were written. Their loss not only infuses this book, but also marks the end of a poetic era that began in the mid-twentieth century and will, of course, never really "end" if the overplus endures.

While I'm committed to such lyric synchrony, I continue to believe that these first decades of the current millennium were important ones in the life of American poetry. In part for that reason, I have organized these essays in chronologically bound sections, though the essays themselves are not always in strict chronological order of publication or delivery *within* those specific sections. This is because I intend for certain essays to speak to and across one another, the way proximate poems do in a book of poetry. But for me, chronology does not equal teleology. My diorama metaphor is spatial, and indeed there is no temporal end-point here—no conversion of the voice, and no decision for or against essayistic approaches either discursive or personal. In a manner that is similar to the poetry I read and think about, I hope that the plurality of these essays resides in doubts and mysteries, to paraphrase Keats, and that they offer no verdict on how best to write an essay about poems. And as a reader of poetry, I hope to keep learning from new voices.

Still, I know this book is the product of the somewhat idiosyncratic ear, obsessions, and blind spots that I call (not always proudly) my own. Though I worked for years at a job titled Reader, I am not Everyreader—nor is anyone, really. It is in poems' nature to embrace contrasting interpretations and approaches to reading; this is one of the most moving conceptual beauties within lyric poetry. For me, it is the nearly audible grace note within a poem—a trick of diction, a metrical substitution, a colon where we expect a comma—and not necessarily its nearness to my own experience, that allows it to take up residence in my somatic interior ("Oh tall tree in the ear!," Rilke wrote of this phenomenon—*Sonnets to Orpheus* 19).

Perhaps like other poets, I have a penchant for repetition: songs, seemingly throwaway phrases exchanged in conversation, television commercials, poems. And the more we repeat, the more the repetition changes our understanding of what we think we know. (John Hollander's "Breaking into Song: Some Notes on Refrain" articulates this concept brilliantly.) Thus lyric poetry paradoxically cultivates both insistence and divergence from itself. Its conceptual and tonal contours shape-shift, even as we are looking at fixed lines on a page. In this way, poetry exploits (in the strategic sense of that word) both syntax and sonority. What is spotlit, what is foregrounded, what is backgrounded? Or what is virtual? "Am I hearing voices within the voice?"

That last question was posed by Roland Barthes, who asked it about opera (Barthes, "Grain" 184). (Barthes is a staunch companion in these essays—as an articulator of verbal and musical pleasure, in addition to the cerebration that such appreciative work requires.) What he loved in the opera singer Charles Panzéra was precisely Panzéra's ability to articulate prismatic voices within the voice. It is also what we find in the lyric poem: the multifariousness of what poets ourselves call "voice," or speaker, which is consonant with ghosts and the overplus. It is a quality that is nonbinary, in consonance with our current understanding of plurality among genders. It is no limitation on our being-human, but it spelunks the human, as it were: poetic voice expands it, detours from it, stores it, carves sinuous rifts through its supposed center. None of these movements precludes the others. As we've already seen, the lyric poem's nonsingularity is connected to its penchant for allusion and echoing—the ventriloquisms and looking back that makes many of our poems throughout the ages "Haunted," in Dickinson's sense (*Poems* 188). And this is the way that "lyric time," in Sharon Cameron's terms, is necessarily geologic and circular (*Lyric Time* 23)

Circular: absolutely. But poems are more than geometry or clockwork, though the best of them may borrow (or ruin) some symmetrical elements from both. In addition to their participation in systems—this, at least in part, is what formal and metrical verse has always done—I believe that poems encourage and enable some of the most valuable nonlinear thinking possible to us. Perhaps this is because, if we read closely and attentively enough, we can witness the poem thinking about itself and its own identit(ies), much in the way that Teju Cole has described fabric folding in *Blind Spot*:

> A folded drapery is cloth thinking about itself. Under pressure from itself or the influence of external agents, a material adopts a topographical surface. A material, around the axis of itself, faces some part of itself, and confounds its inside and outside. (8)

Cole's telescoped description is germane here. "Cloth thinking about itself" becomes an apt metaphor for a poem's nonsingularity and the way that its various voices are simultaneously inside and outside itself, as we saw in the Herrick quotation with which I began this introduction. Maybe such a cloth is even the "Cloths of Heaven" that Yeats wished for (*Collected Poems* 73). And this cloth's Möbius quality also positions and confounds the poem's reader or listener, who may find herself both inside and outside what she is experiencing.

In a similar way, my first-person "I" weaves in and out of the essays that follow. To be sure, I am entwined in the poems I read, and so my first-person pronoun is never fully absent from what happens in these pages. Any "escape from personality," à la Eliot, is illusory at best (Eliot, "Tradition" 787). My readerly and writerly "I" is a female Generation X poet first trained as a literary critic at a time when the writing of literary criticism and the writing of poems were seen as more separate activities than they are today, with requisite differences expected in practitioners' styles, experience, values, and so forth. When I wanted to study creative writing after finishing a doctorate in comparative literature, my mentors discouraged me from doing so, and I was caught between two desires that were presented to me as mutually exclusive.

The earlier essays in this book, dating from 2005, have this divide as a subtext. Whatever else they are doing, they are trying to navigate (and to fathom) a boundary and a set of injunctions that seemed to me, at the time, to define the poet and the literary critic as crisply separate and immiscible entities. But it was as a critical and close reader of poems that I was able to come into my own as a publishing poet. I became a poet as first a "literary" person—a person haunted by lines—rather than someone who had a particular confession to make or story to tell.

My situation as a woman writer, in a time when that category has rightly been mined and made more complex, remains somewhat up for grabs over the course of this book. I consider myself somewhat unusual: when I studied literature as a graduate student—before the existence of VIDA and #MeToo—many of the most powerful intellects I knew, worked with, and were mentored by were women. So the drama in these essays, if indeed there is one, is less a drama of identity (or of "coming to writing" as a woman, in Hélène Cixous's formulation) than a wrestling with how creative and critical modes of writing were read, expected, and perceived, especially by the female writers and intellects I most respected. Interestingly, it was my study of Emily Dickinson's and Elizabeth Bishop's manuscript materials (a portion of which appears in these pages), rather than my own experience as a woman poet and critic in the twenty-first century, that most allowed me to explore the gendered assumptions still in place around the reading of even canonical women's writing in the present day.

As always when it comes to ghosts and the overplus, we continue to revisit and rework our predecessors—sometimes with reverence, sometimes with corrections, but always with the space for contemplation and renovation that the lyric poem allows. It is my hope that these qualities are inscribed and reinscribed in the essays that follow.

2003–2010

This Work Which Is Not One

No Experience Necessary (2005)

"In some poetry you feel there is too little lived experience—here you feel there is almost more than you can take in" (Valentine, cover endorsement). Such was a blurb I found the other day on the back of a first book of poetry. *Read this, and be overwhelmed by experience*: on the face of it, a strange way to recommend poems. But on the other hand, I knew I'd seen that blurb before. Even in a poetic climate that supports the cerebral, ludic peregrinations of *The Iowa Anthology of New American Poetries*, reviewed by Danielle Chapman in the January 2005 issue of *Poetry*, there is still a sizable minority of poets and readers who come to poetry looking for a measure of "experience"—and what's more, "*lived* experience." What, in fact, are they really looking for? Is experience quantifiable? Is it equivalent to an empirically exciting life? Does it drive a red Ferrari, or is it a rambling pedestrian with a long white beard? Is there a difference? And when so many come away from American poetry today—particularly from the work of younger poets—with a feeling of disappointment or outrage, is *experience* what they are really missing?

The category of experience is seldom defined or questioned; as a concept, it's more like a wink or a nudge in the ribs. But those who uphold it as a value seem to want to appeal to a shared sense of humanity—an unspoken agreement that despite our many cultural, racial, gender, and economic differences, we all are born, live, and die. In what it wants to present as a new, graciously multicultural universalism, the category of "experience" seeks to provide a comforting sense that *we're all in this together*—and that we can, at least, agree on what "this" might be. And of course, "experience" wants even more to be the *sine qua non* for writing the type of poetry that will speak to "people" and not "just poets."

But as the messy legacy of the American poets known as the Confessionals—particularly Lowell, Plath, and Sexton—the thirst for experience reveals its own fundamental contradictions. Plath died at thirty: from the perspective of, anyone but the teenaged, how experienced could she really have been? Sexton and Lowell, for their parts, lived the life of economic privilege—which placed them, in Wordsworthian terms, "at a distance from the Kind" (Wordsworth, *Oxford* 328). The writing of both Plath and Sexton was, to a great degree, forged by their struggle with what Betty Friedan called in *The Feminine Mystique* "the problem that has no name": the mind-numbing burden of domesticity faced by women in an America that had yet to undergo the changes brought about by Second Wave feminism (57). Can this be what is touted as "lived experience"?

The category of experience seems to promise a place for everyone: like Walt Whitman, it wants to invite all of us to dinner. But it's clear that many readers simply can't identify with the life stories of Lowell, Plath, and Sexton. And though one could easily follow R. D. Laing and claim that mental illness itself is a voyage of discovery, it's not clear how such a voyage, as articulated in the work of the Confessionals, would feed into the common construction of experience as a shared and democratic value.

Fascinatingly, the contemporaneous New York school, who were chattier than the Confessionals and just seemed to have a lot more fun, played down the role of experience in writing. As Frank O'Hara so succinctly put it, "Nobody should experience anything they don't need to, if they don't need poetry bully for them" ("Personism" 282). Or Ashbery's ruminations in an interview with Kenneth Koch: "We seem to be determined both to discuss poetry and not to discuss anything at all. This is probably what we do in our poetry. I only wish I knew why we feel it to be necessary" (*Selected Prose* 64).

An even better indictment of experience-as-value comes in Ashbery's "And *Ut Pictura Poesis* Is Her Name." There he inimitably asserts that for the poet, "Certainly whatever funny happens to you / Is OK" (*Selected Poems* 235). In this mock ars poetica, "whatever" becomes both everything and nothing—and the wisdom to know the difference. Kay Ryan has seconded this motion by pressing "the importance to the poet of avoiding or ignoring Kodak moments" ("Danger" 330). In an essay that celebrates the habitual or "novelty-free life," Ryan lauds the least entropic state of being: "Your memory will be deep, quiet, undifferentiated as a pool. Change will enter and twist like a drop of ink, the tiniest bit of new per old" (327).

Perhaps it is precisely that near-invisible shimmer in the old that draws me to certain poets rather than others. I admit that I'm often thrilled by the poets of *no* experience: no experience at all, if experience is defined in the popular, unexamined way. For people immune to literature, Emily Dickinson "didn't have a life." After a year at Mount Holyoke, she embarked on what can only be called, experience-wise, an early retirement in her twenties. As for Wallace Stevens, how boring can it be to walk to your job at an accident and indemnity company (in Hartford, no less) year in and year out? From this perspective, both were writing books—or fascicles—on "nothing," much as Flaubert sought to do when he began to incubate the book that would become *Madame Bovary.* Yet we don't fault these poets for their lack of experience, for their humdrum and muted lives, for not having lived enough in the world (wherever we think that may be). For me, a certain contemporary parallel is found in the marvelous work of Charles Wright, which reads as a paean to the limited-experience life. If read collectively, his selected *Negative Blue* paints a portrait of someone who has done little more—experientially— than sit alone in his own backyard for decades.

Still, experience has long provided a dubious litmus test for poetry, and not just in the American tradition. When Rilke's friend Ellen Key told him that his work "smacked of the writing desk," as Judith Ryan notes, she clearly meant that it reflected too little actual experience (Ryan, *Rilke* 1). The poet's aversion to sustained relationships is well known, as is his avoidance of service during the First World War. Isn't it funny, then, that Rilke's poetry has been popularly seen—even prescribed—as the poetry of experience: the poetry of weddings, funerals, and, as Ryan also states, German soldiers' comfort at the front during both the First and Second World Wars (4)?

So the poetry that, for some, lacks experience can be embraced as the quintessential poetry *of* experience by others. And the poetry forged in what we might consider to be genuinely hefty experience—manual labor, for example—can also easily become its own template or formula: something just as repeatable as the oft-lamented "academic" poem. If Wright has repeated himself—much as Dickinson repeated herself—the same could be said of a poet like Philip Levine, who is often looked to as a quintessential contemporary poet of experience. Clearly, then, having "experience" doesn't void the risk of repetition in poems. Poetry that is "novelty-free," in Kay Ryan's terms, may be a function of self-actualization in the work, regardless of how much recognizable experience that work does or does not reflect ("Danger" 327).

The longer I look, the more the category of "experience" dissolves before my eyes. I'm happy to see that dissolution, since it's a fitting prelude to another intimately related argument: one for the viability of the reading life as a version of, or a substitute for, "lived experience." Italo Calvino's *If on a winter's night a traveler* provides a good model for what I'm talking about. There, the allegorical Writer and Reader are two separate people: the first male, the second female. Lately I've envied this Reader her fly-by-night quality, her ability to lose herself so irresponsibly in books. But if I superimpose the one allegorical figure upon the other, I end up with a viscerally viable, albeit cartoonish, prescription for who the writer is—or should be, or could be. Might it be that what is missing in the work of some younger poets is not "experience" at all, but reading that is deep enough to effect changes in the self?

Here is where the university, the proverbial elephant in the room, comes in. Many believe universities fail poets, particularly younger poets, by depriving them of experience. This is said categorically of the MFA and other graduate degrees, as well as of academic positions that now support many poets as teachers and writers. Academia becomes, in this model, a sort of double Procrustean bed. We're told repeatedly that graduate programs in creative writing produce poets who crank out the same experience-challenged, cookie-cutter verse. But do education and "lived experience" have to be so ineluctably incompatible? That question is almost never asked. And few, if any, seem to wonder whether universities are failing poets by not educating them *enough*, or widely enough—or later, by requiring them to teach only in the workshop model. What if experience were not the missing ingredient after all?

I've thought a lot about this question because, though I'm hardly leading the escapist life of Calvino's Reader, I too am a Reader of sorts: Reader for *Poetry* magazine. As such, I see an enormous quantity of work by poets who are hoping for publication. Ironically, it often seems that an inability to get *past* one's own experience causes many of these poems to founder. For the beginner, it's the rather narcissistic belief that, to switch

Ashbery a bit, "whatever melodramatic happens to you / Is OK." But even in certain, yes, more "experienced" poets, there can be an impulse around the anecdotal—around travel, around the family, around "events"—that, if not reworked in what Veronica Forrest-Thomson called the "internal expansion" of the poem, burns as the steady flame of ordinariness (*Poetic Artifice* xii).

What's missing in some of the work I see is an ability to distinguish experience from *occasion*: what I'll define here as the prime mover of the poem, be it based in the poet's empirical life, in imagination, in the jurr of language, in literary texts. Yes, it can even be anecdotal, as in Stevens's infamous "I placed a jar in Tennessee" (*Collected Poems* 76). It's the opening, the antechamber of the poem that invites us into the occasion that will, we hope, master us as readers. Consider these openings—how they *happen*, and how little you can resist them: "I heard a Fly buzz—when I died" (Dickinson, *Poems* 265); "Again last night I dreamed the dream called Laundry" (Merrill 114); "My black face fades" (Komunyakaa 107); "Yes, it's a joke—in the florist's dictionary" (Teare 12); "*flower is becoming the graph*" (Willis 33). Infinite, the snares of occasion. And polyglot. One of them is even taken from the book whose well-intentioned but ultimately misguided blurb I quoted at the outset of this essay.

Though the term may seem old-fashioned to some, occasion manages to crash the party of even the least referential of poetic schools. The best way I know to get a feel for this—what others might call integrity or bloom or motor—is not necessarily to go out and have an exciting life that you can write about in your work. Instead, I think, it's the ability to read widely enough to know which poetic occasions stir you—be they empirical, imaginative, aleatory, linguistic, discursive—and how various and transhistorical are poems' *means* to stir. So to argue against the litmus test of experience is not necessarily to argue, as did Eliot, for the extinction of the personality. It's also not to claim that I wouldn't drive the red Ferrari, if I had a driver's license. Instead, it's to note that poetic occasion may not always be the result of "lived experience" per se. Understanding this will open the door to the younger poet who, like Mark Yakich, "divides his time between the bedroom and the kitchen" ("Letter" 470). At the risk of coining yet another new universalism, maybe this is precisely the sort of experience we should all want to have.

Instinctual Ballast

Imitation and Creative Writing (2008)

In his *Handlist of Rhetorical Terms*, Richard A. Lanham defines mimesis as "imitation of gesture, pronunciation, or utterance; self-conscious role-playing, as when a rhapsode reenacts the poem he is reciting" (102). As defined by Lanham and discussed by thinkers from Plato to Erich Auerbach, mimesis and imitation are inseparable from the endeavor of representation itself; most creative arts are distinctly mimetic in their practice. In our contemporary landscape, however, creative *writing* is almost never taught with mimesis at the forefront of students' or teachers' minds. Instead, the pedagogical method in many workshop courses seeks to enable the student to "discover" her own voice, as if she existed in a form of literary vacuum. Students in such courses might be asked to do an occasional imitation exercise, but the serious practice of imitation is seldom pursued in any focused manner in most creative writing programs.

Even in a literary culture that continues to prize "originality," however, imitation is a viable apprenticeship for a writer. In the past few years under the auspices of the Northwestern University creative writing program, I have taught undergraduate creative writing courses that consisted *only* of reading and imitating a handful of major American poets: Robert Frost, Elizabeth Bishop, Louise Bogan, Gwendolyn Brooks, and James Merrill. Though this type of course goes against the grain of many curricular expectations, I have been astonished at the caliber of poetic work that imitation yields from students.

Because the imitation course is an amalgam of what we might, in other circumstances, think of as discrete "literature" and "creative writing" courses, it rejects the way that institutions cordon off complementary aspects of the mind into separate disciplines. This helps students, in turn, to begin to reject the myths and clichés of who the scholar and the poet should be: those discrete and supposedly mutually exclusive perimeters that determine how we identify ourselves as producers of literature, whether "critical" or "creative." The course thus cultivates the writer, to parse Luce Irigaray, "which is not *one*." It's built upon a radical valuation of the writing act itself—what Stevens called "The poem of the mind in the act of finding / What will suffice"—and the ways in which such an act emerges both steadily and unpredictably from a lifelong act of reading (*Collected Poems* 239).

The task of the writer who is not *one* writer, then, is to reinscribe disciplinary boundaries that are fluid as well as rigorous. Often the traditional workshop format, as practiced in some programs and institutions, can relegate the reading act to the not-said—almost to the realm of the unconscious. A poem might have been "influenced" by another, and we may learn as much over the course of workshop discussion; but that influence is thought to lie, almost indiscreetly, outside the artificial boundary that contains what is thought to constitute creative production. In such courses, reading is ground but not figure; the assumption, but not the task at hand. Yet this is precisely the task that writers need to consider in their own work, since text necessarily generates text. Many creative writing courses may not actively ask how to read as a writer: how should I be reading; what can I be reading; and especially: how, in this culture of images, can I line my life with words, with print? These questions are not only crucial for undergraduates, who are still very much in the stage of formation, but also should be vital to any writer for whom the re-formation of self and work remains a perennial value. By making literary texts the centerpiece of our courses rather than the background, we can teach our students not only to read as writers—"poetry is an art that reading, at its best, can imitate," Mary Kinzie explains (*Poet's Guide* 2)—but also to write as readers. This is a viable practice that literary critics from Helen Vendler to Judith Ryan have discussed. (Indeed, Ryan's *Rilke, Modernism, and Poetic Tradition* recreates Rilke's writing desk.)

Italo Calvino knew quite a lot about the Reader, whom he allegorized as a character in *If on a winter's night a traveler*. The male writer goes in search of this female Reader, Ludmilla by name, who keeps a crowd of picture frames in one corner of her wall:

> The frames are all different, nineteenth-century Art Nouveau floral forms, frames in silver, copper, enamel, tortoiseshell, leather, carved wood; they may reflect the notion of enhancing those fragments of real life, but they may also be a collection of frames, and the photographs may be there only to occupy them; in fact some frames are occupied by pictures clipped from newspapers, one encloses an illegible page of an old letter, another is empty. (144)

What is the import of that last, superfluous, melancholy frame in the Reader's house? Perhaps it points to a moment of transformation that Calvino did not fully envision—in which the reader, steeped and saturated in text, opens a portal to her own writing. The empty frame becomes incipience, or the blank page. Then the beautiful distinctions— man/woman, writer/reader—must themselves be blurred, be productively confounded, and all the genders mixed up. For the reader can only be courted by the writer *within* the self that is not one.

Saul Bellow said that the writer is a reader moved to emulation. Certainly the performing arts place a high value on emulation, or imitation, as do many pedagogical practices in the visual arts (think of aspiring painters who copy the masterpieces hanging in museums). Despite the perennial literary-critical debates regarding the role of mimesis *within* literary representation, however, few educators think of literature as a practice that a writer must learn by performing mimesis of previous writers. Nevertheless, the ballet student learns his art through a muscular, bodily mimesis of the teacher's equally muscular gesture; and here the analogy becomes more than strictly conceptual: because we need to feel poetic meter in our breath and heartbeats, we can't write iambic tetrameter without learning to walk in tetrameter first. Imitation forces us to confront the poem not as an ethereal emanation of our personal wish, but as something distinctly material—that is, something we make through the labor of arrangement and rhetorical manipulation.

A comparison to the other arts can often bring this pedagogy home to skeptical students in the early days of an imitation class. That, of course, would be the time when they learn the course requirements: reading and discussing five twentieth-century poets, as well as writing both a weekly imitation poem and an analytic paper that makes an argument, via close reading, about one of the poet's poems. This is serious work—and the imitation poems are serious imitation, not parody. They are, in other words, what Nicholas Delbanco calls a "sincere imitation" (*Sincerest Form* xxvi). As Delbanco elaborates, such an imitation can never be accomplished without intensive reading and study of the work to be imitated:

> You cannot copy what you glance at nor remember what you speed read nor repeat what you half heard; the reason one writer chooses semi-colons, or another elects an apposite comma, or a third prefers the absence of standard punctuation marks, has a great deal to do with the world view expressed, and a complex or compound sentence or parenthetical observation (such as the one we're engaged in) will represent a different way of looking at the linkages of things—the way the past impinges on the present as does the present on the future in an unbroken line of descent or argument if represented with a dash—than does a simple or short. (xxvi)

Delbanco aptly describes the way that imitation poems necessitate—are, in fact, constitutionally impossible *without*—intensive and some-times self-changing reading of the poet to be imitated. *Put on the nerves and musculature of the poet before you begin*, I have told the students. *This is not about biography, the poet's or yours.* Instead, it's about taking your life into the poem—a different way of taking your life into your hands. For one quarter, the students learn to be sibyls—to let the poet in question speak *them*. This is not a mystical transformation; it is instead the natural outgrowth of attentive reading.

Moreover, it involves much more than retaining a certain meter or line length, though it does require that, too: it also involves assimilating the ways in which a certain poet builds sentences incrementally, syntactically, across lines; the wild geography of what I call that poet's "diction-universe"; what the poet would include or exclude from a particular poem. In one particularly memorable class discussion, we debated whether James Merrill would have used the phrase "reality TV" in his work, had he lived to see it. Contrast, too, is paramount: the precise degree of microscopic sheen in Bishop's "The Bight" or "Sandpiper"—what Richard Wollheim would have described as "seeing-in" ("Spectator" 105)—is unthinkable in a poet like Frost. Only by dwelling within the poet's work can we access the caul of preverbal synergies that Seamus Heaney called the "instinctual ballast" of a particular poet: "What kinds of noise assuage him, what kinds of music pleasure or repel him, what messages the receiving stations of his senses are happy to pick up from the world around him and what ones they automatically block out" (Heaney, "Makings" 62). For Heaney, instinctual ballast is what causes the later Yeats to clatter with consonants while Wordsworth remains the smooth and receptive oar in water, the glittering circles inscribed by the young boat-thief in Book I of "The Prelude."

Kinzie has also eloquently discussed the timbre of reading that imitation requires, as well as the primacy of the literary material at hand:

> Perceiving how shape emerges from the half-shaped background provides the reader with a lens, or vantage, similar to the writer's. But this does not require us to say much about the lives of the poets or how they went about making their works; I am more interested in how the poems themselves wrestle with their tasks and occasions. For task and occasion arise only from a clear sense of poetic mission, a mission that articulates itself most strongly when responding (among other spurs) to a poetic tradition. (*Poet's Guide* 14)

By its very nature, then, imitation challenges the received notion that writing must arise from, or be somehow ratified by, personal experience.

All of this certainly flies in the face of such credos as "Write what you know," "Find your own voice," and "Your experience is the best subject for writing." But as someone who came to writing through and with a doctorate in literature, none of those instructions seemed right to me in the first place. With so much of my life vested in reading, in writing, how could I separate it into book and nonbook? What of my voice, or my plural voices, really belongs to me, and how would I be able to gauge the degree or percentage of that ownership? Perhaps because I did study literary theory, these ideas don't reduce me to despair; instead, they may have actually given me permission to write in the first place, despite so many creative writers' indignation over even the very title of Roland Barthes's "The Death of the Author." If I had ever found writing to be an act of the ego alone, I think an inchoate sense of modesty—or a certain love of privacy—would have prevented me from doing it at all. (In an essay entitled "The Uses of Doubt," Stacey D'Erasmo has written forcefully against the often-unspoken assumption that writing must be ego-driven.) If indeed there is a way that poetry can function as Eliot's "continual extinction of personality" (Eliot, "Tradition" 785), can it also be a concomitant enlargement of what we consider to be the singular, limited personality as such? "Enlargement" is, of course, a world away from "inflation."

Keats's notion of negative capability is closely related to such enlargement. For him, the ability "[to be] in uncertainties, mysteries, doubts, without any irritable reaching after fact and reason" (Keats, "Negative Capability" 70–71) is what Shakespeare possessed in droves, and a capacity that every poet should cultivate in herself. Negative capability is certainly a marvelous description of the writing process, but isn't it also a dead ringer for the reading act? We could say much more about the play between agency and self-dissolution in the case of the reader who is also a writer; but considered in the light of negative capability, the seeming strictness of the imitation assignments is revealed as something more than literary apprenticeship: it can constitute some of the most vertiginous artistic freedom imaginable.

An imitation course thus refines the boundaries of what we categorize as "the creative." It requires a student to do something more dangerous than to trust his own experience or to tell the story she thinks she wants to tell. Imitation unmoors the writer from her comfort zone of familiar syntax, diction, and line. If there is a philosophy subtending imitation, it is surely globally similar to that of deconstruction: both practices suggest that writing is never transparent, or innocent, or a straightforward means of self-expression.

Does anyone own his writing, then? Are imitation and plagiarism commensurate? At first blush, I'm inclined to separate them—to agree, that is, with Christopher Ricks's admonition that "Plagiarism is a dishonesty" (*Allusion* 223). Clearly, however, plagiarism has a much more ambiguous role in the creative arts than in criticism, as poets have incorporated other poets' lines into their own work for millennia. The genre of classical poem known as the *cento*, which comprises one hundred borrowed lines, is an excellent example of what we might now call naturalized plagiarism. For some, Eliot's "The Waste Land," despite its footnotes, also constitutes plagiarism writ large. The imitation course, however, does not ask students to incorporate actual lines from the master poets' work. Instead, students are asked to put on strategies and verbal proclivities, as opposed to "lifting" pieces of text from the poet to be imitated; cutting and pasting would interfere with the generative writing—in another's voice—that they are being asked to do. If plagiarism has any role at all in the course, perhaps it would be the creeping and paradoxical sense of *self*-plagiarism described by William Gaddis in *Agape Agape*: "I've never even seen my, seen this plagiarist because I am the other one it's exactly the opposite, I am the other" (22). I am the other: the writer who is not one.

Lastly, pedagogy seeks practical outcomes. Some might wonder how such concentrated imitation affects creative writing students and whether such a course really allows them to remain "creative," in the popular sense of the term. In my experience, it does. Some students told me that they came to depend on the imitations: that they took great pleasure in that relinquishing of self. Many of these students also went on to write senior thesis projects in creative writing—projects that may have germinated in some of the imitation poems, but that grew in ways that exceeded the strict boundaries of the imitation course. What's more, the students also learned enormously from their own resistance to imitating particular writers. Clearly, some imitations feel easier or more seamless than others, and these experiences help students to begin to unearth and to articulate their own "instinctual ballast," in Heaney's terms. If imitating Frost feels like the proverbial walk in the park, it's almost certain that Merrill will be more of a struggle, and this very contrast will reveal something important about the student's emerging goals and capacities as a poet.

Perhaps most importantly, the challenge of imitation spurs students (in an almost Bloomian sense) to produce poems that are fine poems in their own right, even if taken out of the strict imitation context. A couple of years ago, one of my students wrote a superb Frost imitation that was later published in a small but nationally distributed literary magazine. Thus imitation doesn't always announce itself as such to the reading public; neither, of course, does an imitative inception disqualify a work from standing as its own autonomous entity. Robert Lowell's *Imitations* volume, for example, famously troped the boundaries of imitation and "autonomous" artistic conception. More recently, Susan Stewart's *Columbarium*, winner of the National Book Critics Circle Award for poetry in 2003, has been discussed in the greater context of imitation.

But a result of publication is not precisely what the imitation course is striving for. Instead, imitation allows undergraduate students to be what they are: apprentice writers. When they imitate, these students are apprenticing to the very best and are thereby slowing down their own writerly gestation process—in an age when the rush to publish is infecting even the undergraduate population. Writers are not made in an instant; and no matter what form our writing may eventually take, there is a very real sense in which we are the verbal concatenation of what we have read: whether our work be experimental or traditional is immaterial. Imitation recognizes and mobilizes this essential element of literary learning, and it allows students to learn viscerally from the tradition in which they strive to make their mark.

On Sonnet Thought (2010)

As a poetic form, the sonnet is small but notoriously demanding. Its traditional fourteen lines require both an extreme condensation of language and a heightened degree of emotion and intellection. Many of us, whether readers or writers, also know that living with sonnets can take us to unexpected and feverish places. In that sense, this essay was written from the inside out: over the course of writing a book of poems loosely inspired by sonnets, I came to identify something I called "sonnet thought" or, alternately, the sonnet "mind-set." By the phrase "sonnet thought," I mean to refer to the sonnet's necessarily economical formal harnessing of expansive, complex (or hypotactic) syntax-as-thought, thus incorporating a capacious amount of often recursive mileage, contrast, and change within the small poetic space of fourteen lines.[1]

Many would argue that poetic form instantiates the thought that it concurrently constrains: that the two, in other words, are inextricable. Though I have an intuitive sympathy for this perspective, I discovered that sonnet thought, or sonnet energy, may be separated from the metrical norms and rhyme schemes that have constituted the traditional sonnet in its various formal mantles. T. S. Eliot famously proposed that a "ghost of some simple metre" must hover over free verse; in the case of sonnet thought, however, such a ghost may be more syntactical and conceptual than residually metrical (Eliot, "Reflections" 187). It is the manner of thinking that the sonnet form has enabled or inaugurated, even if the more tactile scaffolding of that form has fallen away.[2]

---

1. In *A Poet's Guide to Poetry*, Mary Kinzie discusses poetry as the productive play of sentence-syntax against the countervailing, sometimes dividing, energies of poetic line. See also James Longenbach, *The Art of the Poetic Line*.

2. This is not to claim that formal sonnetry is anything but alive and well in the present day. See the marvelous contemporary formal sonnets of Seamus Heaney, Marilyn

I hope to show how sonnet energy, or combustion, may be harnessed from the traditional formal sonnet and reignited through the modality of economical free verse that utilizes certain aspects of sonnet manner. In the context of my own poetic work, this meant an articulation of sonnet "thought" in single verse paragraphs containing free-verse lines, as opposed to strict sonnet formatting in fourteen lines of iambic pentameter arranged by specific rhyme schemes. I am certainly not the first to have written free-verse sonnets; the endeavor sometimes seems ubiquitous, so often can we find unrhymed poems that cluster almost organically around the thirteen- to sixteen-line mark. Contemporary poets such as Gerald Stern and David Biespiel have profitably adapted the formal sonnet's predilection for wide-ranging conceptualization—as well as incorporating, and sometimes pluralizing, the sonnet's traditional volta, or turn.[3]

What is it that continues to draw so many of us to the sonnet? It was not supposed to be this way. In 1948, William Carlos Williams dismissed the sonnet form as static and anachronistic, "a form which does not admit of the slightest structural change in its composition" ("Poem" 57). Yet early twenty-first-century poetry reveals that interest in the sonnet is, if anything, waxing. This interest may indicate that a certain stripe of poetic ambition is still alive within us, a habit of mind that the sonnet retrenches and articulates. In a manner rivaled only by the epigram, the sonnet requires us to think big. It asks that we expand, even as it contracts the stage on which that expansion must occur.

As a result of this contraction, we can experience both transport and devastation. And as a free-verse poet who derives incalculable inspiration from formal poetry, I have long been interested in the sonnet as a peculiarly discrete verbal ordeal, an ordeal exemplified by the densely allusive yet unforgettably moving plight that Milton limns in Sonnet XVI ("On his Blindness"):

Nelson, and Anne Winters, as well as Karen Volkman's recent book of formal sonnets, *Nomina*.

3. Plural volte are part of the tradition: see, for example, John Donne's use of elements from both the Petrarchan and Shakespearean templates for his Holy Sonnets, with multiple volte. As Donne demonstrates, the sonnet is remarkably suited to reversals and reconfigurations—including changes of mind, distractions, detours, and palinodes.

When I consider how my light is spent,
Ere half my days, in this dark world and wide,
And that one Talent which is death to hide,
Lodg'd with me useless, though my Soul more bent
To serve there with my Maker, and present
My true account, lest he returning chide,
Doth God exact day-labour, light denied?
I fondly ask; But Patience, to prevent
That murmur, soon replies, God doth not need
Either man's work or his own gifts, who best
Bear his milde yoak, they serve him best, his state
Is Kingly. Thousands at His bidding speed,
And post o'er Land and Ocean without rest:
They also serve who only stand and waite. (85)

At the outset, we hear a speaker who fears the worst of the worst: that his blindness will cost him his eternal salvation. Indeed, "Doth God exact day-labour, light denied?" may seem more a cry than a question or "murmur." Yet across fourteen lines, Milton's blinded speaker moves from a despair that we might, with Hopkins, deem "world-sorrow" to a resting position that the protracted and tortuous sentence of the octave cannot foresee: the state of being comforted (Hopkins, "[No Worst]" 106). (Due to the constraints of the sonnet form, this comfort must remain an implicit rather than stated reaction to the voice of Patience.) In the course of this reversal, Milton's sonnet exemplifies the centrifugal energies that this highly compressed poetic form both articulates and reins in. We can perceive these in its musical management of call and response, in its swift yet incremental movement from despair to implicit assuagement, and in the heartbreaking resonance of talent as both a biblically valenced coin to be invested and a gift—for writing—that the speaker fears his blindness has stolen from him forever.

Startlingly, in concert with the speaker's implicit emotional transformation, we have also witnessed something like an antipodal change of value system here. Over the course of fourteen lines, the sonnet moves from an investment model of worship (Matthew 25:14–30 instructs that the coin, or talent, be spent rather than buried) to the quietist, nearly Zen-like practice of "standing and waiting" in service to God, which the personified Patience figure prescribes for Milton's blind speaker.[4] Of course, the metaphor of "yoke," despite invoking the "ease" of obedience ("For my yoke is easy, and my burden is light" [Matthew 11:30]), also suggests enforced labor, and thus something other than "patience." This complex resonance troubles the poem's outcome in a fascinating way.[5]

The point remains, however, that while the philosophic and theological reversal in Sonnet XVI is capacious enough to be treated in an epic poem containing hundreds of pages, it happens here almost in the proverbial blink of an eye. For this reason, we might say that Milton's lyric speaker is, at least generically, greater than himself. If Keatsian "Kingdoms" and "realms" may be traversed and redrawn within the scant space of fourteen lines ("On first looking into Chapman's Homer"—*John Keats* 5), it is no wonder that we may feel at once passionately roused, intellectually braced, and even physically "spent" by Sonnet XVI (35).[6] Imbued with the heightened, contrastive energies of sonnet thought, the sonnet is indeed an ordeal—often an exquisite ordeal, but an ordeal nonetheless.

The scope of sonnet thought writ large, however, is often not limited to the space of a single sonnet. Since one sonnet often begets another, sonnet thought can be infectious: the scope of disparate energies may readily be multiplied in the sonnet sequence; and it is partially this phenomenon that has interested Joel Fineman. By introducing the volatile "dark lady" into his later sonnets, Fineman argues, Shakespeare has cre-

---

4. Although the movement from octave to sestet is often interpreted as a repudiation of Hebrew Bible values for New Testament ones, Tobias Gregory perceptively argues that the reversal cannot be so neatly understood. While the sonnet is "full of Biblical echoes because Milton's mind was, . . . its prevailing picture of God does not derive from a specific Biblical place. The octave's vision of God as an irascible master who will destroy a slave who doesn't make him money is supplanted in the sestet by a broader vision wherein the poem's 'I' is included among countless servants of a God so mighty that he needs none of them" ("Murmur" 25). Nevertheless, I would suggest that even this more muted theological change is world-altering for Milton's blind speaker.

5. As a rejoinder to this seeming paradox, Gregory proposes that we think of "the readiness suggested as like that of a co-pilot or a second-string athlete on the bench, ready to step in at a moment's notice if called. For Milton, standing and waiting is service; that is the point of the famous last line, and in it lies such consolation as the poem affords" ("Murmur" 28).

6. This quasi-physiological response may be what Louise Glück has in mind when she discusses the opening of Milton's fourth line: "'Lodged' is like a blow. And the next words make a kind of lame reeling, a dwindling" (*Proofs* 40).

ated a new and divided tenor of poetic subjectivity that opposes the idealized, static, and mirroring rhetoric of praise animating the earlier sonnets to the young man. This divide is in keeping with the sonnet's role as a vehicle for psychological and linguistic difference: the "subject of Shakespeare's sonnets experiences himself as his difference from himself" (Fineman, *Shakespeare's Perjured Eye* 25). While Fineman is less interested in how sonnet form abets such quintessentially divided subjectivity, his argument maintains the status of the sonnet as a discrete container of internal incommensurability.

Thus a "narrow room"—Wordsworth's phrase for the paradoxical freedom of a nun's cloister, analogous to "the Sonnet's scanty plot of ground"—can enable remarkable varieties of migration, transformation, and allegorical self-splitting, as the figure of "Patience" may function in Milton's sonnet (Wordsworth, *Oxford Authors* 286). As David Mikics and Stephanie Burt note in *The Art of the Sonnet*, "Rapturous praise, bitter exclamation, and step-by-step reasoning frequently intertwine in [the sonnet's] concise shape" (5). Such antipodal movement—often accomplished in lush appositive motions and swaths of figurative language—can be emotional, conceptual, or even geographic, as in Keats's world-spanning textual travel incited by Chapman's Homer. And more often than not, as in Milton's sonnet, it is accomplished by complex syntax as divided by a necessarily compact set of poetic lines.

I'm convinced that it is largely by virtue of hypotactic (subordinate) syntax, often expressing qualification or hesitation, that many sonnet-arguments intentionally do not present themselves as "true" or "proven" as such: these arguments may cave, snake, whirl, sublime. The sonnet thrives on the flamboyantly untrue syllogism, the rhetorically transparent interpersonal ploy (as in many of Shakespeare's earlier sonnets to the young man), the self-consciously fictional self-comforting: "And, yes, how like my mind / To make itself secure," wrote Thom Gunn in an observation that could easily describe a certain strand of "sonnet thought" (*Man* 67).

I am much more interested in how protracted syntax—measured by lines—can contain contradiction and difference than in the use of short, declarative sentences juxtaposed as non sequiturs, which is often the more fashionable approach to complexity of thought in contemporary poetry (perhaps popularized by Ashbery's heirs, as distinct from Ashbery

himself). Why is complex syntax more appealing than a sequence of stac-
cato feints? Perhaps because it is more mimetic of the way some of our
minds really do seem to work, particularly when we are ruminating on
a problem or issue. "If," "then," "but," "and yet," "however": all of these
crucial yet often overlooked nodes of syntactic tissue seem custom-built
for the perennial contemplation of an insoluble dilemma. The textural
inconsistency of protracted, emotionally charged argumentation also
enables a certain kind of beauty; as Mikics notes of Shakespeare's sonnets,
"never has insecurity seemed so glorious" (*Art* 14). Often, too, syntactical
complexity can allow us to explore the limits of the language more fully:
Roman Jakobson's axis of combination seems intuitively more infinite
than his axis of selection.[7] In other words, grammatical combination
affords richer possibilities than the continual regeneration of new grammatical subjects—or the perennial "restart," as it were.

There is also a sense in which "making the mind secure," or the psychic
condition that makes such reassurance necessary, finds an emblem in the
very structure of the Shakespearean sonnet. By necessitating that the
volta or turn appear belatedly—just before its final couplet—the Shakespearean sonnet is infamously susceptible to ending on aphoristic, uni-
versalized statements that may not seem fully proven by what has come
before. Thus the finished Shakespearean sonnet, despite its drive toward
pithy closure, may still enact Clarice Lispector's plea for more language:
"So long as I have questions to which there are no answers, I shall go on
writing" (*Hour* 11). The multiplication of sonnets in sequence, then, may
be a formal reaction to this phenomenon of subterranean nonresolution
in a form that boasts, on the level of sound, an almost officious musical
closure. If only by dint of its formal definition, Shakespearean sonnets
may elicit more Shakespearean sonnets.[8]

Addressing the closing couplet, Helen Vendler argues that since
Shakespeare's sonnets move from "personal" narration to a final "prover-

---

7. Jakobson's famous formula is that "the poetic function projects the principle of
equivalence from the axis of selection to the axis of combination": words selected gain
new functions in poetic formation—by meter, rhyme, syntax, metaphor, and so on
("Closing Statement" 350).

8. J. Paul Hunter has suggested that extended couplet poems, especially in the
eighteenth-century, might be a form of historical corrective to the closing-couplet
"problem" of the Shakespearean sonnet (Newberry Library lecture).

bial" couplet, they enable "intrapsychic irony in the fictive speaker" or, more precisely, the speaker's "self-ironizing turn" (*Art* 26). Yet such irony, she adds, may also be built into the quatrains:

> Unless one senses the reason for the speaker's turn to the proverbial, and of course "hears" the proverbial tone lurking "under" the "personal" language of the speaker, one is at a loss to know how to utter the couplet. It should be uttered with implied quotation marks around each of its proverbial sayings. (26)

For Vendler, then, the entirety of a Shakespearean sonnet is flecked with irony and citationality, which clusters more densely in the couplet than in the quatrains. Her argument suggests that since one modality must fold formally into the other, the volta serves to disclose what subtended the quatrains all along. While this point of view tends to demote the role of the volta as a catalyst for localized poetic change, it also suggests that the Shakespearean sonnet form, at least in Shakespeare's own hands, has a propensity to abstract the speaker from himself; this is arguably characteristic of Milton's sonnet as well. Such abstraction reflects (and inflects) the conceptual drives to which the sonnet, among discrete poetic forms, is almost uniquely suited.

Vendler's observations also spark more questions about the nature of the sometimes-elusive volta within the sonnet form in general. What is the exact degree or cant of the turn, and how does it reconfigure the sonnet's microscopic unfolding? Whether it occurs before the closing couplet in the Shakespearean sonnet, before the sestet in the Petrarchan scheme, or elsewhere in a sonnet, the volta's often breathtakingly indefinable pivot remains a vital component of the governing structure. The volta even thrives on its own variousness. As Paul Fussell shows, in sonnets by Santayana, Keats, and Wordsworth, the volta is characterized, respectively, as "a logical action" (answering a question posed by the octave); "a moment of sheer metaphoric power"; and, more indexically, "something like a literal turn of the body or the head" (117–18).[9] This capacity

---

9. Fussell's observation points to the important role of questions (and their sometimes surprising answers) as a source of redirection throughout a sonnet—not just in the volta. This is another strategy that my own poems have employed. See the opening of "Eidolon" in my *Grains of the Voice* (52).

for rhetorical shape-shifting—perhaps its only indissoluble "property"—makes the volta a metonym for the surprising elasticity of sonnet form over the centuries. One need only name the often eponymous variations across literary history: Petrarchan, Shakespearean, Miltonic, Spenserian, or the curtal sonnetry of Gerard Manley Hopkins. Though all of these forms have particular relationships to the modality of "sonnet thought," such plurality of "sonnet-ness" suggests that the resiliency of the template transcends the strictures of any single rhyme scheme or prescribed placement of volta.

In light of this resilience, I would suggest that with the right combination of hypotactic syntax, volta (or volte), and economy of lineation, a nonformal poet may productively partake of sonnet manner and sonnet thought. If sonnet thought is democratic in its dispensation, as I believe it is, a poet should engage it without needing to question whether his or her or their poem "qualifies" as a sonnet. This is because sonnet thought is not a toggle switch for the free-verse or the formal poet. Its perambulatory yet crystallized modality may be either heightened or downplayed, depending on how a poet chooses to showcase a cross section of cerebration or emotion in its prismatic possibilities. Even if we don't travel as far as we do in Milton, sonnet thought may still be quietly operative.

For example, Frost's "Once by the Pacific" (composed entirely of couplets) shows immense power within a lesser conceptual circumference, seamlessly maneuvering a description of shoreline into prophetic, apocalyptic, and even disturbed rumination:

The shattered water made a misty din.
Great waves looked over others coming in,
And thought of doing something to the shore
That water never did to land before.
The clouds were low and hairy in the skies,
Like locks blown forward in the gleam of eyes.
You could not tell, and yet it looked as if
The shore was lucky in being backed by cliff,
The cliff in being backed by continent;
It looked as if a night of dark intent
Was coming, and not only a night, an age.
Someone had better be prepared for rage.

There would be more than ocean-water broken
Before God's last Put out the Light *was spoken. (Collected Poems 229)*

"Once by the Pacific" may present as a simple seascape. But in Frost's hands, description quickly becomes ideation, then allusion—to "Put out the light," Othello's instruction before his murder of Desdemona, as well as a reversal of *fiat lux* in Genesis. Despite the implied scope of the poem's ending proclamation, we don't see the conceptual switchbacks or grand reversals of Milton's Sonnet XVI. Frost's doomsday scenario, such as it is, builds steadily rather than switches. At the same time, his showy recourse to personification early on ("locks blown forward in the gleam of eyes")—whose efficacy has been critiqued by Robert Alter—necessarily gestures beyond the scope of realist description.[10]

Indeed, the stately couplets belie the extreme susceptibility that characterizes this poem's speaker. We may readily question the judgment of someone who notes the "lucky" shores and cliffs—whose pointedly colloquial personification has been only ostensibly pre-neutralized by the disclaimer "You could not tell, and yet it looked as if . . ." This hesitant syntax counterbalances the poem's tendency toward judgment-as-proclamation ("Someone had better be prepared for rage"). The final couplet, audibly "broken" by the only feminine rhyme, therefore becomes suspect in its very surety—a situation often felt in the closing couplets of Shakespeare's sonnets as well.

The difference, however, is that Frost's sonnet is all couplets, importing the sound of Shakespearean "ending" as a building block for every two-line increment that this poem's rhyme scheme enacts, and thereby ironizing the aphoristic bent of the Shakespearean couplet itself. The finality of *Put out the Light* deepens that critique in its use of allusion as an even more explicit—here, italicized—citationality. Such formal irony is not entirely identical to sonnet thought as I've been discussing it. Yet the effect is in keeping with what Mikics calls Frost's characteristic "combination of hard-mouthed Yankee proverb and visionary fulfillment" (*Art* 241), a comment that recalls Vendler's observations about the relation-

---

10. "Perhaps the pronounced personification somehow justifies the rather strange image of the clouds as locks of hair, though I am not so sure of that," Alter proposes (*Pleasures* 45). This moment may also be related to what Mikics calls Frost's "innovative awkwardness" (*Art* 241).

ship between the "personal" quatrains and the "proverbial" couplet in the Shakespearean sonnet. In "Once by the Pacific," then, sonnet thought may conjoin with formal irony in order to allow Frost to be himself. If, in the strictly formal sense, Frost's sonnet is not quite a sonnet, it does exhibit sonnet thought—though in a more subterranean manner than Milton's Sonnet XVI.

"Once by the Pacific," however, retains rhyme and meter. What happens to sonnet thought when those strictures have disappeared? Clearly, I've been making a case for the hardiness of what I've been calling "sonnet thought" even in conjunction with loosened formal holds. In an unrhymed, untitled poem by Eamon Grennan, for example, sonnet thought is illustratively pursued through the modality of perception, though a different tenor of perception from what we find in "Once by the Pacific":

When the small hulking rock on my path along the early morning dark started
To be the skunk it really was and waddle an undulant shuffle away from me,
> *showing*
Its chiaroscuro self by the luminous leftovers of a full moon and stars, I startled

For a second or two, brought up short by the uncertain solidity of a world that keeps
Falling back to a fluency that's just the simple fact of things being plain as day
And enigmatic—that clear core we say we see in Being being merely the opaque
> *itself*

But seen without its mask for a moment, telling a truth clean as the swoop-lines
A suspension bridge has: such stolid mystery they make, and we walk on water.
> *Water*
Is like that, hitting the back of your throat with nothing but its wet cool, nothing

In or beyond it—distinct as the invisible dawnbird or a voice inside *a voice, inform-*
> *ing you. (Quick 42)*

In this ten-line poem, Grennan's 3-3-3-1 organization reduces (yet also, in a sense, retains) the Shakespearean sonnet's three quatrains and closing couplet. It is therefore with sonnet manner that he considers the deceptive solidity of the world—wherein a perceived rock is revealed to be a diaphanous chiaroscuro skunk that then embodies the Heraclitean flux of all things. Much like Milton, Grennan uses a protracted first sentence that ushers us into a world in which this degree of change is not only possible but microscopically observed, both empirically and conceptually. The journey from inductive percept (the gestalt of the perceived rock) to the speaker's self-correction depends on both "fluency" and relentless paradox. This is exemplified in the "stolid mystery" of the suspension bridge, whose "bridging" is dramatically enhanced by the enjambment introducing it ("the swoop-lines / A suspension bridge has"). Since all the poems in his aptly named *The Quick of It* comprise ten lines rather than fourteen, Grennan multiplies curtal sonnet-ness into what becomes his book's formal norm.

Here and elsewhere in *The Quick of It*, Grennan has also amplified the pentameter line of the traditional sonnet into something capacious enough to transcend metrical recognizability altogether: his approximately nine-beat lines veer off the metrical map and begin to sound similar to Whitman's expanded free verse. But this expansion doesn't prevent us from responding to the lines' patterning, particularly in their endings—as "started" (line 1) becomes "startled" (line 3); or the line break of "Water" (line 8), after ending the sentence with "water" just before it: this repetition closes an octave-of-sorts before a severely diminished sestet-as-couplet.

These two instances of "water"—the stop-and-start of *anadiplosis*—mobilize the volta. In the phrase "we walk on water," the bridge-supported "we" is imbued with miraculous, Christlike power almost at the very instant it transforms into an act common enough among persons—the act of swallowing water—as to go almost unnoticed in quotidian life. So the volta corrects bombast ("walk on water") by a rhetorical deflation ("Water / Is like that") that nevertheless celebrates the body's infrequently celebrated phenomenological experience. Tellingly, the one who knows the quotidian miracle of the water's "wet cool" is also the one who can walk on water only with the help of a bridge's "stolid mystery." This human presence is a far cry from numinous; it is the same fallible persona who could mistake a skunk for a rock in the poem's beginning—and who perhaps has also learned, with Wallace Stevens in "The American Sublime," that the sublime ultimately resolves in questions such as these: "What wine does one drink? / What bread does one eat?" (*Collected Poems* 131).

With its hypotactic syntax, its contemplation of antipodal oppositions (here, solidity and flux, finally shown to be inseparable), and its self-limiting economy of lines, Grennan's inductive and recursive journey is not unlike the other journeys we have seen in sonnet thought. As Grennan's work shows, the sonnet's peculiar twining of syntax and economy may prove profitable for a free-verse poet. This works best when the poet is pursuing a tenor of thought that necessarily chafes against—while never exceeding—the discreteness of formal limits, even if those limits are not defined as rhyme and meter.

Thus while the free-verse sonnet cannot be reduced to particular subjects or tonalities, it also cannot be content with simple narrative or description. It has to exceed itself—"almost successfully," in Stevens's terms—at the very moment of its own limitation (*Collected Poems* 350). As we have seen in sonnet thought from Milton to Grennan, this "almost-success" is indispensable both to the sonnet and to sonnet-inspired poems in our tradition. It is the lure that keeps poets returning to the sonnet as a source of challenge, inspiration, and a variety of poetic thought that the sonnet form makes possible. Clearly, as we move forward into the twenty-first century, the fascination of the sonnet both resides and builds—to the profit of those poets who continue to engage the synchronic modality of sonnet thought.

Humor Anxiety (2006)

Where is humor in the geography of contemporary American poetry? Some would say that the humorous poem has simply fallen off the map. While this may be an overstatement, it's clear that few of us come to the poetry of our age expressly looking for a laugh—or would admit to it if we did. We equate humor with entertainment and are more likely to seek it in *Curb Your Enthusiasm* than in a book of poems. Even Billy Collins's success inevitably points to humor's relative rarity in our frame of reference; many see his work as welcome relief from a poetic culture that takes itself too seriously. In short, humorous poetry remains something of an oxymoron in our increasingly hermetic literary landscape. I admit that it's still a work of prose—the maniacal description of a presumably ordinary cooking pot in Beckett's *Watt* ("it was not a pot of which one could say, Pot, pot, and be comforted")—that takes first place in my top-ten list of literary humor (81).

This is a curious state of affairs, and one that goes against the grain of what makes a poem a poem. As we know well but also sometimes forget, poetry has a bottom line, literally, that is custom-made both for complex thought and for humor; and this fact has remained unchanged over the centuries. Since the line is both the principle of organization and the vehicle of expectation in poetry, the line break—when invested properly, like money—is the tipping point, as seen in the following stanza by Sir John Suckling:

Out upon it! I have loved
    Three whole days together;
And am like to love three more,
    If it prove fair weather. ("Out upon it!" 271)

Suckling's first line break enacts a certain mock hesitation; it creates a nearly inaudible split-second of silence before the next line's deadpan deflation of the "love" in question. Similarly, the second line's ending of "together" lays the groundwork for the feminine-rhyming punch line of "If it prove fair weather." Though Suckling's work in particular is packed with comic energy, any poem is by definition a succession of stops and starts; with its seemingly limitless capacity to begin all over again at the left margin, the poem becomes an ideal micro-vehicle for what Susanne Langer calls "comic rhythm" (*Feeling* 326).

Suckling's "Out upon it!" is, of course, formal; and at first blush, formal verse would appear to be beautifully suited for humor. The French philosopher Henri Bergson thought that we laugh whenever something natural becomes mechanical—think Charlie Chaplin—and metrical poetry is a case in point (*Laughter* 39). Quite simply, it harnesses the spontaneity of speech into a predicted number of stressed syllables. But in the case of humor, not every meter is equal: if you really want to laugh, try tetrameter. According to Derek Attridge, speakers of English seem to have a visceral affinity for this songlike shorter meter, akin to 4/4 time in music, which lends itself irresistibly to nursery rhymes and other comic poems such as Andrew Marvell's "To His Coy Mistress" (Attridge, *Rhythms* 81). In the brisk clip of tetrameter, Marvell aims to show a smitten yet chaste lady what might happen if her long-term delaying of the sex act were taken to its logical extreme:

My vegetable love should grow
Vaster than empires and more slow;
An hundred years should go to praise
Thine eyes, and on thy forehead gaze;
Two hundred to adore each breast,
But thirty thousand to the rest;
An age at least to every part,
And the last age should show your heart.
For, Lady, you deserve this state,
Nor would I love at lower rate. *("To His Coy Mistress" 966)*

Here an energetic (and thus ironic) vehicle for Marvell's comically slow hypothetical blazon, tetrameter is much more than just another meter. Attridge shows it to be our basic instinct: even the solemnest of blank verse may be on the verge of breaking into rollicking four-beat song. We itch for tetrameter, Attridge suggests: when it comes to formal poetry, we want to laugh in spite of ourselves.

So where is the comedic undersong in the formal poetry that's being written today? It might be more useful to ask exactly what it means to write in form at this late date, or at the beginning of this millennium. Certainly there's a sizable and sometimes vocal minority out there that remains committed to writing metrical and rhyming poems. Yet much of that work takes very few risks on the humor front, perhaps because the formal enterprise itself has taken on a high seriousness, rather like a campaign to save an endangered species. A radical ecology may be at work here, and there's not much humor in ELF or PETA either.

Ultimately, though, it's Bergson who best diagnoses what ails contemporary poetry in this regard, regardless of the formal choices of particular poets. In order for the comic to work, he notes, we must divest ourselves of pity and empathy—emotion, in other words. "*It must not arouse our feelings*," Bergson says in italics (*Laughter* 126). Apparently we can't laugh at Beckett's hapless, ineffectual, allegorical characters if we feel empathy for them. Humor, then, blunts our humanity; it's Prozac for the soul. Couple this with post-Confessional poetry's obsession with emotional expression—what Mary Kinzie calls the "Rhapsodic Fallacy" (*Cure* 1)—as well as the worry about demoting poetry to the status of entertainment, and you've got a recipe for poetic "humor anxiety," something that might well be classed alongside "math anxiety." (Of course, these distinctions really do beg the Aristotelian question as to whether tears can be a form of entertainment in themselves.) Humor anxiety is not unique to formalist poets: it has currency nearly everywhere in contemporary poetry, with the surprising exception of the Language poets ("Within 'the problem with language' lurks a comedic element," writes Lyn Hejinian) and those who are influenced by them (Hejinian, *Language* 78).

Even so, it seems counterintuitive that the poets who do make me laugh aloud—Mark Halliday, Dean Young, and John Ashbery, to name a few—are not writers of formal verse. A classic Ashbery line like "She approached me / About buying her desk" showcases the split-second hesitation of comic rhythm that enjambment is uniquely suited to effect (*Selected Poems* 235). As postmodern and essentially speakerless as some want to claim Ashbery's work is, I would argue that his humor depends on a wicked torsion of John Stuart Mill's conception of poetry as an overheard soliloquy (Mill, "What Is Poetry?" 539). How to imagine the speaker who would intone in such an imperious and then anticlimactic manner? Ashbery's juxtaposition of mock-sanctimonious and throwaway lines—soldered by those pointed enjambments—makes us jerry-rig a character who's a hybrid of Lear's fool and the loudspeaker injunctions of the Chicago Transit Authority.

Ashbery shows the hilarity of subjectivity itself—he's the joke on solipsism. But there's another approach to humorous poetry that is anti-subjective, that divests us of personality in much the way Eliot prescribed in "Tradition and the Individual Talent." These are the poems that make use of the metapoetic: the moments in which we look to the poetic tradition with hilarious results. Such poems depend on prior knowledge of an antecedent poem, as in Kenneth Koch's infamous riff on Williams's "This Is Just to Say" ("I chopped down the house that you had been saving to live in next summer. / I am sorry, but it was morning, and I had nothing to do / and its wooden beams were so inviting"—Koch, *Collected Poems* 135) or X. J. Kennedy's "Famous Poems Abbreviated," published in the July–August 2006 issue of *Poetry*, that socked the question "Who Goes With Fergus?" right back in the younger Yeats's face:

Who will go drive with Fergus now?
You lazy cocks and cunts,
I thought I'd ask you anyhow.
Well don't all speak at once. (284)

When I first read this poem, I laughed because it diagnosed something: we *do* often feel impatience for the stripling Yeats and his Celtic twilight—his Pre-Raphaelite roods and wandering disheveled stars—long before the rough majesty of Byzantium was even a gleam in his eye. Only by knowing the older Yeats can we call the younger one funny. In such moments of laughter, then, we are serious students of the poetic tradition, almost in the way that Eliot had in mind.

And though Eliot's valuing of poetic "impersonality" does have a certain lure, it seems to me that the best humorous poems in the metapoetic tradition are the products of love—even a form of reverence. They are, in fact, the flip side of reverence, and they gainsay many of Bergson's claims about humor and its requisite deadening of emotion. In Koch's poem, we still love Williams; we're just going to have to love him differently.

Can we love our tradition well enough to laugh at it? What would be the cost of relinquishing expressivity for a while and standing a little longer on the shoulders of giants? At the very least, we have a lot of untapped resources in the realm of humor—many of which require us to look backward, even as we look ahead to the next incipient page.

Allusion and Context in Contemporary American Poetry (2010)

When I think about the role of allusion in contemporary poetry, I invariably consider the convention of the poetry *reading*. Poets know that readings are not just about standing up and reading poems. They are as much about what some call "banter," or the talk between poems, as they are about the poems themselves. Sometimes poets' banter can resemble stand-up comedy. But often, poets use this time to convey information that they want the audience to know before the poem is delivered. Though I have not done a statistical study on this phenomenon, I would wager that a large percentage of what we might call "*informational* banter" is centered on the discussion, or decoding, of allusion. This is because "banter" can do something that we often consider to be prohibited in the actual poetic act: unlike a poem, banter *explains*. It fills in allusion where the poem cannot; it foregrounds the particularities of allusion in cases where, in Erich Auerbach's terms, the allusive poem is destined to remain "fraught with background" ("From *Mimesis*" 1037).

For our purposes here, I am considering the word "allusion" in an inclusive sense in order to refer to any (intentional) textual pointing to another text or, in the words of the *New Princeton Encyclopedia of Poetry and Poetics*, "a poet's deliberate incorporation of identifiable elements from other sources, preceding or contemporaneous, textual or extratextual" (39). I am focusing on the textual in my discussion here, but with the understanding that such incorporation can consist of quotation, paraphrase, a reference to a character, or any similar modality. My concern, therefore, is not so much with the morphology of allusion but with the problem of textual reference that allusion presupposes, particularly in the present day of literary life. It may be that allusion—not syntax, form, resistance to narrative, or any other literary strategy—has cornered the market when it comes to the notion of "difficulty" in contemporary American poetry.

What I'd like to consider is the phenomenon of counteracting difficulty by "importing" lyrically articulated explanation into a poem in order to build context around allusion within the confines of the poem itself: a practice that may, in some cases, render banter obsolete. These poems may also find themselves becoming "about" allusion, as allusion and its attending narrative have a tendency to conflate. We'll see this in David Barber's "Masters of the Florilegium," from his collection *Wonder Cabinet*. At the other end of the allusive spectrum, we can find poems that eschew context and render the allusion more free-floating, as in C. D. Wright's *Deepstep Come Shining*: a long poem in which Wright has placed quotations or references almost paratactically through the work, without the protracted embedding that contextual discussion may provide. The questions, then, become the following: How much context does the reader need? How much context does *which* reader need? What is the poem's responsibility to tell the story of another text—to be an allusive storyteller? And to what degree does the poem importune the reader, instead, to become a researcher in her own right? To what degree, in other words, is the poem a goad to extratextual discovery?

These questions are particularly acute in contemporary American poetry because as poets, we cannot really assume the existence of one knowable audience with one set of literary and cultural associations. Additionally, we are such belated comers to literary history that we are dealing, even more directly than did Wallace Stevens, with the cultural extinction of allusive meaning: in other words, the diminution of a set of communal references that make allusion intelligible. For Stevens in "The Noble Rider and the Sound of Words," Plato's charioteer of winged horses in the *Phaedrus* had become, for the twentieth century reader, "antiquated and rustic" (*Necessary Angel* 4) because, in his terms, "the figure is all imagination" (6) and lacks the necessarily tempering pressures of reality that the modern reader needs. As Stevens tracks changes in the role of the imagination from Plato's time to his own, his essay necessarily raises the question of historical and cultural desuetude and the attendant difficulty of keeping time-honored allusions and references alive.

In "Masters of the Florilegium," David Barber revivifies medieval monastic reading and copying practices in what I've just defined as the explanatory mode. His poem accomplishes this by translating its own central allusion and by providing an illustrative recreation of what medieval copying entailed:

Lectionis igne—"fervent reading."
Candle-tremble and cramped longhand.
Leaves of scripture, tendrils of parable.
You bound your gleanings into vellum booklets.
You wet a fingertip and found your place.

Little anthologies, anonymous garlands.
Florilegium—"from flower to flower." (Wonder Cabinet 22)

In case there is any doubt, I want to emphasize that what I am calling "explanation" is emphatically *not* prosaic or documentarian in Barber's poem. Through poetic music, Barber dramatizes the reading process that is inseparable from a copying process. First translating *lectionis igne* as "fervent reading" for the reader of his own poem, he then goes on to illustrate what such fervent reading entails, namely "Candle-tremble and cramped longhand." In Stevens's terms, he is revivifying the "antiquated" by imaginatively inhabiting the metonymies that are attendant upon that antiquation. In a certain way, the entire poem is the definition—or dramatization—of the phrase *lectionis igne*, which was currency in the works of the church fathers. The reader has learned exactly what such activity physically entailed—as well as that "Transcription begets inspiration. / What you parse becomes a part of you" (22). And when Barber quotes the church fathers at the end of the poem, those secondary allusions further enact the process he is describing.

By defining and dramatizing *lectionis igne*, then, Barber has led us to a theory of allusion-as-creation that is both supported and gainsaid by the monks' activity. While they are able to "intermingle / Spontaneous lines, original images" when they write marginalia in the religious texts they copy, such intermingling is also supplementary and thus secondary to that main activity of copying. While it is arguable as to whether the monks' copying would constitute allusion as such, it's clear that Barber's poem does: it proceeds to dramatize, almost phenomenologically, "language shared between two literary works," in the words of Joseph Pucci (*Full-Knowing Reader* 31). Most importantly for our purposes, however, it is the totality of Barber's poem—not just the allusion or allusions themselves—that enables us to inhabit the historical context that makes the allusion intelligible.

At the other end of the spectrum is an approach that downplays rather than dramatizes the context attendant upon "language shared," and this is what we see in C. D. Wright's *Deepstep Come Shining*. Wright's progression is as follows:

Like the man who made whirligigs who said his daddy taught
him to shoot rabbits in the rocks. Maybe he meant actual rocks.

Why would anyone choose the absence of chlorophyll. Is orange
really your favorite color. Don't you just love a trumpet vine.

And if thy left eye offend thee pluck it out.

I don't know about a chicken, but a cat will eat a cast-off eye.
Chicken love. Cat eyes (come shining). (41)

Wright's entire poem progresses via ostensible non sequiturs that nevertheless prove to be eerily, inchoately connected. Here, the *almost* verbatim insertion of Matthew 5:29 ("If thy right eye offend thee, pluck it out") is unattributed, undistinguished from the rest of the passage (rather than appearing in italics, for example) that is written in Wright's voice. The humor here is that Wright's skeptical, nonplussed-yet-jaded speaker has imagined the literalized aftermath of Jesus's allegorical command to pluck out an offending eye: "I don't know about a chicken, but a cat will eat a cast-off eye." This is in keeping both with earlier lines in the passage ("Maybe he meant actual rocks") and with her poem's preoccupation with the medicalization, and therefore literalization, of the seeing lyric "eye."

As Wright insists on rendering the parable literal, as opposed to allegorical, she also necessarily removes it from the New Testament context in which it teaches a lesson on adultery. Certainly one might argue that the biblical text, especially in the demographic of the American South that implicitly underpins *Deepstep*, is well-enough known not to need the kind of contextualization that Barber provided for *lectionis igne*. Yet one could also argue this question in the opposite way, by asserting that this passage dramatizes what happens when the context of allusion is elided from poems in our current day and age. When that happens, according to this potential reading, the allegorical import of the original is lost. This is because a reader who cannot read allusively is doomed to read only literally; in that sense, decontextualization might mean the enforced emptying of allegorical meaning. Wright is amused by this possibility (and when we read her poem, we might be too), but there is another way the passage rings sinister—or at least rings disquieting: that is, the Matthew text is presented and responded to *as if* it were not an allusion at all. While Barber uses allusion both to idealize and to concretize the metonymic practice of a certain kind of writing body, Wright literalizes an allusion that is meant to be read allegorically—thereby voiding the separation between texts that, in some sense, makes allusion possible in the first place.

At this point in the discussion, you might be expecting me to pronounce judgment on one allusive modality or the other: to laud Barber's Virgilian guidance of the reader or instead to prescribe Wright's knowing wink as a more democratic mobilization of reader activation. Unfortunately, I don't think the question is that simple, nor can it be settled by an appeal to the difference between lyric (more traditional) and experimental poetic practices. Both Wright and Barber are, to my mind, profoundly and genuinely allusive poets who are implicitly addressing and incorporating the reader in different ways. Both perceive themselves and their work as gateways to other texts. We can see this in Wright's list of intertexts that she names "Stimulants, Poultices, Goads" at the end of *Deepstep* (and that also includes the artist fellows at Virginia Center for the Creative Arts in 1996—109). For his part, Barber provides a copious set of "Notes and Sources" at the end of *Wonder Cabinet*. Clearly, however, the two poets construct their gateways in different manners, and they build them from different materials.

The greater question, then, becomes this: How are we afforded access to the poet's discrete set of allusive knowledge? Such a question necessarily transfers our attention from poem to poet—as, after all, this essay began with a consideration of the poet as public reader. On the one hand,

I instinctively resist such a movement: one wants to see allusion as textual, intrinsic to the poem itself. But as Tobias Gregory has said of Milton, "Sonnet [XVI] was full of Biblical echoes because Milton's mind was"; and that statement may be even more germane today, since allusion is more privatized and less communally "owned" than it was in Milton's time ("Murmur" 25). How, then, do "explanatory" or "paratactic" poets afford readers access to their own cognitive universes of allusion? Today more than ever, poets must grapple with the element of the social or dialogic—the complicated role of the audience or reader—when they work allusively. This means, often implicitly, constructing the role of the reader within the poem.

This idea introduces the last element I'd like to discuss here: the way that allusion is either naturalized or not within the context of the poem in question. The more a poet teaches, marks, or locates the context of allusion in his poem, the more dialogic and social—and the less "naturalized"—the allusive work becomes. By doing these things, in other words, the poet marks allusion as something more than a "given": he stands outside his own textual universe in order to do the deictic or indexical work of presenting it to someone else. When it comes to allusion, context is show-and-tell. Pointing—contextually speaking—implies that there is someone to point *for*, even if there are no first- or second-person pronouns involved in the poem at all (in our case, both Barber and Wright have employed the second person to very different ends). This is the work that W. R. Johnson has considered in the context of Greek monody as "a speaker, or singer, talking to, singing to, another person or persons" (*Idea* 3).

On the other hand, a poet like Wright treats the allusion as naturalized—or as if the poet's universe of allusion is a given: understandable and/or identifiable without the aid of context. This is a large assumption to make—and would be more in line with Johnson's discussion of the modern "meditative" lyric that has voided the "I-You" pronominal relation foregrounded in classical poetic performance (*Idea* 6–7). Wright's practice also echoes what Barbara Johnson has found in Mallarmé. For Johnson, Mallarmé's repetition of Baudelairean "L'Azur" was more of an intertextual tic than a full-fledged use of allusion; Mallarmé was a poet who could not necessarily separate his own diction from that of his predecessor, but this would hardly make him unique among poets (Johnson, *World* 120). Barber's poem addresses precisely this phenomenon by noting that "What you parse becomes a part of you" (*Wonder Cabinet* 22). There is thus a fine line between the intentionality of allusion and a more free-floating intertextuality; and the less-explanatory allusive poet necessarily straddles that line. In its very refusal to explain, the more paratactically allusive poem, no matter how experimental its strategies, can fall prey to the age-old Language critique of lyric as privileging the subjectivity of the "speaker" over the multifarious desires and experiences of the reader.

In these ways, allusion can become a test case for how poets, and poems, select and construct their readers in the present day. I hope to have suggested here that although allusion can be allied with the notion of difficulty in contemporary poetry, there is nothing intrinsically difficult about allusive practice as such; what is paramount instead is the manner in which a poet incorporates allusion into her poem. In the microscopic perspective that a single allusion affords, we can catch a glimpse of the way that a poet constructs an ideal reader: either one who submits to being "taught" by the poet's inclusion of allusive context; or, on the other hand, one who either (1) shares the erudite set of allusions attendant upon the poet's work or (2) relishes the opportunity of research and further discovery that the poem provides simply by virtue of having *not* provided the context that would render the allusion fully intelligible to most audiences. Is the latter a more "active" reader? Perhaps so, but that activity may come at the expense of the pleasure afforded by a more immediate understanding. Or perhaps pleasure migrates away from the perimeters of the poem itself. Or perhaps, in Barber's terms, we must study hard in order to perform "fervent reading" (22). But however we choose to value the reading process, it is clear that allusion is a portal not only to other texts, but to a poet's ideals, concepts, and fantasies about the reader's role.

Ed Roberson's Inward Lyricism (2008)

"There is no one else like Ed Roberson," reads the book jacket description of Roberson's *Voices Cast Out to Talk Us In* (1995)—"certainly there is no other poet like him." Seldom has a book jacket spoken so succinctly and so truly. Roberson's poems leave you with the ineffable feeling that they are simply sui generis, bringing together areas of concern that are not usually found under one rubric: ecological systems and Black history in the United States; biology and questions of "inspiration"; pointedly vernacular and arcane scientific diction—all articulated by way of an infallible ear, and with an inwardness that casts a spell strangely reminiscent of Yvonne Rainer's choreography in *Trio A*. (Interdisciplinarity is essential, in fact, to the Atelos publishing project, which is edited by Lyn Hejinian and Travis Ortiz.)

Roberson is a seeming oxymoron. Though his fractured syntax and page divisions make for something that looks and smells and tastes like experimental writing, it is worlds away from the punning and playful experimentalism decried by Tony Hoagland in the March 2006 issue of *Poetry*. Unlike the poets for whom sense and signification ebb quite happily away, Roberson's linguistic experiments are rooted in a very concrete and knowable world of historical and ecological reference. In his seventh collection, *City Eclogue* (2006), he has once again given us poetry that is both beautiful and necessary—as misunderstood and misused as those evaluations admittedly often are.

In order to begin explaining these judgments, let me turn to another book jacket. Roberson's author biography on *City Eclogue* reads like this:

> Ed Roberson was born and raised in Pittsburgh, Pennsylvania. In addition to writing poetry, he has pursued a variety of remarkable interests. He has worked as a limnologist (conducting research on inland and coastal

fresh water systems in Alaska's Aleutian Islands and in Bermuda), and for a period he was employed as a diver for the Pittsburg Aquazoo (training porpoises, among other things). . . . Twice Ed Roberson was a team member on the Explorers' Club of Pittsburgh's South America Expeditions, in which context he climbed mountains in the Peruvian and Ecuadorian Andes and explored the upper Amazonian jungle in eastern Ecuador. He has motorcycled across the USA.

Though I've argued elsewhere against putting too much stock in poets' life experience, I must admit that there's an unusual pleasure to be had in reading, even briefly, about a poet training porpoises. In a generic sense, though, I read Roberson's thumbnail biographical sketch as narrative; and in my mind, this presence of narrative—even as a Derridean parergon to the actual "text" of the book—acts as a necessary counterweight to the aspects of his poetry that legitimately resist narrative teleology. In short, Roberson's poetry has not abandoned narrative. Instead it hears, and speaks, narrative *as* experiment. This strategy seems to show that certain narratives—the collective narrative of Black people in this country, for example—are traumatic enough to resist closure or univocal representation, and so they need to be revisited recursively. Roberson must revisit and reinhabit these stories from inside, and in his own brilliantly scuttled idiolect.

What remains, even in poems that are dense and intellectual enough to resist the "pedestrian" reader, is the human and very serious necessity of narrative resistance as a form of cultural resistance. Despite an ear for the elliptical—and one that results in an oblique, conceptual music that is often antilyric in feel—Roberson is not an Elliptical poet, in Stephanie Burt's formulation (*Smokes* review 58). Ed Roberson's worldview is not one in which language eclipses, or unmoors itself from, world or story or history. Despite—or perhaps because of—his idiosyncratic ear, he has never abandoned the referent, even while giving voice to the breathtaking cerebration that allows him to commingle image and concept in unexpected ways.

In *City Eclogue*, Roberson turns his eye and ear to the razing and dubious renewal of city neighborhoods. Though he is concerned with the effects of demolition and gentrification on Black populations, Roberson also places racial experience within the confines of an encompassing

ecology, one that includes the nonhuman. The oxymoron of the title
City Eclogue itself, in which pastoral abuts the urban, speaks to the capacious and eclectic worldview that drives these poems. Roberson's interest
in ecology, and the ecological implications of social and demographic
movements, has carried through his last few books and is encapsulated
in such remarkable lines as the following:

The buildings stood, a bunch of
garbage odd-size barges

lashed together between the currents
of the railroad and river, scuttled

sinking upend into an oily sky,

they are made   into land people pour into
to colonize   as artificial reef is

sunk next to dying corals
on the sea floor   such housing. (City Eclogue 41)

In a way, "such housing" is the twenty-first-century offshoot of Gwendolyn Brooks's "kitchenette building," in which the inhabitants of
Bronzeville—a Black neighborhood in Chicago's South Side—cannot
recognize a personified dream even as it sings an aria, fighting with the
building's garbage (*Selected Poems* 3). (Perhaps not accidentally, Roberson's city is elsewhere populated by "twisted / chrome-less tubing of
cheap kitchenettes"—*City Eclogue* 74.) But Roberson's world is less peo-
pled than Brooks's and more tectonic in scale. He sees urbanization itself
as colonization; in the context of this poem, it is Black Americans who
colonize the buildings' "garbage barges," whose startling internal rhyme
heaps metaphor upon metaphor: "they are made   into land people pour
into / to colonize." Unlike the intimacy and volubility of Brooks's hall-
ways and bathrooms, the sense here is one of reserved documentary. If
there are no named characters left in Roberson's universe, what we feel
instead is the import of the human figure emptied out—in a gesture, or

geste, that is stylized yet consonant with many empirical aspects of the postmodern world as we know it. Within the abandoned or condemned buildings in *City Eclogue*, the human body is continually splintered as synecdoche. For example, "Someone Reaching through a Window" is a sketch of two hands in a window, as seen from the street (124).

Ghosts of buildings and of populaces: in many ways, *City Eclogue* embodies what Ilya Kutik describes (in a conversation with Reginald Gibbons) as Russian metarealism's "vision that is *both* epic, in that it is impersonal rather than lyric, *and* yet subjective, in that it evokes feeling" (Gibbons, "Russian Meta-realist Poetry" 23). Roberson's epic-yet-subjective representation portrays a disposable culture that makes and unmakes with impunity, as seen in his use of the white space that injects visual pressure into the metaphor of the building-garbage-barges "made into land." This instance of "making" is more sinister than its etymological origins in *poesis*—the poetic "making" in which Roberson apparently still has faith, as seen in a poem like "Painting from Science for Hui Ka-Kwong" (*City Eclogue* 90). Yet much of what the poet makes in *City Eclogue* is a regretful, elegiac, and necessarily discontinuous catalog of a culture that itself makes artificial reefs—another form of colonization, this time of the biosphere—that for Roberson become metaphors for the garbage-barges that one can colonize but never truly inhabit.

Roberson has long used white space within his lines as super-acute and magnified caesurae, and such spaces uniquely inflect the urban and demographic concerns that drive this volume in particular. White space formally demarcates the aftermath of demolition, especially when used in conjunction with such rhetorical figures as aposiopesis, or the unfinished sentence. In "The Open," Roberson describes the sublimated emptiness that accrues after buildings are razed:

Their buildings razed.   they ghosts
*   their color that haze of plaster dust*

their blocks of bulldozed air opened to light
*   take your breath as much*

by this kind of blinding choke as by the loss felt
*   in the openness (63)*

"They ghosts" immediately acts as anacoluthon: it twists into vernacular, flown loose from any moderating punctuation, in a startling mark of what's gone. The passage enacts the peculiarly modern, and not simply postmodern or post-9/11, specter of urban openness; the "haze of plaster dust" becomes a metonymic and literal ghosting of familiar buildings. Roberson's cities are living organisms, partially brought into being by the workings of metaphor; but like the artificial reef I discussed previously, their fates are in the hands of a capitalist oligarchy, or what Roberson calls "the scrub of money" (65). This is a ruthless cleanness that situates itself in opposition to the ubiquitous garbage that colonizes the volume. Clearly, the notion of the "open" has a certain aesthetic currency; but in the context of an urban environment, Roberson sees such openness as both unnatural and economically determined. Openness, then, signifies what has been razed and the people who have been displaced: "People lived where it weren't open / a people whose any beginning is disbursed / by a vagrant progress" (63–64). And importantly, it's in "the most recent open field I've crossed" that "Black people get stopped regularly / to show they have university / I.D." (88).

Such is the return, in *City Eclogue* as so often in Roberson's poetry, to the primal scene (or the Lacanian Real) as it inflects Black history in America. In "Sit in What City We're In," Roberson employs the trope of the mirror to describe a lunch counter in the South during segregation, morphing sinuously into the "sitting" of demonstration:

> we are
> a nation facing ourselves our back turned
> on ourselves   how
> that reflection sat in demonstration
> of   each face
> mirror reflecting into mirror generates
>
> a street cobbled of the heads of
> our one
> long likeness
> the infinite regressions.
> The oceans, themselves one,   catch their image

> *hosed by riot cops down the gutter into*
> The sphere surface
> river
>
> > *looked into   reflects*
> > *one face.   (27–28)*

This passage captures the simultaneous empathy and impersonality of the worldview articulated in *City Eclogue*, as the mirror becomes the oceans that unseeingly capture the images of the protestors' heads "hosed by riot cops down the gutter," thus enacting the obverse of poetry's predilection to "give face" in the rhetorical figure of prosopopoeia. The torque of dropped lines and imploded clauses enacts the horror of seamlessness: during segregation, race was seen as monolithic, without differences within it, or "our one long likeness"; here, unspeaking nature "sees" it the same way. This is, ultimately, the scope of the epic. But Roberson's recasting of a Lacanian mirror remains far from any quietist version of "conceptual."

Throughout *City Eclogue*, the apparitions and fallouts of cities and history come preternaturally alive in Ed Roberson's hands. Since he is a master poet cross-hatched with a hard-edged conceptual thinker, Roberson is uniquely suited to present systemic concerns through a complex lens. He has a visceral sense of the drift and heft of language—the resistance that language, in its various guises, poses to the world, and yet the way that history's exigencies necessarily prevent a poetry that is "all language." The result is poetry that creates real music while unflinchingly reflecting—as in the ocean's reflection of the protestors' heads—the demolitions of history. *City Eclogue* is a great achievement, both monument and cenotaph, by a poet whose distinction is incontrovertible and from whom we can only hope to hear more, and more.

Light in Nagasaki

Catherine McCarthy's *We Walk on Jewels* (2003)

"This is the light of the mind," wrote Sylvia Plath, "cold and planetary" (*Collected Poems* 172). Plath's words might well describe Catherine McCarthy's painting *Cold Comfort*, in which an imminently galactic region is hosted by X-rays of flowers, mad seahorses, and carp. But *Cold Comfort* is only one province in McCarthy's greater geography of light. Her work charts the light of the mind as it changes: lambent or theatrical, gilding or shadowing. Each of her paintings is a plural world that is fluid and syntactic, jeweled and eidetic, crabbed and musical.

Over the past decade, McCarthy has navigated a nether region of thought, dream, and interior monologue: the bed in which Van Eyck might lie down with Revlon; the shores where sieves and hoopskirts commingle. She casts a painterly net, and her catch becomes symphonic. Her use of the copied image—whether a landscape painting by Kensett or a silhouette from a children's reader—relocates familiar sights to idiosyncratic sites, much as a page of poetry renovates words we thought we knew. (We have seen them all before, surely, but never *here*.) And her titles themselves are poetic exhalations: phrases from poems written or unwritten.

McCarthy's use of paint is formidable. But her art is also preternaturally verbal, since her mind echoes even as it stencils. In this way, we can reimagine Roland Barthes's equation of text and tissue in *The Pleasure of the Text*. McCarthy creates a painterly tissue of borrowed images and words whose fibers interweave to create a climate of intricate beauty, strange yet familiar in the way that Freud spoke of the uncanny, or *Unheimlich*. This is our necessary sense of strangeness in the home space: the artist's inchoate and fruitful alienation from her or his or their own history.

And this, too, is the splitting from the everyday self that makes art itself possible, as well as enabling the ideological and cultural critiques that art can render. Hence the figure of Nagasaki Moon, McCarthy's Japanese alter ego who inhabits some of the paintings in *We Walk on Jewels*. Nagasaki is a figure whose bearing is borrowed from nineteenth-century Japanese painting, and she has put on the white guise of the geisha or the Noh mask. Yet Nagasaki, whose name sorrowfully echoes the ravages of the Second World War, is also a character divested of narrative. In these paintings, she is a pawn or a cipher, as seen through Western eyes: coifed, clothed, and ripe for transport.

A rhythm of departure animates these paintings. In the sinuous lines of its bridge and waterways, *We Have Always Lived in the Castle* directs the eye in a small journey, even as Nagasaki rises statue-like between the snows. The boats in *Sayonara* and *The Letter His Wife Is Writing* are echoed poignantly in *Greener*, as Nagasaki Moon soberly examines a miniature boat. And the melancholy nature of the miniature recalls Rimbaud's drunken boat transformed into the coveted, impossible toy at the end of that famous poem: "un bateau frêle comme un papillon de mai" [a frail boat like a May butterfly] ("Le Bateau ivre").

The explorers and sailors of McCarthy's 1999 *Upon a Lilac Sea* series have implicitly reached their port in Nagasaki, the culmination of colonialist enterprise. Yet other delicate boats are still on course—as in *Sayonara*, which is a valediction with shoes. Here women's pumps crest upended on the waves, much like talismans. Stiletto boots become whimsical compasses, pointing Janus-like in opposite directions as a boat arcs away toward the greener shores of the painting's background. Such is McCarthy's invitation to the voyage as orbit: transport without destination, eternal delight. *Metaphor*, we remember, is neither more nor less than etymological *transport*. And Barthes is not wrong about pleasure: these are the dreams we would have if we could.

As in the most filigreed of dreams, these painted surfaces are densely and exquisitely composite. Wide swaths of paint serve to curtain or to clothe the pristine outlines of hillocks, huts, and trees populating Japanese landscape paintings and woodblock prints. McCarthy both requires and represents two modalities of vision: focus and wash. The latter is the grazing eye, while the former names the eye engaged in what Richard Wollheim has called "seeing-in" ("Spectator" 105). For McCarthy, paint can mime the kaleidoscopic verbs implicit in vision, as well as its objects.

In *We Have Always Lived in the Castle*, named after the Shirley Jackson novel, Nagasaki Moon foregrounds a stylized landscape in which white paint drips as icicles on pine trees. The ceremonial curve of her parasol and her coat's fur collar have also been lavished as unapologetic strokes of paint—a gesture that would be absent from the intentional flatness of the nineteenth-century Japanese tradition McCarthy is invoking (an association not lost on Lichtenstein, as he aged). We sense the flourish *within* the borrowed elements. And the underside of the parasol is pure gold, Byzantine in its inflections.

McCarthy's paintings speak in dialects—not one, but many. Her rich sediment of verbal and painterly signs has always occupied the hinterland between legibility and opacity. In her earlier work, letters stutter; print "copies" of never-before-seen words such as *eitherandible* and *brideness* wink in mock authority. Her paintings have long enacted the ululation of our preverbal flight into language, the longevity of the Kristevan *chora* (*Revolution* 25).

Of course, Asian art has for centuries recognized a necessary permeability between text and image, and the guise of the Japanese character—character as writing, not to mention character as persona—feels organic for McCarthy. In several of the paintings that comprise *We Walk on Jewels*, the artist's own haiku has been transliterated. Opaque to those who are not Japanese speakers, this haiku hovers in the visual field, invested with the same dignified mobility that characterizes McCarthy's use of the Roman alphabet. Still, the Japanese character may be more acrobatic than our letters, straddling the fluent line between picture and word, image and syntax. And now a tentacle of black ink scribbles over the Nagasaki figure in *Greener* with the unmistakable velocity of writing.

But as in McCarthy's larger body of work, paint is also commensurate with the artist's love for the fabric, the liquid, the tactile: the pools and cambric catching our eye and hand as we move as bodies through the phenomenal world. And these become the swatches that we wish returned to us at night within our own private theaters of dreaming. And now the lush curtain of paint opens in *The Letter His Wife Is Writing*, releasing birdsong as it ripples. We are suddenly privy to a lucid and lapidary dream we cannot forget.

"Some Chant I'm Working At" (2009)

Read in its entirety, Jane Mead's new collection *The Usable Field* has a texture that is reminiscent of both unbroken dream and of the perceptual field experienced by someone who is almost too awake. It is on the cusp of such a distinction that this book's considerable value resides. Mead's voice, with its sometimes impoverished and always ravishing frequencies, reveals this liminal place—located, incidentally, on a vineyard in Northern California—as home.

The Usable Field is not quite a dream book, not quite a landscape book, nor exactly a book of elegies—though in another sense, it is all of these. It is first and foremost a book about the phenomenology of personhood finding its integrity and often its literal bearings in a world that, though familiar, feels perennially unmapped—a place in which persons must search not only for the content of the soul, but also for the delineation of its very boundaries. There is a certain sort of phenomenological, not to say philosophical, motion sickness at the core of Mead's work; and it invariably governs the way the poet perceives the world, whether as landscape or as human relation. The insistence (and morphology) of her search for boundary and delineation may be found in two passages from two different poems:

—*your*
deer-colored dog

is loping in the
deer-colored grass
in the morning. Nowhere

are you where we are not. *(Usable Field 56)*

And:

In grief the pilot knows you—
no need to say take me to my so-called soul—
she is your so-called soul: she knows
you will be waiting when she lands—she wants
you to be with her if you drown. (63)

In the first passage, the metonymic spillage of a deer's color creates a gestalt wherein the observed animal—the dog—becomes indistinguishable from its surroundings ("your / deer-colored dog / is loping in the / deer-colored grass"). This collapse of figure and ground is emotionally borne out by the authority of the italicized insight that follows: any geographic or conceptual distinction between the "you" and the "we" has dissolved. In the second quotation—so eerily reminiscent of Adrienne Rich's "Twenty-One Love Poems," in which the pilot keeps "*keeps / on steering headlong into the waves, on purpose*" (*Dream* 31)—the female pilot not only "knows you" but "*is* your so-called soul," as proximity becomes a disquieting transitivity-as-intimacy: "she wants / you to be with her if you drown." In both of these instances, the self, even while on the verge of dissolution, retains its strange perspicuity and indeed its skepticism ("so-called soul") in the face of the categories that define itself and its relation to others, whether human or nonhuman. This is a voice that, as we are told elsewhere, was given "to believe in nothing // before [it] believed / in the jay" (*Usable Field* 50).

In the preceding passages, we can also hear the plain style sounded out in dissonant notes. With her paradoxical combination of stuttering and oracular sureness, Mead is echoing and yet resisting the musics of several women poets before her: Dickinson, the H.D. of *Trilogy*, and even Louise Bogan (Mead's "High Cliff Coming," for example, is very reminiscent of Bogan's later "Night" and "Morning" poems—*Blue Estuaries* 130–131). It is most gratifying to hear the poet listening so intently to this aspect of her voice. The pitch of this book is consequently higher than in some of her previous work, which sometimes erred on the side of flatness; but I also sense that her distrust of high lyricism abides.

Such distrust reveals itself most often on the micro level—for example, in the occasional obstreperous diction choice such as "bleep," which can intentionally ruin a higher and more musical pitch of declaration. Though these moments can jar, I am convinced that this infinitesimal ruination is what keeps Mead's poetry in an authentic relation to itself. So much contemporary poetry lacks precisely this sense that the line, and the poem itself, must function apotropaically (as a formal and materialized defense against other possibilities of verbal incarnation). Helen Vendler makes this point when she writes the following of Whitman: "[O]ne ought to mention as well the temptations that the poet's mind encounters along the way . . . and how these are staved off or (in some cases) yielded to" (*Poets Thinking* 39). In Mead's own words, we may discern in her work "a cavern of darkness / where the phrase is missing / at the bottom of music" (*Usable Field* 28). The traces of the unwritten, even (or especially) as resolved in the often harmonic surfaces of high lyricism, are what make poems worth reading; otherwise, they become simply machines or verbal exercise.

It is also unusual to find a book of poetry that is not explicitly "themed," narratively or otherwise, exhibiting the degree of tonal cohesion found in *The Usable Field*. In this way, Mead finds her model in Louise Glück, who has always known how to materialize a mental state symphonically in a succession of poems. The poems in *The Usable Field* unapologetically reflect emotional extremes (Mead addresses the heart directly, in a poem titled after it) as well as the slow deliberation attendant upon ratiocination. Mead heightens this effect with a consciously anachronistic use of doubled punctuation such as a comma coupled with a dash; even the poems' titles incorporate this strategy at times. "Same Audit, Same Sacrifice" is how one poem's title encapsulates the book's characteristic duality of shrewdness and lyric drama (57). In short, the impression we get is of something driven, something true—not "true" in a confessional sense, but true in the sense of Glück's own argument "against sincerity" (*Proofs* 33). The poems are not worked up; they give the impression of having emanated directly from a particular insistence of thought and—much rarer—of emotion as well, no matter how alloyed the nature of that emotion might be. It need hardly be said again that the effect here is often Dickinsonian.

"This is some chant I'm working at—" writes Mead in her book's first line after its proem (3). Chant and work: two words that don't necessarily dovetail in the mind of the reader. Yet Mead has coupled them to make a truer trajectory. I would also suggest that Mead "trues," as carpentry—in the material, emotional, and intellectual senses. How beautifully she has inaugurated a collection that is infused throughout with the combined and paradoxical virtues of simplicity, lyricism, and unstinting thought.

An Elegy for Dancing (2010)

> In the modern sense of the term, the elegy is a short poem, usually formal or ceremonious in tone and diction, occasioned by the death of a person. Unlike the dirge, threnody, obsequy, and other forms of pure lament or memorial, however, and more expansive than the epitaph, the elegy frequently includes a movement from expressed sorrow toward consolation.
> —*NEW PRINCETON ENCYCLOPEDIA OF POETRY AND POETICS*

Is it possible to write an elegy in prose? And if so, could it be an allegorical elegy? An elegy, that is, for an aspect of the self that has been lost, or for one in regression or remission? This essay—this *attempt*, to paraphrase the French *essayer*—will try to be just that: a prose elegy for a dancing self, replete with some small measure of sorrow and a motion toward self-consolation. Because I never chose not to dance; chronic pain and injury chose it for me.

The kinesthetic sense of dancing is something I've only tried to describe in poems (though more often, my poems have included the vocabulary of dance rather than the so-called "experience" of it). But by definition, a poem may have what Lucie Brock-Broido has called an "autistic" quality: "I think of poems as autistic, in the sense that they're trapped in extremity's small room—they're large thoughts that don't get to speak in prose" ("Conversation" 146). Though we might question or quarrel with Brock-Broido's precise definition of *autistic*, it's clear to me that she is referring to something like the preverbal synergies that animate the best poems: what Kristeva discussed as the *chora* (*Revolution* 25). Such energy also makes for some salutary conceptual blindness, a blindness not unlike the kind that fascinated Paul de Man (*Blindness* 106). But even when I write in prose about my experience, I'll probably never see it clearly—especially since I'm trying to recreate something as performance-bound, as ephemeral in time and space, as the act of dancing.

· · ·

I remember the beauty of the open studio, its floor a smooth black tarp called Marley. Doubled by the mirrors, it became a broad and virtual terrain—but sprung so the balls of our feet were rendered torque, traction, instrument. The quality of the floor is paramount for the dancer: too hard, and jumps become belly flops. And the risk of injury is that much greater.

We would all warm up, stretching before class. I was very flexible, as I am today: *hypermobility* is what a doctor recently called it. But despite my flexibility and high extensions of the leg, despite my training and smallness and devotion to class week after week, I was not a good dancer and never would be. I could not learn combinations—the nuts and bolts, the stitching together of steps in muscle memory—and couldn't figure out why, since I had taken classes for many years. A teacher once said on this subject, "Either you have it or you don't"—and for the first time, I had wondered whether there might be something constitutional or synaptic that was getting in the way of such learning: something different from but analogous to dyslexia, for example. (One of my best friends from college has had no sense of smell from birth. Even at the age of twenty-one, he tried to keep it secret. He was ashamed: he thought he'd failed to learn something essential as a child.)

But I had dancing in the blood, and so I chose to struggle—or more aptly, to remain in a chronic state of nonmastery. My favorite teacher, Cheri, was fond of sinuous combinations; according to her professional biographical statement, she was interested in *dynamic physicality with lyrical phrasing, and the dancer's relationship to space.* I had never encountered someone so exacting and yet unflappable, someone with so much public equanimity. She could sense the precise lay of vertebrae beneath a sweatshirt. She grabbed my hips and manhandled me across the Marley. She moved my head one inch to the left. I never spoke to her in the personal way, as Louise Glück puts it in "Matins" (*Wild Iris* 13). But her smile, true and impersonal, really could carry a whole room of bodies. I came to see the way her muscles moved. The delicate weight of the head on those shoulders. And I stored that persona somewhere for future reference.

I talked very little, in or after class. I had the requisite sharp ribs and hipbones, but none of the physical or social ease of the other dancers:

that garrulous love of surfaces that characterizes so many who live the life of theater and performance. One famous choreographer claimed that dancers are stupid: indeed, from the point of view of a dance creator, they can be as pawns on a board. Objects. In *Stupidity*, Avital Ronell calls the dummkopf "a creature of mimesis" and goes on to say that "the only thing that the stupid have over the smart is mechanical memory" (16–17). Movement memory, unthinking mimesis: it surely wasn't stupidity in the usual sense, but successful dancers really did seem to have something that I didn't. I might call it now a sustained capacity for self-relinquishment: some talent for askesis or self-emptying, in the Christian and Bloomian sense, that allowed them to move as complexly disciplined, regulated bodies unfolding and changing in space.

Conversely, I could see my own movements only as a static sequence of flat poses: there was something vaguely Cubist about it all. I had the vocabulary, but I couldn't get the syntax. I was stupid, but in a different way. In Roman Jakobson's structuralist terms, I was an aphasic dancer: I had contiguity disorder, or "impairment of the ability to propositionize, or generally speaking, to combine simpler linguistic entities into more complex units" ("Closing Statement" 85). And my teacher kept adjusting the back of my neck, the spot at which the head connects to the rest of the body—the trapezius, I believe. If you think "trapeze," you might imagine where my mind was then as I rode the buses in Boston. A trapeze of consciousness unmoored from flesh. Evidently I was trying to be two places at once, and not succeeding. As Peggy Phelan says, "The body does not experience the world in the way that consciousness does" (*Mourning Sex* 52).

My brain works. I can think on my feet. And my body is light and quick. But it was tough to get them all together; and that was what I needed (to paraphrase Irigaray). The struggle to learn kinesthetically, so natural for some, was for me a continually and somatically articulated version of stage fright. There's no faking what your feet won't do.

As graduate students, we learn how to parry, how to inhabit the position of mastery until it feels natural. When I attended talks during my PhD program in comparative literature, I heard nonanswers to questions that would continue for minutes upon eloquent minutes. That mantle of mastery was something I was learning to put on during the day, but at night it was all drum and piano—putting my body out there and hoping some beauty, some articulation, could come of these muscles. And as in the academy, the demand was always changing. I could practice at home, but that would never really prepare me for the new movement phrases I would have to learn the next week.

Once I heard my teacher speaking before class started. "Why is it that no matter how long I've done this, I always feel like I'm starting all over again?" she said with a small laugh. It sounded like me—or it sounded like what I would have said if I could. At that time, I was always looking for people who seemed to have access to what I was sure were universal secrets, the secrets that I had never been told. But I know now that she was referring to the terribly mundane task of remaking the self every day, as we make beds: to take ourselves in hand over the blank page, for example; to keep prodding what intrinsically wants to rest on the side of the road; to keep exposing what wants to cover its face, to turn to the wall. "To write is to take a retest every day," Ronell says (*Stupidity* 26).

What we need, in order to do this successfully or at least consistently, is something like the opposite of multitasking. Dance class with Cheri required nothing less than my every stray cognitive faculty: a concentration that left no room for anything else. This was fight-or-flight, a tincture of everyday panic. There was no room for what Sven Birkerts has deplored as our current state of "distracted absorption" (*Gutenberg Elegies* 206) in the face of electronic media, as opposed to his description of the *print* reader's near-beatific and bodily focus, a state of being "bathed in the energies of the book" (84). This is a beautiful and untranslatable concentration that is necessarily operative in the reading act, as Wallace Stevens knew in "The House Was Quiet and the World Was Still":

The words were spoken as if there was no book
Except that the reader leaned above the page,

Wanted to lean, wanted much most to be
The scholar to whom his book is true . . . (Collected Poems 358)

Even in its circumscription, Stevens's poem describes a bodily lancination: that *leaning* wherein the book as vehicle disappears so that the world becomes the reader who has become the reading act associated with askesis and, not coincidentally, with the act of leaning itself: "the reader leaning late and reading there" (359). No less absorbing is the movement-learning process, the ways we marshal our muscles into performance. Perhaps my version of askesis didn't result in the performance I saw in other dancers, but I too forgot myself in the very effort. All of this seems related, as well, to the process by which we learn poems "by heart," or the ways that we manage to put poems into the body.

But any story we tell also censors another, and my elegy for dancing must also include a second narrative. In college I had taken a workshop with a dancer who taught the work of Isadora Duncan and Mary Wigman, the German expressionist choreographer. In Boston a few years afterward, I had the opportunity to see the Duncan choreography again, performed by a two-dancer company called Dances by Isadora. It's fair to say that I was transfixed by these brief dances to Chopin and Schubert pieces, performed by two women who were exquisitely attuned to each other's every glance and arm movement: one curly-haired with a round body; one slender and dimpled, with long hair. Their movements were both expressive and imitative: of spring and joy, of sleeping and waking, of mythological figures such as the Muses. Though neither of these dancers has ever become famous in the dance world, I still count their performance as one of the genuinely awe-inspiring things I have seen in my life; and I was fortunate to be able to take class, eventually, with both of them.

At the beginning of the twentieth century, Isadora Duncan positioned her new technique in opposition to balletic virtuosity, though ballet dancers are sometimes drawn to it for reasons of aesthetic and gestural similarities between the two approaches. Nevertheless, there's an intentional check on virtuosity in Duncan: the feet are not stretched to a full arch in point, the arms are not held in poses, and students practice simple steps such as walking and running. It wasn't virtuosity as such that moved me in the performance of Dances by Isadora, but instead the nuance of each movement: the grace note, the eye contact. The miracle is in the transition, as Susan Foster describes:

> [I]n her *Waltzes* (ca 1913), a series of short dances to music that Duncan described as the "many faces of love," the dancer *resembles* innocent adoration, sensuous pleasure, playful flirtation, and other aspects of love during individual phrases of the dance by moving with the sustained weight

of reverence, the quick lightness of play, or the shimmering undulations of sensuality. Transitional phrases between these individual sections, however, show the dancer as a person experiencing love in its various manifestations. During these transitions the movement flows from the center of the body out to the periphery, suggesting a progressive development from "inner" feeling to "outward" form and an organic relationship between one emotional experience and the next. (*Reading Dancing* 71)

This ritual rediscovery and treasuring of another person, dramatized again and again in the choreography, amounts to both a romance and an ethics. As I wrote several years later in a poem that did not directly address the subject, "The slowly lowered head / means more than virtuosity" (*Restoration* 14). The technique is also a latter-day oral tradition, passed down from the girls Duncan adopted and taught.

Duncan class was very different from Cheri's (which I took concurrently). In Duncan training, the barre exercises were the same every week: the same music, the same movements. Once you had the basics down, learning combinations was not an integral part of the practice; the order of the day was repetition rather than combination or innovation. We learned a repertoire of dances—some of the same ones that I had seen Dances by Isadora perform.

With the movements explicitly yoked to the breath in a way that doesn't happen in most modern dance classes, the Duncan technique was, in some sense, more like meditation than dancing, though we moved and ran and executed a whole barre in addition to fully choreographed dances. Maybe it's more accurate to say that due to its familiarity, the repertoire allowed for more serenity and contemplation than had been possible for me in class before. It became a known quantity. I brought my shyness to those studios too, but I was also aware of my own happiness in the execution. From time to time, I would realize that these experiences could not last forever—that I needed to be mindful of their rarity, their enormous value. And I was, sometimes; but as is the way with any genuine practice, the repertories became a way of being in the world—on some level, they became internalized to the point of being taken for granted. You cannot imagine yourself without them. And then it is difficult to be grateful, simply because you cannot imagine yourself alive and not dancing.

Duncan class put no limit on emotional experience. It placed a pre-Balanchine premium on expressivity. I can remember our plié combination marshaling the whole body—initiating the arch of the upper back from the solar plexus, that space located between the breasts. All movement in the Duncan technique is initiated from this spot, where the heart resides. I remember the precise prescription for melting the foot—toe, metatarsal, and the delayed heel—into the floor. This is a process by which the dancer kneads each bone, feeling the entirety of the foot's complex construction. *This is where I want to be but am not. I can express the wish, but it will remain on the page as a wish—identical to any other you can imagine.*

This is both the difficulty of writing about "writing process" and the likely reason that "dance writing" is almost always written from the subject position of the observer—even if that observer is also concurrently a dancer. The diary of Toni Bentley, a young corps dancer in New York City Ballet during the eighties, becomes instructive in this capacity. Trying to describe the performance of Suzanne Farrell in Balanchine's *Diamonds*, Bentley finds herself at a loss for words, or at least at a loss for the dance vocabulary that is ordinarily at her fingertips:

> Suzanne just finished another *Diamonds*, and frankly I cannot put any words on paper to describe her magnificence, her giving. I watch her face and can only think of a love she has greater than I could ever contain. She is from God's world—a direct disciple, I think . . . I suppose the first reaction to such a sight and emotion is to define it. Isn't that what critics do? By defining and attempting to explain her we attempt, I'm sure, to submerge and put aside the sadness that her simple self evokes. She is not to be explained—she cannot be—but it is hard to bear such a sight. Surely any of our mortal words put down to explain her or describe her are absurd. (*Winter Season* 30–31)

Bentley's sense of the incommensurability of dance and writing—exemplified in her jejune but uncannily eloquent hero-worship of Farrell's performance—is a theme that continues throughout her diary: "[Y]ou have to be an unhappy dancer to write at all. If I were totally at peace dancing, I would have nothing to say" (133). It is a commonplace that dancing resists the verbal. But if this resistance applies even to the observer of the dance, it becomes that much more difficult to parse, and to recreate through language, exactly what is lost when these experiences are no longer in the body of the dancer herself.

One loss, surely, is that sense of complete body-mind expenditure that one has after dancing, particularly after a class with someone like Cheri. My own struggle with kinesthetic learning—probably because it was, of necessity, abjectly focused—was a purging of any other thoughts that might have been in my mind during the rest of the day. And perhaps I needed to clean my mind of thoughts: not only to dance, but also to write—to continue the process of discovery in my academic work.

Everyone has different ways of accomplishing this. I had a friend who had to watch junk TV from eleven each night until one in the morning just to be able to continue his writing on Heidegger and Gibson from one until dawn. But for me, television is far from a complete emptying of self: I am still there; I am the one who is watching it. Reading, particularly novelistic reading, can accomplish that emptying, as Stevens and Birkerts variously articulated—but it's also fuel and spur for my writing, energizing and buttressing the identity of the known self. It can become, at least in part, a means to an end. For years, I've loved how Roland Barthe articulated the phenomenon of intellectually *productive* distraction:

> To be with the one I love and to think of something else: this is how I have my best ideas, how I best invent what is necessary to my work. Likewise for the text: it produces, in me, the best pleasure if it manages to make itself heard indirectly; if, reading it, I am led to look up often, to listen to something else. (*Pleasure* 24)

Barthes's last sentence constitutes the dilemma and joy of the poet—to whom, as Frost said, knowledge sticks like burrs (*Collected Poems* 78). But dancing was a part of my experience that was, in most senses, disconnected to the work that comprised "my best ideas," that forged my identity in the world.

I find now that there is little escape from that self: from the one who is identified with the work. As someone who no longer takes dance classes but who "exercises," I can easily tell you the difference. As I swim laps, I am certainly "working out," in the common parlance; but I am working out my schedule, my responsibilities, my preoccupations. The "work" is by its nature repetitive; the body understands what to do; there is no input from the mind, so it's free to go off on its usual independent per-egrinations. The body is quantifiably benefited, I suppose—our annual physicals may tell us that—but there is no respite from self. There is no opportunity to engage some part of the mind differently—to light up, as it were, a different aspect of the brain. It is all numbingly familiar. The way I manage the task of it is to try to forget that I am there doing it.

Isn't this the way with nearly all of the exercise that qualifies as such for Americans today? No wonder so few of us want to do it. The treadmill, ubiquitous contraption, is also an apt metaphor for the way that most exercise functions for us: duty, numbers, rounding the bend, distracting ourselves from it by any means possible—headsets and magazines and anything that will trick us into thinking we're not actually using our bodies. The state of super-alert mental receptivity required in the dance class is not necessary for the sorts of physical endeavors in which we're all told to engage—in order to live longer, feel better, be a better specimen of body. Thus the exercise that we do, if we do it at all, is emphatically *non*-transformative in any kind of genuinely integrative psychosomatic manner.

If this is a digression from the elegiac narrative at hand, I digress only to illustrate what I loved about dancing and what I miss about it now. The Duncan classes were not a panacea for me, insofar as they did not afford me some magic strategy to become better at learning combinations. But they did incrementally manage to put a different type of knowledge into my muscular memory, and they enabled me to start performing work that I had known for years. The classes were about neither newness nor one person's always-changing choreographic vision. Instead, they were pre-servative and conservative, in the sense that they preserved a historically circumscribed and putatively unchanged body of work. I say that with a bit of hesitation, since choreography is always open to interpretation—particularly the sort of choreography that has been handed down orally from generation to generation. And yet it is also a known quantity, partic-ularly when one has been dancing and performing it for a while.

These days, I think a lot about mimesis in the arts. Some days, that is the only way that I can think about the ambition and practice of art and my own place in it: not as a mimesis of the empirical world—Stendhal's mirror in the street—but as an inescapable intertextuality that renders all of our work conservative of a prior tradition. If my poems can conserve some aspect of Donne or Dickinson in an inchoate way, I have done my job as a historically belated poet. But these have been my concerns for years: my dissertation was centrally focused upon issues of mimesis in the ekphrastic lyric, and I have taught in a writing program whose pedagogical model was imitation (that is, training undergraduate students to write by teaching them to imitate major poets).

The issues in dance class were, for me, very connected to these concerns. What dancers must experience, and what I experienced for years in Cheri's class, was a necessarily imperfect mimesis. We all must fall short—of our teachers' movements and bodies. The margin for error is so much smaller in a dance class, in which one must literally do what one sees. And realizing one cannot fully approximate it, and continuing nevertheless. Perhaps this is always the fate of the nonprofessional in any artistic medium. It's possible that being a perennial amateur in some field gives us a different perspective on the field in which we are able to excel.

It may be too simple to make an equation between dancing and writing for publication (to take the obvious example). My writing is something I do by myself, with no audience. I have tried to perfect it before sending it out anywhere. Let's just say that I have had a million hours to rehearse: to fidget with the line break, the semicolon, the comma. To mouth again the precise way that I want the stress to fall before the enjambment. But in the dance studio, it was only me and the present moment: the imperfect instrument of my body trying to learn what was put in front of it anew, every time. Me and the crowd of dancers—no props, no crutches, no footnotes. (When I lock my locker at the pool, I'm often startled by how free I feel without my book bags and laptop: my hands are so light that I wonder how I'll ever be able to do *anything*, so unfettered.) Do I ever feel that I hit the mark, with poems? Yes, I do. If I didn't, I would never send them out for publication. It may not be anyone else's mark—but it is my own, and only my ear knows when I have reached it.

Teaching writing is different, because nothing I can do will be able to replicate that feeling for students. I may give them assignments with mimetic components, but I can never delineate the trajectory through which they can achieve that mimesis. I can advise, but I can't enact. Strangely enough, one of the best things I can do for them is to be a version of Cheri, with her capaciousness and equanimity and energy. Dance class, more than any class in graduate school really, taught me the persona—not the curriculum—I would need as a shy person who wanted to teach. I learned that energy is something one can assume and indeed, something one owes to one's students. I also learned that it feeds on itself when you're doing something you love.

Though it may sound utopian, or Puritan, I do believe that we can self-create through work. When Cheri was preparing to have major surgery, her persona was indistinguishable from what it was on any other day. I took note of that. I was starting to learn the virtues of a public persona: something I had never managed to learn from my family. Probably without ever intending to, Cheri had taught me an ethics of teaching—as well as the ethics of teaching someone who can never, constitutionally, hit the mark of what is put in front of her. In a larger sense, such failure is both literary and ontological, as Rosanna Warren has written of Dante: "Failure is, of course, written into the literary, if not the religious, endeavor, as human and divine can never be commensurate, however analogous" (*Fables* 214).

I return to the elegiac nature of this essay. We don't just want to learn lessons from what we love doing, we want to be able to keep doing it; and a certain strain of modern dancer assumes that if we simply keep up the practice, we can do it all our lives (see Graham; see Cunningham). During a recent stay at an artists' colony, I found myself in conversation with Elizabeth, a photographer who asked what I had been working on that day. She was interested in the topic of this essay and told me that chronic pain had forced her out of competitive martial arts practice when she was in her mid-thirties. Young, we think now.

"But you know, that's the age when people traditionally retired from competitive practice," she said. "We think we should be able to keep doing everything and don't understand anymore that we need to do different things at different times in our lives." Now she surfs out in Rockaway, and that has steadied her. I realized that my chiropractor had said similar things to me five or seven years before, and I had reacted with nothing but silent outrage. I wanted to dance, no matter what.

But somehow in the course of writing this essay, I was able to listen to Elizabeth differently. Perhaps because writing the essay was helping me to put a certain part of myself to rest. Or because I wanted once again—

endlessly—to turn to someone who seemed to have more wisdom than I thought I would ever be allowed. I don't know, but that brief conversation meant a great deal to me as I was trying to put this narrative in perspective. It is hard to give up parts of the self that we have treasured, even in their failures—but a large part of living must require us to do just that.

In my life as a professor, I try each day to bring the energy of my dance teachers into the classroom with my students. I stretch, and I exercise, and I swim: even without class, I maintain the life of the body—that state of *hypermobility*, which I think I actually like, even though I couldn't tell if the doctor approved of it or not. And I still want to think, unscientifically, that parts of the mind light up like Christmas trees. I lean, with Stevens, over the book.

2011–2015

Gravity, Images, and the Hand

On Nonconformists and Strange Gravity (2013)

> So you write him a letter and say, "Her eyes are blue."
> He sends you a poem and she's lost to you.
> Little green, he's a non-conformer.
> —JONI MITCHELL

What ever happened to nonconformism? It must have gone the way of flower power and the sit-in. So Joni Mitchell's lyrics from "Little Green," on her 1971 album *Blue*, may read like a reliquary. In them, the singer laments that her absent lover (and the father of her child) is both a poet and a "non-conformer." Her description may seem quaint or superannuated; but the relationship between poetry and conformism, or the related question of poetry's status as a nonconformist art, still resonates. To what degree is a poet defined by social or political groups of other people—whether other poets or just others? And to what degree must the poet be—or should the poet want to be—"the only Kangaroo among the Beauty" (Dickinson, *Selected Letters* 176)?

These questions were sharpened for me by the recent death of the American poet Paul Petrie, my best friend's father, from cancer at the age of eighty-four. In my eyes, he was the original nonconformist—probably because he was the first poet I ever met. With his gray hair over his ears, his horn-rimmed glasses, his slow and plangent voice and perennial glass of milk, he was the unwitting personification of poetry for a teenaged proto-poet unwittingly in training. Paul's first book of poems had been published twenty-five years before, in 1963, and it was titled *Confessions of a Non-Conformist*.

The title poem suggests, yet deflects, his difference:

I eat carrots
in public places.
I carry spiders
out-of-doors
on the Sunday paper.
I am unfriendly with my banker.
But still wonder.
God-fearing? Free? White? Thirty-one? (Collected Poems 101)

Far from the flamboyance of a Beat or even an early hippie, Paul's non-conformist gestures are nearly invisible. There's a vestigially Buddhist feel to these lines: the poet is a carrot-eating, spider-rescuing young man who, unlike the more self-dramatizing poets thought to be "Confessional," quietly brought his inner life indoors, to a house in Rhode Island, and grew it there.

The lines are also humorous, of course. On the subject of bankers, Paul uses a prefix to reverse our expectations of a familiar prepositional phrase: the implied locution of "friendly with" becomes "unfriendly with," as a negation of social nicety. When bankers were people and not beeping machines, one was apparently expected to make small talk with them. But Paul sounds proud not to do that. (Though he seemed to live on another planet from the sedate Petrie, the high-octane, über-friendly Frank O'Hara also sped past an uncool Miss Stillwagon, the banker who didn't check his balance "for once in her life," on "The Day Lady Died"—the day of Billie Holiday's death in 1959, which was the same year Paul began his teaching position at the University of Rhode Island—*Lunch Poems* 25.)

But the message of this poem is also serious. By his own lights, the least-conforming thing Paul ever did was to be a poet. As he says in the first stanza of the same poem,

At fourteen
I decided to be
unorthodox,
a man
who sings for his bread,
and likes bread. (101)

Yet, as the poem continues to wonder, what kind of unorthodoxy is even possible when one enjoys so many trappings of the mainstream? He was the recipient of white privilege in an America that hovered at the cusp of the civil rights movement. He was married, with children. He actually liked bread. How could he be a nonconformist?

The answer lies not only in the banker, but in Auden. His oft-quoted "Poetry makes nothing happen," from the elegy for Yeats, is not the end of the story (*Selected Poems* 82). After the colon ending that famous clause, Auden continues: "it survives / In the valley of its saying where executives / Would never want to tamper" (82). Thus poetry doesn't really make nothing happen; executives *think* it makes nothing happen, if they are able even to think such things in the first place. Poetry is therefore illegible—no, imperceptible—to those who live their lives by the dictates of the bottom line. Despite their differences in demeanor and aesthetics, then, O'Hara and Petrie staked out similar territories just by being unfriendly with their bankers. ("We must be the last couple in America not to have a credit card," Paul's wife Sylvia said with rueful humor, sometime in the 1990s.) In so doing, both offered up an antidote to determinism, positivism, capitalism, and—yes—conformism. That antidote was lyric poetry.

Someone will object, of course, that these notions are too idealistic. What of the literary marketplace? Even with fewer publishers and book prizes, significantly fewer MFA programs, and much less hype, there was still a skeletal market for poetry when Paul came of age. But he didn't pay much attention to it. O'Hara might have said that Paul Petrie was busy making his own days. He woke up every morning, put on his favorite down jacket, and wrote his poems in bed. (This was before the age of the laptop: his lap had a spiral notebook on it.) His inner life articulated like branches on a winter tree, or the "wintry theatricals" he described in one of his poems (*Collected Poems* 204).

He published widely in both formal and free verse—including ten books and two dozen appearances in *Poetry* magazine alone—but had little to do with poetic trends or with the "schools" that can become a safety net for artists and writers. He didn't apply for fellowships because he thought they should be awarded to poets who didn't have the good fortune, and the financial security, of a teaching job. He was prolific but not public.

Thoreau said, "To affect the quality of the day, that is the highest of arts" (*Walden* 65). Paul excelled at this, in addition to writing. But, as in the poem above, he "still wondered"—about his own place in the literary and metaphysical scheme of things. (The slant rhyme between "banker" and "wonder" is telling, much as Paul Fussell locates the irony that can sometimes attend rhyming words: "[T]he sound similarity 'says' that they resemble each other, while the rhetoric of the stanza asserts their difference"—*Poetic Meter* 111.) Despite his successes in publishing, I think Paul came to see his work in an increasingly Dickinsonian sense—as his letter to the world that never wrote back to him. And yet it's also true that, like Melville's Bartleby, he himself preferred not to meet social or literary life on its own terms. As the decades passed, he left his house less and less frequently.

How important is it for a poet, in Stevens's words, "to face the men of the time and to meet / the women of the time" (*Collected Poems* 239)? Did Stevens himself even do that? I have to wonder instead about poetry's function as an introverted art: the poetic line can act as a material limit to what would otherwise be unreconstructed chatter. And I wonder, too, if Paul's life and work might allegorize the social and relational difficulty of the poet's calling throughout literary history, as well as poetry's ambivalence around the question of the poet's social role—and by "social," I mean his relationship both to other poets and to others who are not poets.

To be sure, Western literary history provides ample evidence that poets can be acutely social creatures. Ben Jonson and the Tribe of Ben. The slightly manic sociability of the New York School. In our own time, the writing workshop and the MFA program. Or the poetry blog and Facebook, whose digital snapshots and shout-outs render every reading, no matter how local, an instant celebrity bash.

But Paul might have replied that poets should resist these sorts of moorings. From this other perspective, the poet should set herself apart, "at a distance from the kind," as Wordsworth said, in order to create her art (*Oxford* 328). This is because poetry has never completely divorced itself from one salient strand of its root in ancient Greece: whatever else it is, poetry is occasional. Its marking of occasion also marks the passing of time in the duration of our own mortalities. This served a social and communal function in the fourth century BCE, but it may require some tincture of the antisocial in ours.

"Poets are conservative," Paul the nonconformist used to say, hastening to explain that this conservatism had nothing to do with politics. "They want to conserve memory and experience." The drive toward poetic conservation is occasional, I'd argue, whether we're conserving something personal, historical, or neither. It can transform a previously unnoticed moment—a patch of red wing, or television noise, or a sentence in Kant's *Critique of Judgment*—into the occasion for language. Where is the poet, of any aesthetic stripe, who doesn't rush to conserve even a fraction of the spark that might blaze as a poem? This need to preserve moments of a perceptual, emotional, or intellectual life in poetic lines does constitute, again in Paul's words, a "race with time and the devil"—a race that none of us can win (*Collected Poems* 694). As Sharon Cameron says, writing of Emily Dickinson's work in particular, "the poles of death and immortality are thus those states that poetic language shuttles between" (*Lyric Time* 244).

Though we often think ourselves too sophisticated to believe it, this resistance within lyric poetry—its drive to conserve the body, and thus the body's emanations of mind and spirit—can indeed triumph in small ways over Shakespeare's "sluttish time" (*Complete Works* 1462). I'm relearning this by reading Paul's poems aloud after his death: they swim to the surface after his disappearance, or the (figurative) drowning of his person. This phenomenon reverses Eliot's notion that "human voices wake us, and we drown" (*Selected Poems* 16). Instead, we drown, and then the human voices of our verses wake some of those who remain alive after us.

As William Waters has said, reading Shakespeare's Sonnet 81 ("Or I shall live your epitaph to make"—1466), "The 'immortality' of poetry is not in the monument but in the breath and voice of the reader. That means: in ourselves, now and here as we read these lines" (*Poetry's Touch* 121). Waters also notes that in 1926, Rilke was asked to make a recording of his poems and ultimately refused—because he thought the imposition of his own speaking voice might prevent what he wished his poems' future to be (120). He wanted them to live on, not as his own repeated and mechanized voice on the record, but as lines spoken in the plural, disparate, and fundamentally unpredictable voices that would belong to his future readers.

But the work that poets do—the amassing of lines that may live as long as there are others who have breath, voice, and the desire to read—can also become a self-ravaging. As Adrienne Rich asked, "What kind of beast would turn its life into words? / What atonement is this all about?" (*Dream* 28).

Some poets may understand what drives the imperative of their own atonements, but this vocation may be more difficult when we don't. Poetic consciousness is not always adaptive in the world at large, particularly in the world of Auden's executives. So poets may have no choice but to be nonconformists—the squatters and nomads of the soul. Awakened by the mortality of Eliot's "human voices"—the voices of other poets' poems, as Paul's are waking me now—they may retain that curse of wakefulness when nearly everyone else appears to be, in Liam Rector's words, "sleepwalking through the dream of choice" (*Sorrow* 25).

This view of poetry is, admittedly, not very fashionable. It's not applicable to language games, digital technology gimmicks, or hypermarketed hipness. But I find that such consciousness of time and mortality, whether explicitly named or not, imbues every poem that is worth reading, and it can reside as readily in the comic as it does in the elegiac. I see perhaps the most poignant examples of it in manuscripts that never see print: poems sent to *Poetry* magazine by the very elderly, who have finally turned to poetry as a way to measure—in the best poetic sense of that word—their own deaths.

The burden of time and mortality probably weighs on every artist, but why does it seem to define the poet more? Paul Petrie articulated this phenomenon as "strange gravity":

Strange gravity, that, as I grow,
downwards, toward the earth,
loosens those fingers, one by one,
which bound me from my birth. (Collected Poems 238)

From Paul's perspective, the poet's gravity is what both hobbles and unbinds him. Thus the ineluctable magnetism of growing "downwards," toward our graves in the earth, is also commensurate with the ecstasy of lightening and unbinding: a self-loosening from the fingers of others that bind our persons to the social and relational world from infanthood onward. The poet's gravity is born of "distance from the kind," and Paul knew that the liberation it affords is gained at a price:

Death, dark shadow, walk
always by my side.
In your clear shade all living things
are purified. (Collected Poems 235)

During Paul's last days in hospice, it was his family who stayed by his side. They took turns reading his poems to him, even when they realized he could no longer comprehend what he was listening to. In those moments, I imagine, he might have heard a discontinuous river of sound. He probably didn't remember what his friend Philip Levine had written about his work in 1988: "I believe it is not only possible but very likely that this poetry which has never been fashionable will quietly pass into the permanent body of our literature, much as the work of Edward Thomas, Wilfred Owen, and Weldon Kees has" (Levine cover endorsement, *The Runners*).

That quiet passage consumes me now, as Paul's words make their way among the arteries that constitute each reader. Like Brian Wilson, Paul wasn't made for these times. He made his poems in geologic time, and for a certain subterranean dissemination. I hear them surviving in the voices of nonconformists—near the valley of death, where executives would never want to tamper.

The Emily Dickinsons (2014)

Poetry and ephemera: despite the exhortations in Shakespeare's sonnets, could there be an abiding affinity between the two? It can certainly seem that way when one is paging through Jen Bervin and Marta Werner's *The Gorgeous Nothings*, a (nothing if not gorgeous) new facsimile collection of Dickinson's envelope poems. By "envelope poems," I don't mean poems about envelopes, which is what the phrase would usually suggest in contemporary poetry parlance. I'm referring instead to poems written *on* envelopes, with facsimile versions of the envelopes reproduced—in this case, those that were held and scribbled on by Emily Dickinson herself. These are digitally preserved in almost tactile detail: you can all but smell the musty paper scraps. *The Gorgeous Nothings* has the aura of an earlier century, in which envelopes contained heartfelt sentences of great complexity—or perhaps the briefer, pithier messages of which Dickinson was also fond. Either way, as Bervin and Werner know, the envelope was charged with mystery and incipience in the moments before it was opened. In *The Gorgeous Nothings*, it also transforms to an exiguous writing surface: Dickinson's poems are like graffiti on small paper walls.

There is something going on here that Jacques Derrida called "archive fever," or an infectious collection of things preserved from the past (*Archive Fever* 12). So how could we not catch fire? It can be thrilling to "read" these fleetly scratched poems—even as our eyes keep darting back to Bervin and Werner's discreet print transcriptions of Dickinson's sometimes-illegible handwriting. We can't help but feel that we're in the poet's pocket, as Bervin suggests in her introduction:

> All of the envelope poems are written in pencil. Unlike a fountain pen, a pencil stub, especially a very small one, fits neatly, at the ready, in the pocket of a dress. . . . Dickinson's one surviving dress has a large external pocket on the right side, where her hand would fall easily at rest. (*Gorgeous Nothings* 12)

And if you care about poetry at all, who wouldn't jump at the chance for that kind of intimacy? Billy Collins and Archibald MacLeish certainly would.

But Bervin and Werner want to offer their readers more than just immediacy. They also want to show us "the real deal" of Dickinson's writing project, as opposed to the ways her poetry has been reproduced in print editions. One could object that this point was made back in 1981, in R. W. Franklin's variorum editions of the poet's work. But the envelope or "scrap" poems have not been available in facsimile form until now. It's also true that most nonspecialists are still reading Dickinson in standardized print versions, edited either by Franklin or Thomas Johnson—and the differences between those poems and the facsimiles here can be both fascinating and poignant.

Take, for example, Dickinson's #1292 ("In this short Life"). In Franklin's print edition, it consists of two pentameter lines: "In this short Life that only lasts an hour / How much—how little—is within our power" (Dickinson, *Poems* 502). In the *Gorgeous Nothings* version, Dickinson's lines expand and contract to cover the reverse-triangular shape of an envelope's flap, thus growing to six altogether (and retaining the variant word "merely" under "only"). As the envelope tapers, so too does Dickinson's writing, enacting the "littleness"—and perhaps the tragic truncation—of the "Life" that is at issue. #1478, the congruently shaped "One note from One Bird," provides a similar marriage of paper shape and sense.

These poems can cause us to consider the mutability—and ultimately the adaptability—of a metrical structure we might have assumed was stable. (It has often been noted how metrically "scannable" many of Dickinson's letters can be, thus potentially troubling the distinction between poetry and prose.) This point is well taken and can inspire interesting thoughts about the liberation of meter from line. In other poems, however, it is not always clear what we should gain from the facsimile reproduction, or why it's necessarily preferable to reading a print version. In most cases, as described above, expediency of reading is not the collection's selling point.

So after some moments of pleasure and epiphany, the question becomes one of emphasis: What do we as readers want to take away from poetry? For many Dickinson manuscript scholars today, the interest is not so much in the disseminable or printable poem itself—that is, its repeatability in our voices, books, and lives—but in the way it adapted itself to the material constraints that may or may not have governed its having been physically written in the first place. In this view, the poem is a product of its immediate writerly environment. According to Susan Howe, who wrote the preface to *The Gorgeous Nothings*, Dickinson's poems are "visual productions" that we cannot understand without seeing them in the settings of their original, handwritten forms (*The Birth-Mark* 141). (According to Bervin, it was this directive that guided the production of the *Gorgeous Nothings* edition; to be sure, it seems to have inspired Werner's later description of the envelope-writings as collages, birds, and holographs—10.) For Bervin and Werner, the collected poems of Emily Dickinson straddle the limits, and fray the boundaries, between poetry and visual art.

These claims don't convince me, though, since Dickinson's medium is never the painterly image (what Plato called the "natural sign"), but instead always the alphabet, or the so-called artificial sign, regardless of the poet's chosen writing implements or manner of paper. I'm also too committed to the age-old genre of lyric poetry—and to Dickinson's participation in it—not to think that calling these works "visual productions" effectively squelches or even silences their aural qualities.

Still, I'm sure to be in the minority here among both scholars and poets. Howe has influenced a generation of manuscript scholars who see the idiosyncrasy of Dickinson's handwriting, scraps, and fascicle production as integral to the way we should read her. And such concern with poetry's "means of production" is admittedly timely. It's in line with the concerns of at least two strands of poets writing in the present day: the metonymic bent of Language poets (with whom Howe has been a strange, if enduring, bedfellow), and poets writing "born digital," or hypertext, works. In these ways, Dickinson's gorgeous envelopes underline the power of writers' physical or technological constraints—and suggest that the limits of our material technologies, whether electronic or flimsy as an old candy wrapper, can play as large a role in creative production as the more traditionally "formal" or aesthetic demands of, say, meter itself. (Probably the best twentieth-century version of what I'm talking about is the adding machine tape on which A. R. Ammons typed *Tape for the Turn of the Year*.)

Like poetry, scholarship probably works best when its time is of the essence. It has traditionally been easy—and, of course, inaccurate—to stereotype Dickinson as a recluse and loner. Today, Dickinson manuscript scholars may be overcompensating for their predecessors' mistakes by overemphasizing the social, or epistolary, qualities of her work. And by drawing our attention to these envelope scraps—rather than, for example, to Dickinson's carefully threaded, arranged, and hidden fascicles—some scholars want us to associate Dickinson with the ephemeral and the fragmentary: with the veneer, at least, of the aleatory or unfinished. (In a nod to "archive fever," paper mail delivery is itself going the way of ephemera as I write—it is now almost a thing of the past.)

The delectable appeal of *The Gorgeous Nothings* will be obvious to poets: Dickinson's fragments are visually exquisite, and Werner is the rare literary critic whose writing is beautiful and lyrical enough to be a prose poem of its own. The dangers of the production, in contrast, are much more oblique—and ultimately twofold, in my view. One is that, just as Dickinson's first editors co-opted her work into a "sentimental" role that didn't fit, now the "unfinished" aspects of the envelope poems may come to characterize her entire output. (Arguably, this has already happened.) This critical tack sways Dickinson toward experimental rather than lyric aesthetics. Equally importantly, by "socializing" Dickinson in the epistolary manner, the great poet becomes more stereotypically feminized and more domesticated than the content of her most important work warrants.

You may well ask why contemporary poets should care about these debates at all. The question of how to read and interpret Emily Dickinson may seem an antique scholarly wrinkle that has no real relevance for artists today. Yet Dickinson continues to be among the most indelible of influences in American poetry. We couldn't get rid of her if we tried, and no one seems to want to try very hard to begin with. It's difficult to imagine May Swenson, Jean Valentine, Lucie Brock-Broido, A. R. Ammons, Kay Ryan, and any number of poets without having had Dickinson's work first. At this moment, I'm also remembering a poet who, for a while, used Dickinson's famous portrait as an emblem on his personal stationery. How many others of us superimpose her diction or syntax on our own?

Dickinson is clearly alive and well and still being worked out. But the question remains: *which* Dickinson are we working on? Which one are we fantasizing about? The Howe/Werner/Bervin model is undeniably attractive. She's also the one that is in fashion this season. Given her increasing power, how might we keep the other Emily Dickinsons conceptually—and meaningfully—in play?

"A Lovely Finish I Have Seen"

Voice and Variorum in
Edgar Allan Poe & the Juke-Box (2012)

Who can predict the half-life of a dead poet's unfinished works? And if they are disseminated for public consumption, who—or what aesthetic—is liable to co-opt them? These questions have become more salient after the 2006 publication of Alice Quinn's *Edgar Allan Poe & the Juke-Box*, a volume that features draft editions, variants, and facsimile reproductions of Elizabeth Bishop's unpublished poems. As is well known, Quinn's edition has provoked its share of controversy in the literary world, largely regarding issues of authorial intent and deceased poets' control over unpublished materials.[1] Perhaps the most famous objection to this publication was Helen Vendler's outrage that the "maimed and stunted siblings" of Bishop's published poems should be collected for the public to read ("Art").

I would like to put these questions aside for a moment, however, to address other and more globally aesthetic issues that are raised by Quinn's volume. What is the nature, whether aesthetic or otherwise, of the literary world's investment in variorum or facsimile editions? In what ways do these editions redramatize, recharacterize, or reinscribe our hallucinated relation to a dead poet? Can lyric poems in manuscript format be co-opted by the thrall of the "unfinished" that is operative in a more experimental poetics? And is this experimental aesthetic actually imbued with a heftier conservatism than its proponents might allow, especially when it applies (or is applied) to the works of women poets in particular?

I'll be addressing these questions, in part, by juxtaposing Bishop's

---

1. For a discussion of the nature of these disagreements, see Mokoto Rich, "New Elizabeth Bishop Book Sparks Controversy."

manuscript work with the fascicles of Emily Dickinson and by suggesting that a recent movement in Dickinson scholarship may also affect
the impact of *Edgar Allan Poe & the Juke-Box* on Bishop's reputation.
Specifically, R. W. Franklin's manuscript edition of Dickinson's poems,
published in 1981, has effected a change in Dickinson studies—wherein
critics' concerns have become arguably less "poetic" and more graphic or
archival in their orientation.[2] And although the jury is still out regarding
the lasting impact of *Edgar Allan Poe & the Juke-Box* on Bishop's critical
reception, I will be arguing here that the publication of the variorum
or facsimile edition as such, by canceling the terms and the sublimate
sonorities (or fastenings) of poetic "voice," may paradoxically anchor the
reader in a more conservative relation to the figure of the female poet in
particular.

To address the cases of both Bishop and Dickinson, we first need to ask
whether the dissemination of manuscript materials can be compatible
with the emphasis on poetic "voice" that the lyric tradition both assumes
and promulgates. Is a concern with poetic voice really viable after post-
structuralism? And if it is, can the publication of a manuscript edition
somehow silence that voice? Clearly, the dissemination of handwritten
manuscript work would fall in line with the Derridean exhortation to
treat writing as graphic trace rather than as the logocentric transcription
of (an ostensibly univocal) speech. But even in the wake of poststruc-
turalism, the construct of poetic voice is alive and well in the criticism
of the lyric, as seen in the work of W. R. Johnson, Mutlu Konuk Blasing,
Susan Stewart, and Allen Grossman, to name only a few examples.[3] Per-

---

2. For a discussion of this critical change in the focus of Dickinson studies, see my
"Ghosts of Meter: Dickinson, after Long Silence." Betsy Erkkila's "The Emily Dickinson
Wars" also covers some of this intellectual ground, with more of an emphasis on the
cultural values at stake in the dissemination, publication, and popularization of Dickinson's work.

3. What Johnson prizes in the lyric genre is the modality that he terms the "I-You"
pronominal construction (*Idea* 3). This involves "a speaker, or singer, talking to, singing to, another person or persons" (3) after the model of Greek monody. More recently,
see Blasing's assertion that "[a] convincing lyric subject is spoken by the words she
speaks. . . . what individuates her is not what she says but the particular ways in which
she makes *audible* the shape, the 'beautiful necessities,' of the language" (*Lyric Poetry* 35,
emphasis mine). Blasing draws upon developmental speech theory in order to articulate the role of the mother tongue as it inflects poetic rhythm: "Rhythm is experience in
and as time, as a persuasive movement of the voice" (55).

haps even more crucially, it has remained the coin of the realm for many contemporary poets, especially those who see Elizabeth Bishop's work as seminal for the development of their own. As the late James Merrill wrote of Bishop, "Whether this voice says hard and disabused things or humorous and gentle ones, its emotional pitch remains so true, and its intelligence so unaffected, that we hear in it the 'touch of nature' which makes the whole world kin" (*Recitative* 129).

In Bishop's work, there is a significant relationship not only between voice and referentiality (Merrill's "touch of nature"), but between voice and "finish," as cited in this essay's title. It has become almost a commonplace to call Bishop a poet of assiduously polished surfaces, in which even ingenuous questioning shores up the poet's ravishing rhetorical authority. What is more, her poems often read as if in transparent service to extratextual visual acuity. As Lee Edelman has observed about the poet's critical reception, "They have cited her work . . . as exemplary of precise observation and accurate detail" ("Geography" 92); he goes on to quote David Kalstone's assertion that Bishop was portrayed as a "miniaturist," with all of the attendant enameling that the word implies (92).[4]

If we juxtapose the statements of Merrill, Kalstone, and Edelman, we can begin to understand the unusual ramifications of poetic voice in Bishop's work. By coupling the exigencies of miniaturist detail with the creation of "kinship," we'll see that the poet's enamel-like "finishing" is surprisingly tempered by the demands of communicative, nearly dialogic speech. The conjunction of filigreed, paratactic descriptive work (as seen in "At the Fishhouses" and "The Bight," for example) with "true" emotional pitch, in Merrill's terms, means that the focalized patina of her finished poems is not only commensurate with, but also may in some sense constitute, the sonorities of Bishop's conversational voice. Perhaps the best emblem of this unlikely balance was created by Bishop herself, who noted "the curious effect a poem produces as being as normal as *sight*

See also Susan Stewart's discussion of "Sound" in *Poetry and the Fate of the Senses*: "Keeping time in poetry is exercised through the single voice manipulating duration in such a way as to produce both expectation and surprise" (83). In *Summa Lyrica*, moreover, Grossman notes that "[t]he poem summons the voice of the speaker of the poem to enact the business of the speaking person" (258).

4. Edelman goes on to critique the relationship between Bishop's poetry and a straightforward conception of referentiality.

and yet as synthetic, as artificial, as a *glass eye*" (*Edgar Allan Poe* xi, quoted by Quinn). Here, Bishop has combined the faculty of sight with its prosthetic simulacrum in order to define voice as both natural and artificial; such a paradox becomes the alchemy of what makes lyric poetry "work."

But the publication of poems Bishop chose not to publish—likely, in the poet's mind, "unfinished"—clearly situates her in another arena, in which the visual thrall of the abandoned manuscript-in-progress chafes against the finish created by a mimetic, *extra*textual, referential impulse: the impulse, in other words, that guided her published poetic output. In *Edgar Allan Poe & the Juke-Box*, Bishop's referential visual register has often been exchanged for the "look" of the manuscript page itself. For this reason, it is almost wonderfully ironic that the first poem in the volume's 1929–1936 section is titled "A lovely finish I have seen . . . ," as if the present perfect were to act as an unwittingly elegiac commentary on the inviolability of the work in Bishop's *Collected Poems* and an equally pointed look ahead to the contents of the Quinn volume (11). As if proleptically aware of its own allegorical placement, the poem asks, "Can one accuse of artifice / such finishes and surfaces?" (11). Whether these "finishes and surfaces" refer to the contents of Quinn's volume or to *Complete Poems*, it is telling that the line rhetorically defends the "accused" value of artifice.

At the same time, however, the front matter of *Edgar Allan Poe and the Juke-Box* thwarts any vestigial expectation of "finish" that the reader might have had: the book's facing title page features a handwritten version of the poem "Edgar Allan Poe & the Juke-Box" with its stanzas slashed by a single stroke of ink. Before the book has even begun, then, it has visually allegorized its own title as a cancellation; the compilation has been named after a poem that Bishop "nixed." Such flouting of the poet's manifest intent is striking here—and indeed, it is what most bothered Vendler—but in another sense, it is hardly the point. There is something even more arresting about the title page presentation: it proffers an aesthetic that is antithetical to the purview of Bishop's "live" poetic voice, as we saw above. The canceled poem fairly refutes the linguistic polish of the Bishop whose poems we knew, and yet Bishop herself is the author of it: she is presented, then, as the author of her own undoing. And the title page itself is hardly an anomaly: as Quinn notes in her introduction, the volume contains eleven other poem drafts that were "entirely crossed out by Bishop" in manuscript (xx).

From the outset, then, it is clear that *Edgar Allan Poe & the Juke-Box* necessarily "plays" Bishop differently—almost as a record on a jukebox—from the music of her finished poetry. The erstwhile voice of the *Complete Poems*, which acts as a form of recto to the current volume's verso, is epitomized by the assertion that "The burning box can keep the measure / strict, always, and the down-beat" ("Edgar Allan Poe" 49). If legibility is allied with the productions of poetic voice, then the facsimile productions cannot keep such strict aural measure; on the contrary, they graphically capture one of our most obsessively legible poets in her transitional or self-canceling moments of illegibility. And if illegibility co-opts voice, as we will see in more detail later, then the public presentation of drafts with their variants leaves Bishop vulnerable to co-option by a more experimental code of aesthetics than what she embraced in her life as a publishing poet.

At this juncture, I want to clarify that my concerns are not so much with Quinn's manifest intentions around the drafts, as her stated goal is to "provide an adventure for readers who love the established canon, enabling them to hear echoes and make connections based on their own intuitions and close reading of both the finished and the unfinished poems" (xv). Instead, I am more interested in the way in which our current critical climate supports the aesthetic choices implicit in the very enterprise of facsimile dissemination—and thereby opens the way to a set of receptions and co-options of the lyric, and of poetic voice, that we can see most saliently in the recent critical history of Emily Dickinson's work.

As I noted above, Franklin's facsimile publication of *The Manuscript Books of Emily Dickinson* in 1981 significantly redirected the study of Dickinson's poems. Since then, Dickinson criticism has turned away from questions of poetic voice and has instead embraced the problematics of the visual mark, cancellation, works perennially in progress, and the limits of legibility. Portrayed by critics as exemplary of writerly flux and resistance to finish, Dickinson's poems-as-manuscripts have become a newfound experimental "open text," in the formulation made famous by Language poet Lyn Hejinian: "The 'open text' often emphasizes or foregrounds process . . . and thus resists the cultural tendencies that seek to identify and fix material and turn it into a product; that is, it resists reduction and commodification" (*Language* 43). In resisting "fix," the open text also necessarily resists what we have been discussing as poetic "finish."

Due both to this advent of textual scholarship and to experimental poets' recent interest in her work, it is fair to say that Emily Dickinson's lyric output has been reborn as experimental: as visual marks that foreground process as such, much as Hejinian formulated. In particular, the criticism of Susan Howe, a poet often associated with the Language movement, has established Dickinson as a foremother of the experimental project; she ultimately allies the poet's work with "the space of silence" (*The Birth-Mark* 170) rather than treating it as communicative speech or song. This is partially because, in her words, "These manuscripts should be understood as visual productions" (141).

And in her tellingly titled *Choosing Not Choosing*, Sharon Cameron has attributed a poetics of nonclosure to Dickinson, based largely on the way in which the poet's fascicle poems, in their presentation of variant words as foils and counterpoint to poetic lines, resist the choice of a "finished" line as such:

> In Dickinson's fascicles . . . variants indicate both the desire for limit and the difficulty in enforcing it. The difficulty in enforcing a limit to the poems turns into a kind of limitlessness . . . for . . . it is impossible to say where the text ends because the variants extend the text's identity in ways that make it seem potentially limitless. (6)

There is a strong connection between Hejinian's openness and Cameron's "limitlessness." Yet to ascribe limitlessness to poems written in common and short meter is to ask that the reader's eye be trained away from the patently limiting circumscription of rhyme and metrical structures—those structures that, in a global sense, help to determine "voice" as it is usually conceptualized in lyric poetry. Here, then, Cameron interprets the fascicles' variant words as destabilizing the very foundations of prosodic construction. This move is very much in line with the current direction of Dickinson studies, which have often myopically focused on microscopic aspects of the manuscript work, thus portraying it as a form of perennial Kristevan genotext, or text-in-progress, and eliding the components of prosody and sound that are indispensable aspects of poetic voice.

By taking Cameron's move as emblematic of a certain kind of reading, my purpose is to ask what happens when the values and modalities of "voice"—values often congruent with, but not fully identical to, prosodic structure—are exchanged for the more graphic values of "limitlessness" within the boundaries of the *same* poet's work. How could the notion of "limitlessness" speak to the poems in *Edgar Allan Poe & the Juke-Box*, for example—and how would such redressing serve to silence Bishop's recognizable voice?

For Cameron, as we've seen, Dickinson's retention of variants serves to create the limitlessness that then becomes representative of her oeuvre as a whole. Perhaps not surprisingly, the Quinn volume also includes many variants. In suggestive lines like "The chic dog and the not as chic   leak / peak / street" from "Rainy Day, Rio.," Bishop is imbued with a veneer of experimental—even if rhyme-driven—undecidability that, when printed, transforms the finish of her published poems into a different poetics altogether (133).

This line also recalls Sally Bushell's discussion of Dickinson's structural "creative optionality" in her manuscript composition, wherein "The fixed frame establishes a factual structure of event and narrative, syntax and meter. The optional parts are limited to nuances within that frame and to subtle changes of tone and emotional register that affect the overall meaning at the level of feeling" (*Text* 198). Even though Bishop seems primarily to be playing with assonance and near-rhyme here, the variants also proceed from nonsense to something approximating referential meaning: the singsong "(not-as) chic   leak" becomes, over the course of sequential wordplay, the almost referential "(not-as) chic street"—which could begin to describe a neighborhood that is not quite Fifth Avenue, for example. So if we decide to read these variants sequentially, they may indeed reveal something about the poet's aural process of composition. But the process itself would not have remained integral to the completed work; as we know, the "finished" Bishop was not a poet of wordplay, though she was also not averse to playing occasionally with prosody.[5] For

---

5. See, for example, her line break truncating the proper name of "Glens Fall/ s" in the cross-rhymed "Arrival at Santos" (*Complete Poems* 89). This enjambment playfully acknowledges the exigencies demanded by perfect rhyme, as well as the humble speaker's prosodic "imperfections." Thus when Bishop does play with sound in her poems, she enacts this play within (and sometimes as a metapoetic statement about) the formal confines of the poem in question. We can see this as well in the following lines from "The Map": "Shadows, or are they shallows, at its edges / showing the line of long seaweeded ledges" (*Complete Poems* 3). Here, the wordplay of "shadows" and "shallows" is

Bishop, then, "creative optionality" would be, at best, a momentary arti-fact rather than a viable, process-driven poetics.

Thus the preponderance of variants in *Edgar Allan Poe & the Juke-Box* must read differently for Bishop than for Dickinson, who after a certain point chose to retain her variants as an integral part of her fascicle pro-duction. For this reason, the graphic attention extolled and practiced by Dickinson's most ardent textual readers has an opposite effect in the case of Bishop's poetry, since publishing the poems in *Edgar Allan Poe & the Juke-Box* does militate against Bishop's de facto intentions—and some-times even overrides her textually manifested choices within the drafts themselves, as in Quinn's statement that "I feel that there is nothing to be learned from omitting punctuation where it is clear she *would have* employed it" (xix, emphasis mine). Though the volume spotlights the unfinished, there are evidently moments in which Quinn's editorial agency provides more "finish" than do Bishop's drafts.

More often than not, however, editorial selection and arrangement serves to intensify the appearance of undecidability in Bishop's unfin-ished work. Since the volume presents certain drafts in both print and facsimile forms, sometimes on facing pages, it provides a fascinating window into the aesthetics of editorial choice—which can necessarily "play" a writer differently than she might have played herself. In this case, the facing-page presentations serve to underscore the abyssal relation between each lettered surface and its textual, and technological, "other," thus opening a space for a more experimental poetics to reside.

As we saw in the line from "Rainy Day, Rio.," for example, recalibrat-ing and "pasteurizing" handwritten drafts into print requires frequent use of the bracket and the virgule, diacritics that mark negative space in the manuscripts. Because these marks signify emptiness in the form of lacunae or aporia, they are closer in spirit to the indeterminate aesthetic of the "open text" than to anything resembling the Bishop of *Complete Poems*. In the print version of "Good-Bye—," for example, such a line as "Our eyes bleary & /   /" is proleptically reminiscent of the blanks in Jorie Graham's *The End of Beauty* or indeed of Alice Fulton's doubled equal signs (13). Both of these prominent poets have worked with print diacritics as

---

incorporated into a pentameter line which, as we see, resolves into the inner "folds" of an envelope rhyme.

a way to resist particularization and semantic limitation. That neither of them would be fully claimed as "experimental" only reveals the degree to which aporia and undecidability have become accepted components of the mainstream repertoire that is available to the contemporary American poet.

These conditions necessarily contribute to the ease with which Bishop's unfinished drafts may be imbued with the experimental lure of the "mark." Perhaps we can see this best in drafts that inexplicably resist print recalibration altogether, as in a poem called "The Blue Chairs" (127). Here, we are given only a dubiously legible notebook page in facsimile reproduction, never a print "interpretation." Thus the visual mark was privileged over the poem's sense—with the page's verso ink perceptible in gusting layers of impenetrable hieroglyphs. Moreover, the choice to include the love poem "It is marvellous to wake up together . . ." as a photographed typescript also suggests that Bishop's creased paper and typewriter strokes might afford a more appropriate readerly "embrace" than a print version would allow (44).[6]

I just spoke of an experimental "lure," and at this juncture, I'd like to step back for a moment in order to acknowledge the considerable fascination of these facsimile presentations. Though I am arguing here that Bishop should not be looked on with an experimentally inflected eye, I would also be remiss not to acknowledge the tremendous appeal of the handwritten draft; no person of a literary predilection could be impervious to it. The smudge, the blot, the fold: these are the nostalgic reader's bread and butter, as I'll discuss more later. But it is for this very reason that we should guard against embracing such material too hastily. At the very least, Quinn and her publishers may be sensitive or even wise to such atavistic yearnings on the part of the reader; their editorial choices have considerably aestheticized Bishop's working pages.

When Bushell similarly aestheticizes a fragment from one of Wordsworth's ruined drafts of "The Prelude," we can better understand what

---

6. This choice is resonant with Marta Werner's nearly tactile, sometimes ecstatic, reading of a poem that Dickinson wrote on an envelope ("Flights"). She describes the work as a poetic "collage" which also constitutes a "taxonomy of paper wings": "The unfolding of the manuscript creates a strange visual rhyming of wings" (http://www.altx.com/ebr/ebr6/6werner/Pages/6wern1.htm). Dana Gioia's discussion of manuscript as "relic" is apt in both of these cases (*Disappearing Ink* 48–49).

is at stake in such choices: "When we respond to the page in isolation, it has a kind of beauty, I think, not only because of the evident fragility of the meaning it contains but also because of the unexpected and unintended enactment of its semantic meaning in its visual form" (*Text* 90). This judgment presents as a familiar statement about form and content, but one that is enhanced by the element of uncorrected chance that occurs in the draft; for Bushell, it is the fragility of both letter *and* meaning that makes the draft beautiful. By aesthetically ratifying the values of the incomplete and the aleatory (or what exceeds the author's compositional intention, difficult as that may be to ascertain), Bushell is arguing that draft material can and should be interpreted literarily and not simply as steps in a writer's teleological formation of a work. It seems to me, however, that this argument could only be made in a climate that already supports the aesthetic of the unfinished-as-literary, whose values remain antithetical to the exigencies of poetic voice.

What is ironic in all this, of course, is that Bishop's status as a major reviser preceded the publication of *Edgar Allan Poe & the Juke-Box*—but in a very different capacity. For years, writing programs have fetishized her multiple drafts of "One Art" as a sort of mathematical proof that mainstream workshop pedagogy "works." Indeed, according to the traditional goals of the writing workshop, a student's multiple drafts will culminate in a "finished" poem that shows no traces of the drafting process. The rueful ease of Bishop's often-anthologized villanelle, having "vanished" its many previous draft versions, seems an emblem of those very values.

Similarly, in *The Writer's Home Companion*, Joan Bolker treats Bishop's multiple drafts as a lesson to be learned about a necessary writerly teleology: "[J]udgments of our first drafts, of poetry or prose, are irrelevant . . . what we need to do with our writing is to keep going, keep revising, keep moving the work towards what it is meant to be" (101). This is the second of two philosophies of revision that are driving these pertinent "looks" at Bishop's poetry: revision as synchronous value or limitlessness, as in the previous Cameron quotation or in Bushell's discussion of Dickinson's "anti-telos" (*Text* 196); or revision as means to an end, in Bolker's formulation. When Bolker categorically safeguards the draft from "judgment," she necessarily disqualifies it from the literary-critical judgments that Bushell promotes as appropriate for the reading of unfinished manuscript materials. Consequently, revision "plays" differently in *The Writ-*

er's *Home Companion* than it does in *Edgar Allan Poe*; both texts reproduce Bishop's drafts of "One Art" for divergent purposes.

What we have, then, is a critical impasse regarding the proper status of revision in the literary work. I have been trying to show that due to the current critical climate, and in a manner analogous to Dickinson's rebirth as an experimental poet, Bishop is more likely to be conscripted by an "anti-telos" than to continue being associated with the teleological model epitomized by Bolker's comment. The moments of true illegibility in *Edgar Allan Poe* would go some distance in supporting this contention: illegibility, while only dubiously accessible by discrete criticism à la Bushell, is virtually disqualified from teleological process due to its apotropaic opacity.

There is an important sense, then, in which these moments of illegibility—in which the *non*-transparency of the medium is offered for readerly delectation—become test cases in *Edgar Allan Poe*. Here, the impediment is the message. Consider, for example, the nearly occluded "(Florida Revisited)?," a poem whose title itself contains parentheses and a question mark (177). On the left-hand page, we have a copiously marked-up typescript of the poem that includes circlings, smudge marks, and crabbed ink handwriting. Facing this is a print version of the poem, whose lineation is supplemented by variant material placed close to the right margin. While the presentation reads as a testament to Quinn's voluminous labors of deciphering ("Bishop's handwriting is challenging," she notes simply in the introduction—xviiii), it also shows the very unstable relationship between an effaced text and the necessarily indeterminate process of reading it. Here, transcription becomes the "wild surmise" of interpretation. Indeed, this very juxtaposition calls the distinction between process and product into question since the reader can see for herself how potentially inaccurate any such print choices might be; again, Hejinian's open text hovers over the presentation.

This problematic is palpably magnified in another poem, "Hannah A.," which the book also represents in facing pages of facsimile and print (53). The facsimile shows an inked notebook page that is marked and canceled beyond the point of legibility. The print version of this poem, with only one bracketed stanza—less tentative in its presentation than many printed poems in the volume—opens a chasm of questions about intelligibility, legibility, and the degree to which these print poems have become a product of Quinn's editorial labors. Such questions exist in sharp contrast to Dickinson's editorial history, in which "faithfulness" to the fascicle (or even extra-fascicle) markings is seen as a certain type of accuracy, even if such accuracy is commensurate with perdurable undecidability. According to this line of thought, the earlier and more "finished" print publications of Dickinson's poems are shown to be products of her editors rather than herself. What *Edgar Allan Poe & the Juke-Box* shows us about Bishop, quite graphically, is that the closer we get to "original" mark, the greater the possibility for interpretive editorial largesse. Perhaps most powerfully, however, the volume also reveals the degree to which such largesse becomes the occupational hazard of any archivist interpreting illegible materials. Indeed, the draft of "Hannah A." shows archivist reading as a necessary fiction. One can only think that a premium has been placed on the inability to read.

But why? What is the market for illegibility? What is the real interest in disseminating drafts of incomplete poems that can barely be deciphered? The stock answer is that the ephemera of a major poet should be made available both to a public readership and to the scholar. But illegibility is, as we've seen, a question of degree: the culling and presentation of manuscript material, particularly in facsimile form, necessitates formal and editorial choices. And as we've begun to see, the illegible and the canceled were privileged in the facsimile productions included in this compendium. Quinn herself notes that in certain cases, the facsimile was the most "exciting" means of presenting the work (xv). I am arguing here that the excitement of illegibility is, even if osmotically, the product of an experimentally driven critical climate that fetishizes what exceeds normative grammar and syntax, that is, illegibility and "mark," as emblematized by the transformation of Dickinson from primarily a formal poet to an experimental one. But I also want to suggest that the re-dressing of both Bishop and Dickinson in experimental poetics may result in their critical—and in some cases, popular—re-domestication as women poets. This is a surprisingly reactionary move that would be far from experimental (or at least Language) values as such.

I'd like to develop this idea by looking more closely at the way that visual images and objects have functioned in the oeuvres of both poets. The deceptively marginal role of visual material in *Edgar Allan Poe & the Juke-Box* begins, in fact, to encapsulate some of the richest intersections between the Bishop and Dickinson manuscripts. There are two issues to be considered here: one is the inclusion of illustrative pictures next to facing poems (a problematic that Quinn doesn't take up in her introductory discussion); the other involves drafts of poems on which Bishop has drawn pictures. I am more interested in the latter problematic, in which the poem "Dear, my compass" only appears in *Edgar Allen Poe* as a typescript containing childlike drawings of a barn, a goose, a swan, and a single bed (140). Here, as in similar cases we have just discussed, no print version of the poem has been included.

In the context of the volume as a whole, this presentation suggests that "Dear, my compass" cannot be separated from its accompanying drawings: that something essential would have been lost if the poem had been presented in a nonillustrated print form. Such a view would dovetail with the materialist arguments of Virginia Jackson, a leading critic of Dickinson's manuscript materials. In a trenchant critique of lyric voice, Jackson argues that we cannot interpret Dickinson's letter-poems without the objects (for example, the flowers or dead crickets) that the poet sent along with them in her correspondence. Jackson's complaint is that "the poems in bound volumes appear both redeemed and revoked from their scenes or referents, from the history that the book, as book, omits" (*Dickinson's Misery* 3). Clearly, Jackson wants to critique the ostensible universality that the lyric—and its concomitant "voice"—has foisted upon Dickinson as its unwitting exemplar. But in doing this, she goes so far as to suggest that what Dickinson wrote may not have been lyric poetry at all, at least not insofar as our critical tradition has understood it: "But how do we know that lyrics are what Dickinson wrote?" (17).

I would suggest that there is much more at stake in Jackson's argument than a dismantling of lyric voice. By arguing that critics must take the metonyms and material contexts of Dickinson's poetic composition into account—the paper she used; the mementos she sent to Susan Gilbert Dickinson and others—Jackson relegates Dickinson's writing to the private, domesticated sphere of the poet's historical circumstances. What her argument doesn't address is the fact that such domesticated space has traditionally and often unquestioningly been seen as the domain of women writers. If Dickinson can *only* be viably interpreted in manuscript form, with the reader made aware of the original "props" around her writing, what does this really say about her viability as a major poet? Did Keats and Wordsworth need props?

My point here is that despite all appearances to the contrary, Jackson's argumentation comes perilously close to portraying Dickinson as a manner of "Sunday poet" who sends an editor photos of her grandkids alongside her poem about them—and thus a poet whose work cannot viably be removed from the historical context of her feminized, sociable world.[7] Indeed, when Jackson decries Dickinson's poems' "being taken out of their sociable circumstances" by critics, one can only wonder at the loss to literary history if they had remained *in* them (21).

Jackson's overemphasis on manuscript-as-materiality, in its refusal of a reductive universality, may thus refuse a (woman) writer the baseline universal of creating a text that can be widely disseminated; as Walter Benn Michaels explains, "the very idea of textuality depends upon the *discrepancy* between the text and its materiality, which is why two copies of a book (two different materials objects) may be seen to be the same text" (*Shape* 3, emphasis mine). This is a refusal I have also located in Quinn's choice to reproduce "Dear, my compass . . ." with its faux-naïf illustrations. The issue becomes particularly acute in the case of Bishop's swan drawing since, according to Marilyn May Lombardi, the poet associated the figure of the swan with her "single most vivid memory of her mother":

> Her mother, dressed incongruously in the mourning clothes required of a widow "in those days," sits with the three-year-old Elizabeth in a swan boat on a Boston lake. A real swan comes up to the boat. Her mother "fed it and it bit her finger," splitting the black kid glove and the skin underneath. (*Body* 24)

---

7. Obviously, the "Sunday poet" comparison does not take chronological differences into account. But by applying the habits of writing practices in Dickinson's time to the reception of her work today, Jackson ignores the very limitation of those practices, particularly as they define the "domestic" work of women poets. While Jackson critiques feminist critics such as Sandra Gilbert and Susan Gubar for their focus on the "person" of Dickinson (or their "fantasy of an incarnate literary text"—*Dickinson's Misery* 177), she does not address the ways in which her own argumentation necessarily "incarnates" Dickinson as well, but through different means—namely, by recreating and resuscitating the trope of metonymy as it was literalized in Dickinson's material writing practices.

The metaphoric and metonymic resonance of the doubled swan, as figured both in the actual bird and in the boat's design, has a complicated relationship to Bishop's memory of her black-clad mother (whose clothing stands in archetypal contrast to the whiteness of the doubled swan symbol before it is "eaten" by that whiteness itself). Indeed, one could hypothetically argue that the emotional power of the swan image—as figured here in its striking rhetorical recursivity—would render it an indelible (visual) icon in Bishop's psyche. If we follow this hypothetical argument further, the mimetic swan drawing becomes paradoxically representative of everything that resists representation into language; its very refusal of verbal symbolization would necessitate the reproduction of the facsimile drawing, even as the poem itself describes "swans [that] can paddle / icy water" (140). Standing in for Bishop's personal mythology, then, the drawing would become a subtext or phantom text that the *verbal* poem could never successfully convey.

Although the above argument does not follow the exact contours of Jackson's, it begins to reveal the garden path of biographical (inflected by psychoanalytic) criticism to which her argument opens the proverbial gate. The risk of this approach is redoubled, I would argue, in the case of women poets who have often been the object of a biographical fascination that seems almost to eclipse their poetic output; we will discuss this later in the case of Plath. Yet we can also contextualize Jackson's materialist approach by putting it into dialogue with other recent critical responses to Dickinson's manuscript materials. Take, for example, Marta Werner's seemingly opposing comment about editing Dickinson's fragments: "Never prepared for publication, perhaps never even meant to be read by anyone other than the scriptor herself, they are not so much 'works' as symptoms of the processes of composition, data—aleatory, contingent—of the work of writing" ("Woe" 27).

Werner's transformation of poet into scriptor—perhaps a body even *produced* by its writing—is notable both for its unapologetic universality and its radical commitment to a writing or "marking" that lacks a referential addressee like Susan Gilbert Dickinson; these qualities are precisely what Jackson critiques as the reductive construction of the lyric throughout literary history.[8] If anything, Werner's description creates

---

8. In *Dickinson's Misery*, Jackson has critiqued Werner for reading Dickinson's archival materials in too "lyric" a manner (50–52).

an experimental sheen: far from referential, the *writing* is its own theater. But Werner's perspective also slips a bit: if writing is "symptom" rather than communication, it retains the infectious, self-contained fascination of pathology.[9] In fact, it is a remarkably short road from the "symptoms" of writing to the "weirdness," or worse, with which Dickinson has been imbued by critics and biographers.[10] In most cases, this characterization is a result not of Dickinson's writing but instead of her life choices.

The arguments of Werner and Jackson, I would argue, occupy two paradoxically complementary extremes on a spectrum of Dickinson textual criticism: while Werner's severely abstracted "scriptor" is by definition shorn of biography, Jackson's attention to the manuscripts' referential metonyms and material circumstances necessarily situates critical concern within the domestic or biographical realm. While the latter slippage is a fairly obvious risk, I am also concerned that Werner's super-abstracted, textually created, and even transgressively experimental "scriptor," as generated within manuscript materials, could act as a screen for the retention of a very conservative relation between reader and (woman) poet: it could serve, in other words, to uphold the dubious category of "women's writing," a category that Bishop herself regarded with a measure of suspicion.

This is because even the materiality of writing-as-such, as Werner describes it, often shades into an obsession with the gendered body—and life—that technologically produced that writing; the text is about the writerly conditions of its own production. Though metonymy is not as historicized for Werner as it is for Jackson, it is nevertheless relentless—and metonymy is, as we know, the trope of bodily proximity par excellence. Thus even the neutered "scriptor," insofar as she is identified with marks rather than with voice, can play into the gendered assumptions that I have been critiquing here. The work of both Jackson and Werner shows, then, that the manuscript edition may elicit a reception that val-

---

9. Interestingly, Quinn uses somewhat similar diction to speak of Bishop's drafts in *Edgar Allan Poe and the Juke-Box*: "drafts with phrases that haunted her. . . . drafts with lines written out in a rush but accompanied by a chosen rhyme scheme; fragments that showcase verbal gestures familiar to Bishop readers from the more successful resolution of those gestures in the poems we know" (x).

10. For relevant discussions treating this portrayal of Dickinson, see Adrienne Rich, "Vesuvius at Home," and Sandra M. Gilbert and Susan Gubar, *The Madwoman in the Attic*.

ues muscular, social, or gendered personhood over an attention to lyric poetry as such.

Will this happen to Bishop? One thing is certain: her posthumous publication schedule has increased such a possibility. In 2008, the publication of *Words in Air*, the correspondence between Bishop and Robert Lowell, followed closely on the heels of *Edgar Allan Poe and the Juke-Box* in 2006. If we are to read "props" in conjunction with texts, as Jackson suggests, it is likely that each of these books will act as a material-conceptual prop for the other—thereby increasing the likelihood that *Edgar Allan Poe* will be not only "experimentalized" but also read biographically. Though another volume of Bishop's letters, *One Art*, had appeared earlier, the tête-à-tête "celebrity" aspect of the Bishop and Lowell correspondence necessarily places Bishop in a differential—and in some critics' fantasies, heterosexualized—relationship to the gigantism of Lowell, thereby enabling the type of gendered operations that I have just suggested.[11]

Recent reviews of *Words in Air* suggest as much. Michael Hofmann's comments in *Poetry* fairly exemplify the euphoric tone of many reviewers of this volume, as well as their tendency to overreach regarding the book's significance for gender relations: "It's not least a gender myth more astute about men and women than that of Atalanta and Hippolytus. . . . He is her anchor, she his kite" (359). Here, a friendship between a lesbian woman and a straight man has been handily conscripted into the heteronormative aspects of Greek mythology—specifically, a myth in which a man tricks a powerful woman into marriage. And William Logan focuses his *New York Times* review on the theme of thwarted love between the two poets. Though he acknowledges that Bishop's lesbianism made a consummated relationship between them impossible, he also perseverates on Lowell's attraction to her and finally frames the volume as a love story manqué: "Two poets in love must succumb to the same folie à deux as the actor and the actress, the magician and the fellow magician" ("I Write").

It is notable, to say the least, that such astute critics as Logan and Hofmann would fall into the hackneyed gendering of the male-provider "anchor" and the diaphanous female kite—or a fantasy heterosexualiza-

---

11. My thanks to Jason Roush for first pointing out in conversation that the reviewers of *Words in Air* were heterosexualizing the relationship between Lowell and Bishop.

tion that both critics seem intent on invoking, if only for the reason of lamenting its very impossibility. It is indeed remarkable enough that we should question the nature of the extra-intellectual forces at work in what has become a doubled publication event—and what may become an allegorically doubled, or hallucinated, vision of Elizabeth Bishop herself.

In these ways, then, *Words* has been publicly constructed as *Edgar Allan Poe*'s heteronormative "other half," one that opens the way for a domesticated portrait of Bishop to rise phoenix-like from the abandoned drafts in *Edgar Allan Poe*. Clearly—and unavoidably—the letters treat Bishop as "life" rather than "scriptor." Made to feel vicariously "close" to Bishop much as Lowell was, the reader of *Words in Air* will follow the life around; as Hofmann notes, the volume can almost function as an epistolary novel (358). Thus the publication of *Words*, particularly so soon after *Edgar Allan Poe*, may well tip the scales of Bishop criticism in a decidedly biographical direction—even if the content of this biographical focus has more to do with the fantasies of readers and critics than with the actuality of Bishop's biographical experience. And as I've suggested in my discussion of Werner's perspective in particular, such a direction is not necessarily incompatible with reading *Edgar Allan Poe* as a form of open text.

In *The Shape of the Signifier*, Michaels has critiqued our contemporary tendency to read texts through the lens of identity politics and thereby interpret them as nothing more nor less than bodily emanations of their authors' "difference."[12] While his critique exceeds the narrow field of contemporary American poetry, I might also suggest that American women poets are particularly susceptible to these sorts of readings, even as the percentage of women writing poetry has steadily increased over the last twenty-five years or so.[13] It is arguable, in fact, that readers and poets are more likely to focalize the bodies and persons of women poets; as a purely anecdotal example, Hofmann's review directly quotes Bishop's fleeting commentary on eye shadow—out of a volume totaling over nine

12. I am referring here to what Michaels calls "the fantasy of meaning without representation—the text written in blood, the computer virus, the genetic code" (*Shape* 123). He argues that materialist interpretations often portray texts as identity-determined embodiments rather than as signification.

13. See Jennifer Ashton, "Our Bodies, Our Poems" for a useful discussion of this changing demographic and its impact on the ways in which women's lyrical and experimental outputs have been marketed and critically received.

hundred pages of letters (363). And often body and text are commingled when a poet's idiosyncratic marks, as handwriting, are brought into the mix.

When body becomes confused with text, moreover, the variorum or facsimile edition can act as a sort of textual underwear, much as the ending of Billy Collins's "Taking Off Emily Dickinson's Clothes" suggests. In a blazon of incremental undressing that is reminiscent of Donne's "Elegy for His Mistress Going to Bed," Collins's speaker casts himself as a "polar explorer" who is "sailing toward the iceberg of [Dickinson's] nakedness" (*Picnic, Lightning* 24). When he undoes the poet's corset at the end of the poem, however, the act becomes commensurate with a collective or public reading of Dickinson's works:

and I could hear her sigh when finally it was unloosed,
the way some readers sigh when they realize
that Hope has feathers,
that reason is a plank,
that life is a loaded gun
that looks right at you with a yellow eye. (25)

Here, Dickinson's presumably sexualized "sigh" is compared to the collective sighs of readers who internally "realize," or make real, some of her most famous lines. Thus for Collins, the fantasy of seducing the mythologized Dickinson is analogous to the reading act itself, if only via symptomatology. There is a sense, then, in which undressing the poet— the metonymic act par excellence—becomes a civic gesture on behalf of a discerning ("*some* readers") reading public. If Dickinson's body and poems are interchangeable to this degree, we must venture only a little further to render her undergarments commensurate with the Cavalier "delight in disorder" of unkempt draft formats (Herrick, "Delight" 811). Collins's poem doesn't directly address recent Dickinson criticism, but it does suggest that we are all voyeurs of her irrevocably compounded text-body—whether we are heterosexual male poets or manuscript scholars of any gender or persuasion[14]—and that this perennial undressing is

14. Clearly, to situate Collins in the company of Werner and Jackson is to conflate a popular and even populist poet-persona with the more arcane concerns of textual

not only pleasurable for us, but also what the dead-but-iconic Dickinson "wants."

If Bishop seems an unlikely candidate for such a denuding—or conversely, for such a mythologized assemblage—we might do well to supplement our continuing consideration of Dickinson with a short revisiting of the popular effigy of Sylvia Plath, particularly insofar as the latter was grafted over posthumously published manuscript materials. Jacqueline Rose has described a ubiquitous cultural "haunting" by and of Plath, which is a phenomenon that is also discernible in the Dickinson cottage industry (*Haunting* 1). Perhaps Plath's daughter Frieda Hughes has put it best: "Since she died my mother has been dissected, analyzed, reinterpreted, reinvented, fictionalized, and in some cases completely fabricated" (*Ariel* xx). Of course, much of this attention revolved not around Plath's writing but instead around her personal life and especially around her troubled relationship with her husband Ted Hughes. Plath's posthumously published *Ariel*, the real maker of her literary celebrity, became a battle ground in this arena since Hughes himself had edited the book for publication after his wife's death.[15]

Perhaps not surprisingly, the long-awaited publication of Plath's original facsimile version of *Ariel* in 2004 served to fuel the fire of venom against Hughes. For mainstream critics, as Rose notes, this "restored" *Ariel* has been interpreted as a window into Plath's psyche rather than her writing process or, strictly speaking, her "texts." Indeed, Rose quotes Marjorie Perloff as decrying Hughes for suppressing "nothing less than the 'rebirth of an isolate [female] self'" (71) in his original editing of *Ariel*. And in her introduction to the new edition, Frieda Hughes encourages readers to see the restored *Ariel* as the person of Plath: "This new, restored edition *is* my mother in that moment" (xxi, emphasis mine). Thus the "restoration" of Plath through facsimile publication is seen as a bodily rather than textual one: a healing of the Lacanian "corps morcelé," or the body in bits and pieces, which Hughes's editing ostensibly effected on the anatomy of *Ariel* (Lacan, *Écrits* 72). Yet we know that any such reconstruction is, in Lacanian terms, fictional. The imago in the mirror—the

---

scholars. And yet, again, these disparate approaches may dovetail to produce a "hallucinated" portrait of the woman poet.

15. Rose discusses Hughes's editing of *Ariel* in *The Haunting of Sylvia Plath* (70–71).

outline of Plath's bodily integrity, reassembled via her original manuscript—is by definition illusory.[16]

Some may find it untenable to draw connections between Bishop and Plath in this arena. Indubitably, we are subject to a larger and more formidable "public" Plath than will probably ever be the case with Bishop, due to the circumstances around Plath's suicide and her arguably sensationalized use of historical and personal materials in both her poetry and fiction. For this reason, the publication of *Edgar Allan Poe & the Juke-Box* will probably do little to transform Bishop into such a "haunting" cult figure for the general public. Yet two notable poetry critics, David Orr and Dana Gioia, have accorded Bishop a predominance and a ubiquity in the poetry world that are striking at best, hyperbolic at worst. "You are living in a world created by Elizabeth Bishop," was how Orr startlingly opened his *New York Times* review of *Edgar Allan Poe & the Juke-Box* ("Rough Gems"). And in Gioia's opinion, the posthumous stature of Bishop today is historically equaled only by the reputation of Emily Dickinson (185).[17] If the doubled specter of the blond and brunette Plath haunts the terrain of literary culture—almost as the black and white mother-swan in Bishop's memory—surely Bishop's own work has formed the topography, the very bedrock, on which contemporary American poetry has been built.

At this juncture, I may seem to be suggesting that the variorum or facsimile edition has come to constitute a kind of glass ceiling for women poets—a way of undermining or domesticating women who, to paraphrase Orr, have become powerful enough to create viable literary worlds. But this is not exactly what I wish to argue. Far from wanting to impute invidious intent to any of Bishop's skillful curators, I would suggest instead that our readerly need for intimacy with what Gioia calls "the poet's hand" is more pronounced in the case of women poets, due to a larger acculturation that arguably still holds sway regardless of the empir-

16. Lacan highlights this disjuncture by noting "in the spatial captation manifested in the mirror-stage . . . the effect in man of an organic insufficiency in his natural reality—in so far as any meaning can be given to the word 'nature'" (*Écrits* 4). The imago in the mirror is thus an unattainable visual ideal that can never reflect, much less heal, the baby's *feeling* of the body in bits and pieces.

17. See also Thomas Travisano's "The Elizabeth Bishop Phenomenon" for a discussion of the various factors that have contributed to Bishop's relatively new status as a major poet.

ical gender composition of the present literary world. This phenomenon is not far from what Simone de Beauvoir critiqued in *The Second Sex* as women's association with immanence and the limited life of the body.[18] More surprising, perhaps, is the way that a progressive experimental aesthetic—Hejinian's open text—serves this acculturated need by insisting on graphic mark, or what cannot be separated from the writing hand, rather than on the "finish" of duplicable text. This becomes a way of metonymically writing-in the (gendered) *person* of the writer, who is thereby prohibited from exiting the "footlights" of the text, in Barthes's terms.[19]

But if we let graphic considerations replace or displace voice when we read lyric poetry, or the manuscripts of lyric poets, we do so at the peril of poetry itself—not because we thereby flout the poets' intentions, nor because voice restores some chimerical sense of presence; but instead because the "finish" of a carefully crafted voice—whether formal or otherwise—allows for a necessary abstraction from the immanence of the body and its matter, an abstraction that is necessary for the creation of text itself. This abstraction, indeed, is what W. R. Johnson has called "the transformation of the personal into the impersonal or, better, the tempering of the personal with the universal" (*Idea* 33). While such recourse to the universal has been widely and validly critiqued as exclusionary, we might also consider reintroducing a strand of it as a corrective to the hallucination of too much personhood in the figures of these women poets. A silenced voice, in other words, inevitably leaves a remainder—of too much material matter.

18. What Beauvoir means by "immanence" is encapsulated in her pithy statement at the beginning of *The Second Sex*: "Woman? Very simple, say the fanciers of simple formulas: she is a womb, an ovary" (3). This association with, or reduction to, biological functions constitutes the "immanence" that for Beauvoir stands in stark contrast to the "transcendence" which is associated with male privilege. Though perhaps few would make such a stark statement today, many aspects of our cultural life (including "mommy wars," the repudiation of the very language of feminism, and significant demographic resistance to abortion rights) suggest that women are still constrained by their cultural association with immanence, much as Beauvoir described.

19. "On the stage of the text, no footlights: there is not, behind the text, someone active (the writer) and out front someone passive (the reader)" (Barthes, *Pleasure* 16). My point is that the manuscript edition—even as interpreted by a scholar like Werner—actually does construct the writer in the way that Barthes is critiquing here; it will not allow her to exit her text's "footlights."

Thus an excess of ephemeral writing may lead more toward the trappings of biography—or indeed to a hallucinated imago of the woman poet's person—than toward poetic voice itself. As we began to see in the recent high-profile reviews of *Words in Air*, biography can also collapse into mythology, whether heterosexualized or domesticated (and not least in the case of Plath). What Gioia admiringly calls "the magical nature of the author's hand" (46) may lead to a critical magical-thinking that compartmentalizes the achievements of women poets by inserting them into life-narratives either euphoric or dysphoric. This, I think, is what we should watch for in Bishop's case, particularly in light of any potential dovetailing between *Edgar Allan Poe & the Juke-Box* and *Words in Air*.

More generally, and by way of closing, let's further consider the fascination of the facsimile edition at this precise point in literary history. It is difficult to say if there has been an increase in these publications lately. But if the case of Dickinson is allegorical or even symptomatic of a cultural moment, it is notable that her critics' intense interest in the idiosyncrasies of the poet's very marks in the fascicles or ephemera—what Werner names "strike-outs, underlinings, horizontal and vertical boundary lines, and other kinds of graphic 'noise'" ("Woe" 36), as well as "angled dashes, flying quotation marks, and other pointings" (36)—is happening at the very moment at which handwriting is disappearing as a modality of cultural communication, having been all but replaced by the uniformity of the letters produced on a computer screen. For many writers who compose on the computer today, the recreation of successive "drafts," as in Bishop's "One Art," has become all but impossible. Indeed, when Vendler ("Art") lamented that Quinn's volume would cause poets to "incinerat[e] their drafts" for fear of becoming the subject of a similar compilation, she might as well have been speaking from another era.

In this way, the variorum or facsimile edition, while seeming to support an experimentalist poetics, may be conservative not only of archetypal and outmoded gender relations but also of nearly outmoded and mourned-for technologies, much as the very title of Sven Birkerts's *The Gutenberg Elegies* suggests. This question comes full circle, however, since many manuscript critics view the electronic medium as uniquely suited for disseminating the visual particularities of manuscript production. The website for the Dickinson Archive Project suggests as much in its mission statement:

We take advantage of the computer's remarkable capacity for representing visual material by displaying full color facsimile images of [Dickinson's] manuscript pages and drawing our transcriptions from the manuscript record itself in an effort to further critical inquiry of her manuscripts beyond those featured in R.W. Franklin's *The Manuscript Books of Emily Dickinson* (1981).

According to this discussion, the computer surpasses the book's generic capacity to present manuscript materials—even Franklin's groundbreaking manuscript book, which revolutionized Dickinson studies as such. In a sense, then, the electronic archive paradoxically wants to "out-book" the book.[20] For many manuscript scholars, the electronic field has become the preferred locus from which to reanimate what Derrida calls "nostalgia for the proferred page on which a virtually inimitable handwriting creates a path for itself with the pen" (62) and what for Gioia is the Benjaminian "aura" still held by the handwritten manuscript in an age long past the advent of mechanical reproduction (44).

So the electronic age may usher in a return to biographically based criticism—even if what qualifies as "biography" is the particular moments achieved by the musculature of the hand. This is especially acute in the case of Dickinson, whose marks are often seen as utterly singular and idiosyncratic. It may be the ultimate irony that experimental writing, with its emphasis upon text liberated from referent, may become the most viscerally referential of all—when it cannot be disconnected from the (literally) manual labor of the writing, and thereby living, human body. To hold the work too close to that body may be to deny it the severance that paradoxically lets it live as textually disembodied voice—and thus, as art.

No less a lyric poet than Wallace Stevens said that "[a]ll poetry is experimental poetry" (*Opus Posthumous* 161), and it may be that even the most committed lyric poem can present as experimental if caught as a freeze-frame within the long process of artistic production. Bishop might have seemed the unlikeliest of candidates for such a presentation; but in

---

20. In *Paper Machine*, Derrida writes of "the temptation that is figured by the World Wide Web as the ubiquitous Book finally reconstituted, the book of God, the great book of Nature, or the World Book finally achieved in its onto-theological dream, even though what it does is to repeat the end of that book as to-come" (15).

Edgar Allen Poe & the Juke-Box, her "finished" poems are presented with their versos, and her record plays backward: the values of the finished and the unfinished are necessarily calibrated differently. As revision is always a work in progress, so is the changing tenor of its aesthetic and allegorical value. As we have seen, however, some experimental values are all too familiar. In light of this, we can only hope that the voice of Bishop's published poems will continue to resonate for her readers.

"Arranging, Deepening, Enchanting"

Catherine McCarthy's *Flower Arranging* (2011)

"I like to see flowers growing, but when they are gathered, they cease to please. I look on them as things rootless and perishable; their likeness to life makes me sad." Such are the musings of Lucy Snowe in Charlotte Brontë's last novel, *Villette* (424). And therein lies the paradox of both the empirical bouquet—the flowers we may gather from gardens—and their painterly representations. These representations constitute one moment in the genre of still life, which is known in French as *nature morte*, or "dead nature." As Brontë's character suggests, still life is inflected by both the incipience of living and the micro- or proto-narratives of decay. In her remarkable series of paintings titled *Flower Arranging*, Catherine McCarthy shines both a spotlight and a microscope on such paradoxes, featuring bouquets that are palpably material yet gorgeously theatrical.

McCarthy's source images are taken from instructional photographs in 1960s flower-arranging manuals, from which she also derives titles such as *Hogarth's Curve*, referring to the shape that the arranged flowers form. But while she gazes backward at the showy inscrutability of these photographic images, she also transmutes them through the tactile and mercurial medium of paint, imbuing still life with the variegations of *nature morte*. In McCarthy's hands, the decorum of the sixties' housewife is delivered with the troubling zoom and clarity of dreams. In this way, she invests the small or domestic genre of still life with the looming drama of the imagination or the unconscious—the nearly choral tones of the Freudian death-drive. Sometimes this is accomplished by way of global color: her twinned instances of *Victorian Slipper* are, in the first instance, deathly cool—"Grayed in, and gray," in Gwendolyn Brooks's words—and then fierily hot, as if pressing two sides of a fairy-tale coin

(Brooks, *Selected* 3). At other moments, we perceive such consciousness in the shadows thrown by the flowers and their vases; in the seminal *Hogarth's Curve*, for example, the shadows are nearly animalistic in their provenance, foreboding in their inchoate connotations.

McCarthy's dream, moreover, is foremost a dream of paint. So again in *Hogarth's Curve*, her flowers are painted with the eerie smokiness of a Baudelairean *fleur du mal*; a vase of dahlias is rendered in the black and white of ghostlier photography. But punctuating the diagonal of the flowers' curve are two buttery, flame-tipped, nearly liquidated blooms that foil the formal drama of the black-and-white composition; they are discrete sunbursts within a tonally constrained structure. The curve, of course, remains intact: what exceeds structure also upholds and instantiates it, in a phenomenon that is similar to foot substitution in metrical poetry. For McCarthy, this is the moment of paint's insistence within a formal composition.

It is precisely at such moments of dramatized liquidity, or haze, that the petals speak most directly to the intensity of the artist's aims. These are also the moments in which the artist's brush, or the trace of her hand, is most noticeable. Paint, eye, and hand intertwine: as James H. Rubin notes in *Manet's Silence and the Poetics of Bouquets*, "the 'visual' hand was discovered through the 'handling' eye (and vice versa)—that is, through acknowledging the materiality of human perception" (224). We can perceive such entwinement in *Ledge Hybrid*, a bouquet painted in partial collage, its central bloom outlined in black as the illusion of a cutout imported from a scissored photograph. This borrowed blossom is flanked by others that appear to be in the early stages of what Robert Frost called "the slow smokeless burning of decay" (*Collected Poems* 101): a wilting that is suggested by the reddish, crisping, nearly nervous outlines of their petals. This outlining is another trace of the artist's hand—and another grace note fashioned by *nature morte*.

Sometimes McCarthy's dream is of a more conceptual variety. *Hogarth's Camo*, for example, features an almost photographically rendered white vase that fractures into painterly stripes of navy and green-toned abstraction. Through the medium of paint, we perceive the illusion of two different modes: photography and abstraction inhabit the same field. And it is as if the flower arrangement has splintered through the very abstract energies of its own making; as if the concrete always carried the abstract within it. We can perceive the wildness of hurricanes in these buffeting waves.

There is yet another variety of abstraction that informs McCarthy's dream gaze. Even in her more mimetic paintings, and unlike many traditional works of still life, McCarthy's bouquets are abstracted from the rooms or settings that house them. Sometimes they seem to float; occasionally, as in *Ledge*, we may glimpse the illusion of a mirror or shallow pool placed as ballast underneath. At other times, a vase may hover on the edge of dissolution into its background or support. We see this in both the bright whiteness of the glass heel in the "cool" *Victorian Slipper* and the luminous dolphin vase in *Ledge*—which has either absorbed, or is currently reflecting, the dappled grays and greens of its backdrop and the foliage that populates it. As a rule, McCarthy's shaded backdrops recall the clouded backcloth of schoolchild photographic portraiture: an abolition of the pictorial surround, or a severing of the child from the metonymies of her childhood aura.

So while McCarthy's sourcing is clearly imbued with the decorum of American upper-middle-class femininity, she has also removed these images from the picturability of their attendant domestic narratives. And while she seems to enjoy the nearly camp pleasure these images can transmit—the Victorian glass shoe-vase, for example, is humorously metonymic of an even earlier fashion or mythology of womanhood—there is also a significant strand of seriousness in their magnified theatricality. This is to say that McCarthy is dramatizing not only the material world that is in part these paintings' subject, but also the activity of arrangement itself. This notion recalls "The Idea of Order at Key West," in which Wallace Stevens describes fishing boats whose lights arrange a seaside scene with ordering transitivity, "Arranging, deepening, enchanting night" (*Collected Poems* 129). For Stevens, arrangement is what creates the amplitude of environment—and it is also constitutive of art itself.

Far, then, from the "mental relaxation" that Renoir described as the state he enjoyed when painting flowers, McCarthy's bouquets constitute a work of rigorous double discipline (Rubin, *Manet's Silence* 163). This is in part the discipline of arranging, shaping, and juxtaposition whereby Lucy Snowe's "rootless" blossoms flourish and transform into letters, often the delicately near-illegible rondure of the "S" shape formed by Hogarth's curve; but it is also the discipline of seeing and rendering, in which the painter must speak to both the demands of visual precision and the hungers of the imagination. It is the fruit—or more accurately, the flowers—of such discipline that we enjoy in the ravishing immediacy of these paintings: still life and *nature morte*, offered to us by the doubled singularity of Catherine McCarthy's eye and imagination.

A Farm, Two Spiders, and A Book of Luminous Things

Czeslaw Milosz's Affinity for the Image (2011)

I am only a man: I need visible signs.
—MILOSZ, "VENI CREATOR"

To address the topic "Milosz in and on America," I take as my starting point a small corner in the grand architecture of Czeslaw Milosz's career. In 1997, Milosz published an anthology of poems with Harcourt titled *A Book of Luminous Things: An International Anthology of Poetry*, containing American and world poetry in translation. This project was connected both to Milosz's teaching at Berkeley and his friendship with his translator, the poet Robert Hass; in 1993, the two co-taught a graduate seminar on the poems collected in the book.

Clearly, the editing of any anthology also constitutes a work of criticism—insofar as an editor confers value on a poem when he or she or they include it in a collection. And Milosz is well aware of the tenor and scope of such agency. In his introduction to *A Book of Luminous Things*, he uses the diction of geography and real estate to describe his work as an editor: in his own words, he is both engaged in "the management of the estate of poetry" and, moreover, "carv[ing] . . . a province of [his] own" within it (xv). Such language—fascinatingly elegiac in the first case—clarifies Milosz's sense of his responsibilities, as a Nobel laureate, to disseminate literary values. It also suggests the sense of proprietorship the anthology enabled him to enjoy with respect to those values. As we'll see, the anthology reveals important aspects of Milosz's affinities—with respect to his particular vision of American poetry, his construction of the image as such (or the "luminous things" of the book's title), and finally, the role of both the formal and thematic "miniature" in Milosz's thoughts about lyric poetry. This is a theme perhaps best exemplified by Adam Zagajewski's poem "Auto Mirror" in the anthology: "In the rear-view mirror suddenly / I saw the bulk of the Beauvais Cathedral; / great things dwell in small ones / for a moment" (128). The three strands of my discussion are braided; and to address them, I'll eventually be talking about the significance of Walt Whitman's work within Milosz's volume.

By compiling *A Book of Luminous Things*, Milosz is offering us a particular, tangential, and perhaps synecdochic vision of American poetry—not, as he himself states, through an observation of "revolts," "movements," "schools," or "trends," but by the agency of nonsystematic selection that an anthology project can occasion. By way of his own metaphor, he is an "art collector," with some of the welcome eclecticism that such a role might enable (xv). And here it is difficult not to be reminded of the British poet Andrew Marvell's gallery: "Clora, come view my soul and tell / whether I have contrived it well: / Now all its various lodgings lie, / composed into one gallery" ("The Gallery" 966). For Milosz, the gallery is figured as a book: by definition, an anthology has to be a book of variousness, in Marvell's terms. And while Marvell's beautiful, satisfyingly dissonant rhyme in the second couplet ("lie"/"gallery") gainsays the unity or "oneness" he needs to construct in order to "contrive" his singular soul, the poem goes on to tell us it that it is actually the same woman—the addressed "Clora" of line 1—who provides, disguised and costumed, the subject of the many portraits that constitute his gallery. Thus luminous things, while disparate, may also serve a single principle—or in Marvell's case, a monochromatic obsession.

How is this related to Milosz's own principles and the "luminous things," both emblematic and periphrastic of poems, that populate his verbal gallery? In his introduction to the anthology, Milosz says he has chosen poems that are, in his own terms, "short, clear, readable and, to use a compromised term, *realist*, that is, loyal toward reality and attempting to describe it as concisely as possible" (xv, my emphasis). The choice of the latter term is surprising, as Milosz seems to realize: if we convert *realist* to its attendant noun, *realism*, we have a term more frequently associated with the "mirror in the street" of the nineteenth-century novel than with the more circumscribed and partial shape of the lyric poem; for example, when M. H. Abrams defines realism as "what is said to represent life as it really is," he mentions only novelists (such as Balzac, Eliot, and William Dean Howells) as examples (*Glossary* 174). In contrast to the inclusivity of the novel, the lyric poem's "business [of] circumference," in Dickinson's famous formulation (*Letters* 176), has the generically generated problem of what we might call partial or synecdochic representation of the empirical world that may inspire it; or, in the words of Wallace Stevens, poems represent just "*Some* lineament or character, // some affluence, if only half-perceived, / In the poverty of their words, / Of the planet of which they were part" (Stevens, *Collected Poems* 532–33, my emphasis).

The contrast between the lyric's "poverty of words" and the novel's comparative surfeit of them, if we stay with Stevens's formulation, underscores the generic issues around realism that Milosz must address as he compiles his anthology. And it may be precisely this generic dissonance that informs Milosz's way of describing the poems he terms realist: they are, as he says, "*loyal* toward reality." I am very interested in this description. Why "loyal"? While the OED notes that the word describes the condition of being "true to the obligations of duty [or] love," and that it is derived from the Latin *lex* or "law," I also sense that this word has a narrative of temptation fairly built into it. I want to suggest that loyalty is implicitly created or valued by way of an implicit, or even explicit, overcoming of temptation, or a "testing." For Milosz, as we'll see, the temptation that the "loyal" "realist" poem faces is abstraction, almost as if the poem is always poised, in a sense, to "fly off the handle" of the realism that is nested within its representational project—but, like Odysseus, is always tied to its own empirical mast in order to resist such abstractly Siren songs. Thus in what is still the inchoate personification within the adjective "loyal," we can discern a distinct generic chastening happening within the "realist" poem.

Milosz's own ekphrastic, literary-critical poem titled "Realism" (not included in *A Book of Luminous Things*) expands upon this idea. The very title is a celebration of the mode he most loves in visual art. Here Milosz suggests that, and I quote, "we are not so badly off, if we can / Admire Dutch painting" (*Collected Poems* 606). He continues:

A jar, a tin plate, a half-peeled lemon,
Walnuts, a loaf of bread, last—and so strongly

It is hard not to believe in their lastingness.
And thus abstract art is brought to shame,
Even if we do not deserve any other. (606)

For Milosz, the appeal of the Dutch still life lies, at least partially, in its flattering juxtaposition with abstract art. The "luminous things" comprising the jar, the plate, the lemon, the walnut—in a word, empirical particularities: these are what Milosz shores up in order to best the large category of abstraction, which is itself "abstracted"—that is, presented as a concept, and not particularized into discrete percepts as the still life is. In other words, the abstract is presented as a category, not Rothko's *Earth and Green*. For a poet who is drawn to the sensuous world, how could abstraction not lose in such a stacked contest? And yet this shamed "abstraction" is accorded its necessary place in the poem's argument, as if its materially negative, conceptual space is paradoxically the bulwark against which realism must define itself. (Oddly—and borderline inappropriately—a line from one of my own poems comes to mind: "thus abstraction / shores up ground, lends it (flying / buttress) supreme weight" [Pugh, *Grains* 55].) Moreover, almost comically, the admirers of abstract art become a sort of target anti-audience for Milosz's "gallery," in the introduction: "I act like an art collector who, *to spite the devotees of abstract art*, arranges an exhibition of figurative painting" (xv, my emphasis). And as many of us know, spite can be a strong motivating factor in the creation, or arrangement, of art.

How, then, does Walt Whitman address Milosz's notion of the realist poem and its greater generic struggle? If only through numbers alone, it becomes clear that for Milosz, Whitman is the most "loyalist" (or loyal to reality, as he defines it) poet in American literary history. The collection contains no less than ten poems by Whitman, a quantity that dwarfs the work included by other American poets—for example, Robert Frost (1), Allen Ginsberg (1), Denise Levertov (5), Theodore Roethke (2), and, last but not least, Emily Dickinson (1). (I'll soon have more to say about the unexpected contrast between Milosz's representation of Dickinson and Whitman in the anthology.) The only poets who are more represented than Whitman are the Polish poet Anna Swir (at 12), and the Chinese poets Tu Fu (11), and Po Chu-I (also 11).

While Whitman's sphere of influence is numerically expanded in the anthology, he is also, in a sense, contracted. By this I mean that Milosz has not chosen the "big" or panoramic Whitman featured in "Song of Myself," but the more imagist (avant la lettre) Whitman we see less frequently in anthologies of American poetry: the Whitman of tightly compacted short poems such as "A Farm Picture" (three lines), "The Runner" (four lines), "Cavalry Crossing a Ford" (seven lines) and so on. So while it's a commonplace that our most influential American poetic ancestors Dickinson and Whitman enact contraction and expansion respectively, Milosz has reversed Whitman's position within that dichotomy. Through his selection of Whitman's literally (and numerically) smaller poems, he has "contracted" many of the rhetorically capacious aspects of Whitman's voice (and perhaps not coincidentally, the very aspects of that voice that are most frequently on display in many anthologies of American poetry).

To be sure, every anthology constructs only a partial representation of a poet's work. By way of what he has chosen here, however, Milosz has refocused and even reformulated the popular conception of the Whitmanian lens on the world, a lens that Michael Ryan has described this way: "[Whitman's] focusing lens was the result of a self-transformation that couldn't be faked and would now be grandiose, anachronistic, misconceived, and willfully blind" ("Poetry" 177). Ryan's characterization may seem extreme, but I have chosen his intentionally bombastic portrayal of the Whitmanian lens-subjectivity to show what it is in the poet's reception that Milosz arguably seeks to correct by way of his own selections.

In this context, let's consider Milosz's striking claim about art's propensity to effect a salubrious self-dissolution in the observer:

> Art liberates and purifies, and its tokens are those short moments when we look at a beautiful landscape forgetting about ourselves, when everything that concerns us disappears, is dissolved, and it does not matter whether the eye that looks is that of a beggar or a king. (xix)

This democratization of looking is, then, part and parcel of what he charges the "realist" poem with accomplishing. How better to dramatize this aspect of "realism" than to reduce—again, not by critical discourse, but by *selection* of poems—one of the more capacious (and capaciously inscribed) poetic egos in American literary history?

There is a sense in which "A Farm Picture," anthologized in *A Book of Luminous Things*, dramatizes such self-dissolution if we read it against the backdrop-mural of "Song of Myself" and other large Whitman poems (largeness of poem often equates to largeness of "self" in this poet's work). Here we get a glimpse of a farm, but little if any recourse to the insistent, larger-than-life Whitman persona:

Through the ample open door of the peaceful country barn,
A sunlit pasture filled with cattle and horses feeding,
And haze and vista, and the far horizon fading away. (55)

Comprising just three lines, "A Farm Picture" is, arguably, a miniature. Here, it is as if we have been made to pause at a single relay in one of Whitman's famous paratactic catalogs, prescinding a description from its syntactic sequence and conferring the veneer of "totality" upon an exiguous sentence fragment. In its use of "and," the sentence fragment mimics paratactic sentence structure—in this way, it miniaturizes the additive amplitude of Whitman's long poems—but *in* itself, it is not syntactically complete. For this reason, miniaturization (of Whitman's poems' famous length or "stature") and fragmentation (at least on the grammatical level) are both occurring here.

To what degree is "A Farm Picture," in Milosz's terms, a "luminous thing"? Though short and seemingly simple, it wrestles mightily with both the terms and prohibitions of the "realist" approach as Milosz has conceived it. While the "picture" contains the concrete entities of horses and cattle, the framing barn door also opens to, in Whitman's words, "haze and vista, and the far horizon fading away." This latter aspect of the poem is, at first, deceptive. We might first think that in its evanescence, the "far horizon fading away" is something custom-made for *language*—for sequential representation and for the nonparticular; yet this is also precisely when the titular "picture" fairly names itself as a "tableau," since such a fading horizon indicates the presence of a vanishing point in the way, for example, that Norman Bryson has discussed the Albertian "realist" technique (*Vision* 106–7). Thus the moment the poem departs from realist particularity (of horses and cattle) is also the moment it tags itself as a realist painterly "composition"—indeed, one that employs traditional realist perspective.

This problematic is intensified in the role of the haze. "The role of the haze": that last phrase does sound odd, but such a dispersed entity is much magnified in a poem of this length. Haze is what obfuscates objects, of little substance unto itself—but, importantly, Whitman's paratactic structure renders it equivalent to the "clear" entities of horses and cattle. So Whitman makes a syntactical place for what Milosz says he would like to excise from the volume as such—when he states that the anthology, in its embrace of realist poems, should disprove "the widely held opinion that poetry is a misty domain eluding understanding" (xv).

There is a sense, then, in which "A Farm Picture" exemplifies, via not only its almost pedestrian plainness, but also its realist "planes," both Milosz's realist values and the phantom "temptations," particularly around abstraction, that I discussed above. In this way, the realist project is revealed to be differential—at least when it comes to the lyric poem, or the lyric poem in America. This poem may indeed be "loyal" to the empirical world; but its haze also preserves the faceless "temptations" of the abstract. And here, Sharon Cameron's words may generically apply: "Sometimes the angle of a poem is formed by the disparity between the dimensions of the palpable world and those of a less circumscribed interior" (*Lyric Time* 10). Whitman's haze exteriorizes this notion.

Cameron's statement is taken from a book on Emily Dickinson. And because Dickinson is so underrepresented in *A Book of Luminous Things*— again, she appears in only one poem ("A Narrow Fellow in the Grass")— I'd like to juxtapose her poem 1163 (uncollected by Milosz) with one he *has* chosen: Whitman's "A Noiseless Patient Spider." My aim here is to compare two miniatures—two spiders in two small poems—in order to gain a different set of insights about Milosz's affinity for the image. Though Dickinson's spider was not invited into this "gallery," it (or he), for that very reason, may help us to articulate exactly what Milosz wants to embrace and what he wants to exclude. Here is the first stanza of Whitman's "A Noiseless Patient Spider" (included by Milosz):

A noiseless patient spider,
I mark'd where on a little promontory it stood isolated,
Mark'd how to explore the vacant vast surrounding,
It launch'd forth filament, filament, filament, out of itself,
Ever reeling them, ever tirelessly speeding them. (Milosz 210)

And here is Dickinson's spider (not included by Milosz):

A Spider sewed at Night
Without a Light
Opon an Arc of White—

If Ruff it was of Dame
Or Shroud of Gnome
Himself himself inform—

Of Immortality
His strategy
Was physiognomy— (Poems 465)

Both poems focalize, but differently. These two spiders—Dickinson's spider populating the entirety of her poem, and Whitman's appearing in his poem's first half—are, of course, the miniaturizations of poetic principle; they are ars poetica, much as we also see in Frost's "Design" (*Collected Poems* 275). Why does only one of these spiders make the cut for *A Book of Luminous Things*?

Putting aside for a moment the differences in syntax and line between these two poems—which is not nothing, as I'm very much aware—we can again find a clue in the two spiders' contrasting relationship to the unpicturable or, in Milosz's terms, to the abstract. Whitman's spider explores the "vacant vast surrounding"—the void—by launch[ing] forth filament, filament, filament" (or line, line, line) out of itself. Ever "reeling" the filaments, ever "exploring" the void, the spider is like a fisherman of empty spaces, as Helen Vendler has noted (*Poets Thinking* 56). What it "launches" (fishing line or poetic line) becomes *itself* a very tenuous wisp of visibility even as it searches for what is discernible within the void. The filament is thus the searcher for and the embodiment of the slenderest sliver of visibility—that is, the physiological shaft of discernment—whose mediating "lifeline" will extend until, as Whitman continues in his second stanza, "the bridge you will need be form'd, till the ductile anchor hold, / Till the gossamer thread you fling catch somewhere, O my soul" (210).

So when the spider is delivered to us as metaphor—when it is revealed in stanza 2 as the vehicle for the tenor of Whitman's soul—what happens is that, in the early words of Jorie Graham, "eventually / something catches" in the outside world (*Hybrids* 3). The completion of metaphor secretes a connection from the poet to the receiver of the poem. Indeed, in his introductory comment above the poem, Milosz notes that Whitman is "looking for a response, an understanding, for friends, readers, the perfect opposite of an artist who turns away from people and the world" (210). So Whitman the realist involves himself with the world, as opposed to the poet who turns away: this latter description would epitomize, of course, a set of received responses to Dickinson.

How might this impact Dickinson's spider, and how does it compare with Whitman's? First, Dickinson's "white on white" sonic strategy (strategic if, per Frost, "design govern in a thing so small"—275) precludes *her* spider from the mediating, visually actualizing, and (eventually) unilaterally metaphoric function of Whitman's. This is due to the almost pleonastic quality of the triplet rhyme scheme we find here, in which the sonic brightness of "light, "white," and "night" nearly cancels out the semantic darkness of the last term in that list. Such motility of paradox—inseparable from our somatic reaction to the sunny long *i*'s of the rhyme scheme—is also bound up with the indeterminacy of the spider's sewing. Is it, metaphorically, to be ruff of dame or shroud of gnome?

We don't know. The gnomic spider is keeping this to himself, as per Dickinson's own instructions to him: if we reconstruct what Cristanne Miller would describe as one of Dickinson's "recoverable deletions"—that is, elisions in syntax often brought about by its relationship to meter—we can rephrase "Himself himself inform" as "let him inform himself" (*Poet's Grammar* 28). Again, self-informing is somewhat pleonastic in orientation, as the repetition of "himself" implies. It is not outward-looking communication like the appealing filaments spun by Whitman's spider-become-soul. The "Of" in Dickinson's last stanza suggests that the spider is already engulfed in Immortality: it is inseparable from his physiognomy. So the spider is grammatically and physiologically wrapped up in the abstract—as opposed to Whitman's spider, who will, with the help of metaphor, heal the empty—that is, unpictured and potentially abstract—spaces in which he finds himself.

Looking at an implicitly rejected spider, then, enables us to consider the role of metaphor in Milosz's conception of realism. Both poems employ it, but it is a question of how. The question becomes the following: does metaphor enable or obstruct visual picturability in the reader's mind's eye? In Whitman's case, it enables—to the degree that the "filament" is both the searcher for and the conductor, though of course an exiguous one, of visual empiricism; in Dickinson's, metaphor is both changeable and hypothetical—and like the spider's "sewing," it is "*secret*-ed" at the moment it is "secreted" ("Himself *himself* inform," but not us). Thus for Milosz, metaphor may be a welcome aid to realism, but only when it allays indeterminacy, as in the case of Whitman's spider—not when it supports it (as in Dickinson's). Not every spider is created equal; and Dickinson's spider may not be "loyal" enough to the empirical world to qualify for *A Book of Luminous Things*. Something so fraught with the roil of language becomes a difficult envoy for the empirical or even, in its most stable of senses, for the metaphysical.

In closing, I'd like to suggest that Milosz's selections of American poetry in *A Book of Luminous Things* reveal several strands of his affinity for the image. One is that the realist project, in his terms, often necessitates the miniature, or the reduced poem, as in the case of Walt Whitman. As we have also seen, metaphor is not unwelcome to the realist task as Milosz conceives it—but as Dickinson's spider may suggest, metaphor is welcome only to the degree that it more definitively articulates some aspect of the material world or—as in Whitman's spider—a principle of connectivity from the poet *to* that world, thereby dispersing the obfuscating "mist" or even "haze" that might be representative of abstraction.

Finally, the anthology represents American poetry as a strategy of reduction—not by following the most obvious path of accomplishing this, which would be to represent heavily the short-metered Dickinson, but by shrinking our perhaps knee-jerk assumptions about the panoramic scope of the Whitman oeuvre. Perhaps Milosz feels that Whitman brings the empirical world home to us in a more vital and direct fashion than does Dickinson, and that some of Dickinson's linguistic and syntactic difficulty flies in the face of what he wants to present as "clear." On the other hand, he may also feel a satisfaction in rescuing Whitman from the "temptation" of his grander self and gleaning the discrete moments when this poet enacts the nearly selfless witnessing that Milosz so values in his introduction, and that he connects to the realist project in lyric poetry. Either way, Milosz, in his selection, has put his own unforgettable stamp on our vision of American poetry.

Turning, Troping, Wresting

Michael Ryan's "My Dream by Henry James"
(2012)

"Describe a dream, lose a reader," a beloved mentor used to tell his workshop of aspiring poets. I must have taken that dictum as a challenge, since my second book *Restoration* mostly comprised dream poems. But the most brilliant contemporary dream poem I know is Michael Ryan's "My Dream by Henry James," from *God Hunger* (1989). Far from losing us, and worlds away from the self-indulgence that my mentor rightly tagged as a temptation attending the dream poem as a genre, Ryan's poem holds the reader close. It ratchets her attention to a pitch so breathtaking that she has no choice but to see the poem through to its end. How does the poet do this?

One important way is through a series of expertly plotted poetic turns. This poem's searing empathy-become-memory is rendered in a series of hypotactic turns that transform its single verse paragraph into a sinuous switch of language. This switch—and its constituent microswitches—is neither sensationalist nor satisfied to stop at a simple mimesis of the visual or verbal non sequiturs that constitute the surface life of dreams. The switching is instead part and parcel of a deep integrity that informs Ryan's approach, since the weaving of conscious and unconscious material is necessary for the assimilation of dreams into our waking lives, as Freud knew. Ryan's trajectory is associative, but it is also the product of shrewd, albeit subterranean, reason; here, crystallized emotion cedes to more distanced analysis and back again, making space for both to breathe. The speaker has learned from the dream, and we will too—though this is a poem, after all, and we might not all learn the same thing. But this poem is not content to bask in a dream's cleverness or weirdness; Ryan is too relentless for that. His poem is instead both an expository and an archaeological site.

At times, we've come to see the very notion of the poetic turn as emblematic of the lyric poem itself, particularly in cases like the sonnet's *volta*. It is ironic, then, that this turning is precisely what enables Ryan to do the work demanded of a fiction writer the likes of James employing a "reflector" in the novel: that is, to create a character whose consciousness narrates the action with such articulated, stereoscopic imagination that the boundaries of the self no longer apply. Hence a dream no longer "belongs" to the ego of its dreamer but is instead authored by the dead Henry James, who seems to produce the sentence introduced in the first line (later, we also learn that the dream "came" to the speaker as if activated by an agency outside the self):

In my dream by Henry James there is a sentence:
"Stay and comfort your sea companion
for a while," spoken by an aging man
to a young one as they dawdle on the terrace
of a beachfront hotel. (New and Selected Poems 44)

The plaintive beauty of that sentence—"Stay and comfort your sea companion for a while"—is made ominous by the enjambment ending the poem's third line, when we learn that it is "spoken by an aging man / to a young one" (44). While the sentence's addressee would not be particularly notable if the young man really were a man who is young, we learn several lines later that the person in question is instead probably a boy, since he's traveling on the ship with his parents and refers to their dining table as "his parents' table" (not something an adult would likely do).

Ryan tells us frankly that the line "takes on sexual overtones," thus inviting the specter of pedophilia into the poem (44). But the aging man, much as Aschenbach in Thomas Mann's *Death in Venice*, is treated not with contempt but with compassion; we're told that the young man cannot see "the aging man's loneliness / and desire for him" (44). Still, this younger person seems to know instinctively how to protect himself, and he does so through the work of metaphor: "this odd / old man who shared his parents' table on the ship / seems the merest disturbance of the air, / a mayfly at such distance he does not quite hear" (44). As the boy's mind transforms the old man into a mayfly, this very metaphor protects him both from the perilous beauty of the man's sentence and from its implications as a sexual proposition. The deceptively easeful "turning" of metaphor allows him to "not quite hear" what the older man is saying—to turn away, in other words, from the sentence's urgency and potential violence.

At this very moment of turning away, the poem's larger turning pattern redoubles, creating turns at their most immediate, most complex, and most deeply linked to metaphor. (We might remember that figurative language itself, or trope, constitutes turning.) As we see in the passage below, Ryan's next metaphor begins as a description of the boy's almost fugal inertia, but it soon becomes electric enough to awaken the speaker's own eidetic memory:

Why should I talk to anyone? *glides over his mind*
like a cloud above a pond
that mirrors what passes over and does not remember.
But I remember this cloud and this pond
from a midweek picnic with my mother
when I was still too little for school.... (44)

The pond "does not remember" the passing cloud: true enough, since ponds have no memory at all unless they are personified. And the metaphor (expressed as simile) presents first as incidental to the young man's disaffected, humorously adolescent, yet ultimately self-preserving rhetorical question. After the initial "But," however, not-remembering turns to sudden and visceral memory; not "talk[ing] to anyone" is transformed to the unspeaking gesture of the speaker's mother as she turns her son's face toward the cloud captured in the water. The metaphor-in-dream—whether in the dream itself or in the conscious narration of it—becomes the vehicle for anamnesis and for the potentially overwhelming emotion that is sometimes attendant on a memory of this sort, especially if it had been previously inaccessible.

Crucially, then, the final turn in the poem is the mother's, and she performs it muscularly: "with both hands she turned my face / toward the cloud captured in the water / and everything I felt in the world was love for her" (45). Far from the turning-away that metaphor enables the young man in the dream to do, we see here a forcible turning-*toward*: this is nothing if not mandatory visual attention. Indeed, the old man's sentence and the mother's silent turning of her son's gaze are different but related versions of imperative. Is the mother's turning—wresting, really—imperious or loving? Is the love here sinister, echoing the exchange between the old and young men, or is it pure? (Is "pure" motherly love even possible?) Did the image in the water awaken the birth of the child's aesthetic sense, or did his mother's forcefulness inaugurate his sexual drive? Might all of these unanswerable questions coexist in the poem as they do in dream? Are dream and memory as distinct from one another as the poem's final scene—with its inaugural, turning "But"—first leads us to believe?

It is Ryan's masterful turning that allows us to ask these questions, and to be both disturbed and moved by the possible proliferation of their answers. His journey through turning has allowed the mystery of this final personalized turn—one that would have had less power if it had not been authored, in part, by "Henry James." For a reader, the poem shows the trespass of dream into waking and reading life, the permeability of those boundaries, and the importance of such image and narrative in a culture that would rather read dreams as nonsignifying neural confabulations than as pieces of the arcane puzzle of being human.

"Found Breath"

The Contemporary "Mainstream" Lyric (2013)

In American poetry today, "mainstream" lyric is the school that has no name. Or more precisely, it is the school that is not a school. Since its practitioners include poets as diverse as Jorie Graham, Frank Bidart, and Rita Dove, the "mainstream" lyric is irreducible to a demographic identity, a set of precise aesthetic goals, or a settled-upon technique. Thus the difficulty of defining the lyric "mainstream" lies precisely in the latter's naturalization: like ideology, we feel it to be both everywhere and nowhere. Although its position can appear culturally safeguarded—by institutions like the Poetry Foundation and by presses such as Graywolf and Ecco—the "mainstream" lyric, unlike the Language poem that critiques it, thrives on a certain benign neglect when it comes to the question of stringent self-definition.[1]

We may thus be tempted to define the "mainstream" by all that it is not, much in the manner that Alice Fulton describes Emily Dickinson's poetry: "Dickinson defines subtle states by saying what they are *not*, possibly because no word exists for the emotional realm she's creating" (*Feeling* 145). Indeed, since to write "mainstream" is ostensibly to write with the grain rather than against it—or to swim with rather than against the current of tradition—"mainstream" poetics is monolithic only in the eyes of those who oppose it on aesthetic or political grounds. Language poet Lyn Hejinian, for example, famously critiques the "simpleminded model

---

1. This is not to claim that "mainstream" poets are uninterested in contemplating their art within the confines of the essay or other extended prose. But their books of essays—such as those by Louise Glück, James Longenbach, and Carl Phillips, to name a few—are more likely to place the contemporary lyric in a historical context than to pinpoint what characterizes today's "mainstream" lyric as such.

of subjectivity and authority" that is enacted by the "romantic, unitary, expressive self" in "mainstream" lyric and its predecessors (*Language* 329). For Hejinian and other Language poets, "mainstream" tradition is the intellectual product of a mainstreamed America, regardless of the politics that its practitioners may personally espouse: a way of writing, in other words, that connotes capitalist individualism rather than a set of collective goals.[2]

Thus an arguably capacious range of poetic voices appears "mainstreamed," in the sociological sense, only to those who approach it with the same disregard for difference that afflicted William Carlos Williams's judgment of the sonnet as "a form which does not admit of the slightest structural change in its composition" ("Poem" 57).[3] At the same time, the "mainstream's" deeply conservative, sometimes reverential stance toward literary history does make for an almost autonomic affinity between poets, which often involves the propagation of long-standing lyric values such as emotional texture, musicality, and linguistic sheering or density. Though we are far from Pindar and from the oral poetry that W. R. Johnson celebrates in *The Idea of Lyric*, many "mainstream" poets identify with the work of predecessors ranging from the time of John Donne and before.

Contemporary poets are not, however, simply "mouth[ing] other poets," in Sylvia Plath's terms (*Journals* 92). We can often find colloquial notes in "mainstream" diction, which can be corralled into lyric musicality of a potentially jazzy stripe: in *Black Zodiac*, for example, Charles Wright names "winter's vocabulary, downsized and distanced" (46), thereby transforming corporate language into postindustrial lyricism. The challenge that C. Day Lewis perceived as central to the poetic endeavors of Wordsworth, Dickinson, and Hardy remains a viable goal, then, for Wright and others: "The singing line could be broadened by an alliance with the speaking line: it was, and still is, a fascinating technical problem—how to incorporate some of the roughness, flexibility and down-to-earthness of common idiom into a lyrical texture" (*Lyric Impulse*

---

2. The degree to which such (sometimes celebrated) atomism is either inculcated or counterindicated by the workshop environment, or indeed the "poetry world" as such, would be material for another essay.

3. Even the change from the Petrarchan to the Shakespearean sonnet form proves Williams's contention to be untrue.

17). "Lyrical texture" is key here: the "mainstream" poem strives toward a musicality that is at once topical, idiosyncratic, and linguistically pleasurable. Indeed, a poet like Wright is often more interested in imbuing colloquial language with the pleasure of Pound's melopoeia than in sharpening it to perform explicit political or ideological critique.

Despite their differences in voice, form, and technique, then, "mainstream" poets maintain a preservationist rather than iconoclastic relationship to canonical literary history. In this way, T. S. Eliot's "Tradition and the Individual Talent" becomes more than a delimited paean to high modernism; it also suggests a synchronic aesthetic stance that can be viscerally espoused by contemporary "mainstream" poets themselves:

> [T]he historical sense involves a perception, not only of the pastness of the past, but of its presence; the historical sense compels a man to write not merely with his own generation in his bones, but with a feeling that the whole of the literature of Europe from Homer and within it the whole of the literature of his own country has a simultaneous existence and composes a simultaneous order. (784)

To be sure, the limitations of Eliot's viewpoint have been well noted; he constructs an arguably elitist and exclusionary "Western tradition" to which "mainstream" poets need not be limited. Yet the sense of geologic time—often a sharpened sensibility in these poets—and the role of intertextuality remain indispensable to understanding the work that is inspired by contemporary poets' literary and intellectual forebears. Such projects range from Jorie Graham's homage to Western philosophers in *Materialism*, to retellings of the *Odyssey* by Louise Glück (*Meadowlands*), Thom Gunn (*Moly*), and Derek Walcott (*Omeros*); from Carl Phillips's rethinking of Donne's Holy Sonnets in his "Blue Castrato" series in *From the Devotions*, to Lucie Brock-Broido's reinscription and reinterpretation of Dickinson's "Master letters" in her book of the same title—and the list goes on. To "make it new" today is, ultimately, to keep making it old, even if the cadence of these contemporary voices may have seemed unimaginable before the last couple of decades. Such is the conundrum and the lifeblood of the "mainstream."

How might the above list address Hejinian's critique of the lyric "I" as commensurate with a "unitary, expressive self"? For one thing, its intensive intertextuality would seem to preclude straightforward self-expression as we usually understand it. But more importantly, even a cursory reading through literary history (Shakespeare, Donne, Milton, Keats) reveals that the lyric "I"—or the poetic speaker—has never been unitary or, by extension, "expressive" of anything unitary: for that matter, how could something so one-dimensional have lasted so long? As we'll see, the best "mainstream" poets are those who took neither the Confessional ethos (and its ostensibly referential relation to "selfhood") nor Language critiques of the lyric to heart, but who instead have drawn from a much longer tradition in which the lyric "I"—while not always scrambling or refracting syntax, as in more experimental work—has long been understood to be fictional, rhetorical, and multivalent. "Mainstream" poetics is therefore more than allusive; it also seeks to replicate the most complex speaker-constructions found over the course of literary history. Such complexity is found both in individual poems and in the cross-hatchings that comprise poetic collections.

Indeed, this strand of speaker-construction is nothing new; it is traceable from Donne to Dickinson to Berryman.[4] In the last twenty-five years, we can find it as readily in the formal poems of Thom Gunn as in the dispersed yet indexical Graham: "How the invisible / roils. I see it from here and then / I see it from here" (*Materialism* 3). Now, as in the past, the lyric's "I" is not only incommensurable with the expression of a *biographical* self, but its rhetorical and fictional speaker—whether or not it is posited as an explicit "I"—may not be commensurate with a self at all, at least insofar as the term implies a strong degree of referentiality.[5]

Since the positing of an "I" is often materially central to a lyric poem's unfolding, though, we should consider more deeply what the best lyric poetry—contemporary and otherwise—offers as an alternative to Hejin-

---

4. Along these lines, Glück notes that "Berryman began to sound like Berryman when he invented Mr. Bones, and so was able to project two ideas simultaneously" (*Proofs* 44). But the invention's purpose is not a "true" representation of Berryman's self; instead, its goal is the creation of "distinctive voice" (44), as separable from empirical or understandable selfhood.

5. Even Paul Allen Miller, who sees in the poetry collection the birth of "lyric consciousness" (*Lyric Texts* 1), ultimately refuses to reduce that consciousness either to straightforward psychology or to the creation of "selfhood" in the work: "This ego is not the historical Catullus, but rather is a function of the reader's engagement with the collection" (74–75).

ian's notion of self-expression. While we usually understand the latter as an untroubled one-to-one correspondence between biographical experience and artistic representation, Roland Barthes provides a different context for the word "expression," one whose Latin derivation suggests instead the process of photography: "'imago lucis opera expressa'; which is to say: image revealed, 'extracted,' 'mounted,' 'expressed' (like the juice of a lemon) by the action of light" (*Camera Lucida* 81).

In quoting Barthes here, my intention is not to suggest that poems should have the documentary capacities of certain photographs, but instead to emphasize the etymological association of "expression" with the *technical* properties of extraction and condensation within representation. Thus what the photo does with light, the poem accomplishes with prosody and technique as the agents that "express," or "chemically" enlighten, empirical or nonempirical material into representation; that the poet is, in turn, the agent of technique remains unproblematic in this context.[6] In the "mainstream" lyric of the present day—even in the lucidly crabbed Southern vernacular of C. D. Wright, for example—the values of resonant extraction and condensation have remained constant.

Ultimately, this line of thinking invokes M. H. Abrams's discussion of the lyric "I" and its historical paradoxes:

> Although the lyric is uttered in the first person, the "I" in the poem need not be the poet who wrote it. In some lyrics, such as John Milton's sonnet "When I consider how my light is spent" and Samuel Taylor Coleridge's "Frost at Midnight," the references to the known circumstances of the author's life make it clear that we are to read the poem as a personal expression. Even in such personal lyrics, however, both the character and utterance of the speaker may be shaped by the author in a way that is conducive to the desired artistic effect. (*Glossary* 108)

Abrams's first sentence suggests the time-honored dramatic monologue or persona poem, in which a historical persona or created character is made to speak; such "mainstream" poets as Frank Bidart and Ai are still

---

6. Though the prose writer also can enact extraction and condensation, I would argue that these values are more fitted to the greater generic selectivity of the lyric, due to its historical reliance on line (as opposed to the conceivably unlimited paragraph) and its heightened relationship to cadence and orality.

profitably engaging this lyric subgenre. Yet the final point of this passage is even more instructive for our purposes: while material in poems may surely be taken from actual "experience"—after all, even at this moment of Flarf and Google-induced poetry, persons are still the ones doing the writing—such experience must be subordinate to, and transformed by, poetic structure.[7] "Personal expression" is therefore not commensurate with what Abrams calls the "personal lyric" (even pace Abrams himself). More recently, Mark Strand has articulated this distinction from a poet's perspective: "[W]hen I use 'I,' I'm not reporting on anything that I do. I draw on events and feelings that I've lived through; but I don't feel that I am being autobiographical. The 'I' is a convention" ("Mark Strand" 54).

For many contemporary American poets, the direct line to such convention is the work of their nineteenth-century forebears Dickinson and Whitman, who each created a variously outsized, imminently rhetorical poetic "I." To understand this, one only need juxtapose Dickinson's infamous instances of meiosis ("It would have starved a Gnat— / To live so small as I—"—Poems 205) with her countervailing, sometimes exclamatory grandiosity ("Title divine, is mine"—Poems 92); or recall Whitman's "referential" self-constructions that are transparently identifiable as bombastic rhetorical fictions ("Walt Whitman, a kosmos, of Manhattan the son"—Leaves 47). The actualization of such speakers, who contain more multitudes than any empirical self could reasonably support, is dependent upon the readerly imagination described by Jonathan Culler: "Any speaker whom the reader fills in or imagines will be a poetic construct" (Structuralist Poetics 166).

Indeed, to see the poem as reflection (of the poet's person) rather than artifact is the province and pitfall of the beginner. It is therefore unsurprising that our most successful "mainstream" poets are less concerned with putting the self into poetry—or with the apotropaic, laborious labor of keeping it out—than with transforming strands of intellectual and emotional material into grist for poetic form; as Glück says, "first, I love it. / Then, I can use it" (Vita Nova 39). That poetry sometimes is associated with truth-telling in our culture is undeniable; but this belief is a func-

---

7. In Poetic Artifice, Veronica Forrest-Thomson discusses the nature of this transfer, or what she terms the "internal expansion" of the poem (xii). For another account of how poetic form transforms Milton's (clearly biographical) experience of blindness in his famous sonnet, see Glück's "Against Sincerity" in Proofs and Theories, especially 37–41.

tion of the fallacy that Glück has defined as "our failure to separate poetry which *sounds like* honest speech from honest speech" (*Proofs* 35, emphasis mine). The task is not to remove the poet from the poem, as the New Critics espoused, but instead not to assume the very continuity that such removal was understood to remedy.

As Glück shows in "Against Sincerity," it is poetic form and lineation—which is not reducible to rhyme and meter, though often vestigially dependent on it—that has always enabled the poet to separate the work from the "self," thereby creating a permeable boundary between the personal and the impersonal, the personal and the universal (*Proofs* 39–40). Mutlu Konuk Blasing describes the results of such "formalization": "The poet's personal memories and associations in the mother tongue are formalized and thus socialized as a generic discourse of a *virtual 'I,'* so that other speakers with other, different, memories and associations can recognize their 'own truths' as socialized/individuated subjects in language" (45, emphasis mine). For Blasing as for Abrams above, then, even traceable "personal" material in poems must yield to the depersonalizing effect that poetic form, in its protean possibilities, confers upon it. The movement from the internal self of the poet to the externalized structure of the poem—from the biographical "I" to what catches the eye and reverberates in the ear—is always imminently technical and, to a certain degree, alchemical. This is another way of approaching Barthes's notion of photographic "expression."

But one might object that such theorizing turns a blind eye to diachronic concerns. Why, for instance, is there not more autobiographical "self"-representation in the best "mainstream" lyric after the Confessional poets? Probably because the Confessional label itself was a misnomer in several cases, at least insofar as it implied a direct confession of life events.[8] Though the nature of the work arguably opened the door to new and more daring representations in poetry, the Confessional poets were not writing memoir as we understand that popular genre today. The "confessional" Plath often wrapped her poems in metonymies and metaphors of a distinctly mythological cast (see, for example, "Lady Lazarus"

---

8. Adam Kirsch notes that "in confession, [criticism] found a bad metaphor for what the most gifted of these poets were doing. The motive for confession is penitential or therapeutic. . . . but the poets discussed in this book always approached their writing as artists, and their primary motive was aesthetic" (*Wounded Surgeon* x).

and "Edge"—*Collected Poems* 244–47 and 272–73); the "confessional" Bishop was able to excise her lesbian identity so assiduously from her published poems that they were still being decoded long after her death.[9] As we can see from the sometimes dramatic contrast between their personal writings and their published poems, neither Plath nor Bishop established—or more importantly, cared to establish—an unproblematic, continuous identity between poetry and biographical life.[10] On the contrary, the torrid emotional urgency of *Ariel*, combined with its patently fictional constructions of Plath's "self," is precisely what any poet has license to create.[11]

Partially for these reasons, our best "mainstream" poets have remained largely unconcerned by the misunderstandings surrounding the Confessional work of the previous generation. In "Self-Portrait as Apollo and Daphne," for example, Graham reconstellates Plath's personae by deindividuating the titular "self" into various pairs of characters from Greek mythology and the Hebrew Bible. Graham's further contribution, perhaps impossible before Merleau-Ponty, is to inhabit the always-incipient phenomenology of characters who remain arrested within the webs of their determining story-lines—"sleepwalking through the dream of choice," in Liam Rector's terms (*Sorrow* 25)—yet always conscious of the preexisting narrative questions that implicate their ostensibly private thoughts and conversations:

---

9. In *The Body and the Song*, for example, Marilyn May Lombardi claims that "relevant diary entries and early drafts, often more forthright than the final, enigmatic version of the poem, unveil the flesh-and-blood author behind the poetic personae" (4). Though we may take issue with the efficacy (or even the desirability) of searching for the "flesh-and-blood author" at all, this quotation shows that for Lombardi and others, the supposedly "Confessional" Bishop-as-such was not easily discoverable in the "poetic personae" that inhabited her published poems.

10. As Cameron notes of Dickinson in *Lyric Time*, however, sometimes even "personal" writings, such as letters, are in part the product of a created persona; and the "investment" created by such a persona may be inversely proportional to its referential obscurity: "We lie for the sake of accuracy. In Dickinson's letters we can observe that the more vested the relationship with the letter recipient, the more aphoristic, epigrammatic, and explicitly literary the letters become . . . the letters may, in fact, tell us more about the postures that replace relationship than about the relationships themselves" (12).

11. Nevertheless, as Jacqueline Rose discusses, some of Plath's most frequently anthologized poems (e.g., "Daddy") have been castigated precisely because they misrepresented the "facts" of Plath's biography.

the shards caught here and there—what did you do
before? or will you forgive me? or say
that you'll love me for
ever and ever

(is it a squeal of brakes is it a birthcry?)

(let x equal forever he whispered let y let y ...) (End 32)

Here, Graham's hypothetical "shards" of lovers' speech remain
unanchored to any character: they are attributed neither to Daphne
nor to Apollo. What we see instead is not only self-portraiture as self-
splitting, but the further lyric reduction of these parenthetically "split"
figures: that is, their characterization is subordinate to the magnified
role of inchoate narrative event. By extension, the titular "self" may be
neither unique nor "unitary"; Graham suggests that selves are not limited to fleshly entities but are instead parceled out among the scores
of our inherited cultural mythologies—which, while "mathematically"
unsparing, remain elliptical in what they reveal of their own divisions
and equations ("let y let y ...").

Considering the relationship between formal and conceptual values
in these self-portrait poems in particular, Helen Vendler places Graham
in an ancestral lineage of long-lined English and American poetry ranging from Hopkins to Whitman to Stevens. She also argues that Graham's
poems recall "the cinematic freeze-frame, by which an action sequence in
film is divided, like the flight of Zeno's arrow, into minutely brief 'shots'"
(*Breaking* 80). This reading exemplifies the dual concerns of the lyric
modality that we're considering here: contemporary lyric capacities that
are suggestive of current filmic technology must also be tempered and
filtered through the crucible of Eliot's "pastness" on which the genre also
continues to insist. Moreover, while Graham's poetry presents as both
imminently intertextual and phenomenologically "new," her biographical world—that is, her empirical inhabiting of "self," as opposed to this
splintered set of speakers—remains incidental to the poems' work.

Graham's career trajectory is also instructive for what it suggests about
the role of "mainstream" lyric criticism in assigning poetic value. Though
her synecdochic relationship to contemporary lyric may seem unassail-

able today, such positioning was not a foregone conclusion. Indeed, the very breadth of poets to whom Graham is compared suggests other critical and generic possibilities for her body of work: as Catherine Sona Karagueuzian notes, "Given her displacement of narrative and her efforts to thwart conventional strategies of reading and interpretation, Graham is frequently compared to the Language Poets" (*No Image* 16).

Graham's poetry in *The End of Beauty*, and after, does often enact a tenor of indeterminacy that was promulgated by the Language school. Yet it was Vendler's "siring" of Graham in the lyric family tree—as shown in the very subtitle of her book *The Breaking of Style: Hopkins, Heaney, Graham*—that proved definitive for the poet's critical placement. One could claim that Vendler's influential role in "making" a lyric poet is similar to the ideological process that Virginia Jackson describes in *Dickinson's Misery*: "[H]istory has made the lyric in its image" (15). Though I would not go as far as Jackson does here—I do believe that Graham's work is fundamentally lyric—Graham's reception points to the ways that criticism can fasten a potentially hybrid poetic body of work under the aegis of "mainstream" values.

Perhaps there is no greater contemporary paean to these values, and to the incommensurable tenors of the lyric voice, than Glück's *The Wild Iris*. Here, the poet personifies flower species and a dimly Judaic God figure in poems that are interspersed with others containing a more recognizably human voice—one, indeed, that is modeled on the figure of Glück herself. But these loosely autobiographical poems cannot simply be taken at face value. They are integral to the book's larger, polyphonic project of exploring what Steven Knapp calls both "the nature of personified agency, and . . . the contrast between such agency and the lives of our ordinary selves" (3). It is within this lacuna that the book's power resides, as in Dickinson's "internal difference— / Where the Meanings, are—" (*Poems* 143). And since Barbara Johnson describes apostrophe as "almost synonymous with the lyric voice" (*World* 185), there is a sense in which Glück is also anatomizing the lyric genre as such.

By overlaying personification, apostrophe, and prosopopoeia in these various figures, Glück creates a chorus of monologues—voices that can speak, but never listen or reply: "Certainly / you don't look at us, don't listen to us," says the choral voice of "Field Flowers" to an unnamed human figure (*Wild Iris* 28). By creating a heteroglossic populace that nonetheless cannot achieve dialogue, *The Wild Iris* explores the constitutive, insis-

tent nature of monologism in the lyric, which we see with some clarity
in the book's title poem:

You who do not remember
passage from the other world
I tell you I could speak again: whatever
returns from oblivion returns
to find a voice:

from the center of my life came
a great fountain, deep blue
shadows on azure seawater. (1)

Figured metaphorically as a fountain's water, the liquid voice of the
iris is inflective of the monologic voice as such, much as the "deep blue /
shadows on azure seawater" cast blue on blue: here, shadow is the result
of gradation rather than contrast or the painterly term of *chiaroscuro*.[12]
Voice is therefore a subtler superimposition, not a dark shadow cast in
sun by the self's limbs and lineaments. By extension, a speaking flower
"finds a voice" by likening that voice to a shadowed fountain of which
its own petals remain tenor. While this is, in a sense, an extremely self-
reflexive moment, it is also a figure that is worlds away from "finding a
voice" in the workshop setting (which relies on the dictum "Write what
you know").

Indeed, some of Glück's flowers claim to have no knowledge at all,
thus divorcing lyric speech from preconceived ideation: "The great thing
/ is not having / a mind," muses a red poppy in a poem of the same name
(29). Since many of Glück's flower voices speak at the very moment of
their rebirth in the spring, the wild iris's "oblivion" is always the near
shore of the speeches they make. The human figures in the book are
afflicted by their own oblivions, persistently calling to an "Unreachable
father" (3) rather than listening to the flowers' questions and injunctions.
In this sense, *The Wild Iris* is nothing but a book of address, less uphold-

---

12. Johnson also shows that in Mallarmé's "L'Azur," the signifier *azur* is a sign not only
of poetry-as-such—"a sign that what one is reading is a poem" (*World* 120)—but also, as
Baudelaire's revenant, "an explicit version of the ways in which a text is never its own
contemporary, cannot constitute a self-contained whole" (121).

ing Jakobson's conative function than dramatizing its necessary failure if tested as a communicative device. As Glück creates apostrophe as a system of incommensurate—and perpetually missed—signals between the human and an imaginary or lyrically derived divine, her work also recalls Barbara Johnson's characterization of Gwendolyn Brooks's "The Mother" as a similar reconfiguration of the trope: "[T]he grammatical I/thou starting point of traditional apostrophe has been replaced by a structure in which the speaker is simultaneously eclipsed, alienated, and confused with the addressee" (*World* 189).

To lean so heavily on the trope of personification, especially at the end of the twentieth century, was admittedly a risk, considering that Wordsworth himself was trying to rid poetry of such abstractions back in his "Preface to Lyrical Ballads." But *The Wild Iris* received the Pulitzer Prize in 1993, which suggests that certain lyric tropes should not be dismissed as outmoded when they are employed with both lucidity and passionate investment. There is a sense in which Glück's resurrection of "perennials" is also the perennial and salutary resurrection of personification and apostrophe in the lyric. To claim this, however, is not to say that such resurrection can impart anything like a Christian born-again life: Glück's god is an indifferent one, and the human figures in the book are often melancholic and ineffectual.

In sum, Glück's sequence shows the inefficacy of human experience as a single catalyst for, or determinant of, art. It is in this spirit that we may read Carl Phillips's similar assessment of George Herbert's poetry: "Herbert's poems . . . are an honest and, to a large extent, self-interested inquiry into questions whose answers did not entirely accord with personal experience" (*Coin* 49). One could add that the very insufficiency of empirical experience is the breeding ground for poetic trope. It also inaugurates the move toward impersonality that Sharon Cameron has described in Emerson's "Experience," when "the most painfully intense property of a particular personal experience—dissociation ('it does not touch me')—migrates so that it is recognizable as the property of *all* experience independent of particularity" (*Impersonality* xvii). This is the crux of Glück's disparately invested—and arguably dissociated—voices in *The Wild Iris*.

Such elusive "experience independent of particularity" also characterizes the work of Thom Gunn, whose fixed poetic forms trouble the boundaries of what we might call the empirical self.[13] In *The Man with Night Sweats*, Gunn elegizes his friends, gay men who died of AIDS in the late eighties, thus beginning with a personal relationship to a historic epidemic. But through their very use of poetic form, his elegies also disperse the self into the plural other—into friendship inflected with agape, with sexuality, and often synonymous with the culture of the gay community in the late twentieth century:

Contact of friend led to another friend,
Supple entwinement through the living mass
Which for all that I knew might have no end,
Image of an unlimited embrace.
. . . .
But death—Their deaths have left me less defined:
It was their pulsing presence made me clear. (80)

Gunn's heroic quatrains and pluralization of elegy readily invoke Gray's "Elegy in a Country Churchyard." Moreover, he describes *contact* as both the progress of the virus ("Contact of friend led to another friend") and the deferring of self into relationship not with a single other, but with multiple others (the sexualized "living mass") that could be infinitely extended in a variant of mathematical sublime. Surprisingly, it is the pluralized mass—inevitably both the "pulsing" crowd and the infectious growth—that confers boundaries upon the individualized speaker who fully enters it. While Peter Sacks notes that the elegy traditionally works to "place the dead, and death itself, at some cleared distance from the living" (*English Elegy* 19), Gunn's speaker finds his own contours "clear[ed]" only through the "pulsing presence" of the living mass itself; his very elegy, even in its formal strictures, has rendered him "less defined."

As Mark Jarman and David Mason note, the New Formalists—a group younger than Gunn's generation—have employed fixed forms in order to

---

13. Though born in Great Britain in 1929, Gunn lived in San Francisco for fifty years—from 1954 until his death in 2004—thus qualifying, for some, as an American poet even though he never became an American citizen. His inclusion in anthologies such as *The Best American Poetry 1998* suggests that at least some in the American poetry establishment were more than willing to claim him as their own.

promulgate "a valued civility, putting a premium not only on technique, but also on a larger cultural vision that restores harmony and balance to the arts" (*Rebel Angels* xviii–xix). In contrast, however, Gunn's project is more in line with what we have been discussing as "mainstream" lyric values that are not determined by a single formal choice. As I have suggested here, the contemporary lyric succeeds not to the degree that it is "civil," but to the degree that it "suffices," in Stevens's terms, to create a complexity of speaker or linked speakers who are not commensurate with—or limited by—empirical "selves."

In this light, let's consider Gunn's use of trimeter to describe the direst of medical conditions, a choice that recalls Dickinson's use of the ballad meter to enclose extreme emotional straits:

He still found breath, and yet
It was an obscure knack.
I shall not soon forget
The angle of his head,
Arrested and reared back
On the crisp field of bed,

Back from what he could neither
Accept, as one opposed,
Nor as a lifelong breather
Consentingly let go,
The tube his mouth enclosed
In an astonished O. (66)

The deceptive gaiety of the three-beat line articulates something between a rock and an existential hard place: in order to continue to be (comically) defined as a "lifelong breather" like the rest of us, a dying patient cannot reject the breathing tube that he also concomitantly "oppos[es]." As a result of this philosophic and physiological impasse, his mouth must continuously shape—but not say—the open O of apostrophe, which has now become both a vessel for breath and an occlusion of voice. In this sense, "found breath" constitutes the very vestige of life as medically enforced silence.

In this way, the ruefully "obscure knack" of aided breathing brings up difficult, if now quite familiar, questions about a dying person's agency with respect to his own death: this terrain delimits the very limit of "self-hood" and what necessarily troubles its definition. How can we usefully define "consent"? When, in fact, does one stop being a "self" who can provide it? Yet when figured as trimeter rhyme in the poem, these weighty questions have become inexplicably, dolefully "light." As in the previous quotation, the speaker himself is implicitly redefined through his formal construction—importantly, not just his empirical "witnessing"—of this particular life in a deeply moving, yet also somehow humorous, manner. It is in this sense that "found breath" may be read otherwise: in contrast to "finding a voice" in "The Wild Iris," the phrase is commensurate with "mainstream" lyric's discovery of a form—in this case, a very old folk-meter—to reconsider and to re-dress the long process of dying. For Gunn, this is an ancient theme whose metonymies are ineluctably current.

As we've seen, "mainstream" lyric is nothing if not literarily conservative. But the degree to which literary tradition is itself conservative remains, at the very least, debatable. Despite their differences, Graham, Glück, and Gunn are clearly steeped in the poetics that not only provides pleasure but that also, in Barbara Johnson's words, is "capable of conserving and inscribing messages the radicality of which may not yet have been explored" (*World* 31). This is not to imbue "mainstream" poetry with a radicalism that it doesn't have, but instead to articulate that varieties of linguistic music, or the positing of a lyric "I," do not preclude complexity or new knowledge. In the last two decades or so, the work of these and other "mainstream" poets has revealed precisely that.

2015–2021

Voicing the Overplus

Prosopopoeia

The Throwing of a Voice (2019)

When I was little, our family had a dog named Clifford—named after Clifford the Big Red Dog, for those to whom that text might be familiar. As dogs go, our Clifford was pretty sedate, and he often looked as if he were observing a world in slow motion. But my sister made Clifford talk. By this I mean that she adopted a voice—a trilling soprano, actually—in which she talked "for" Clifford, that is, she talked for him in the first person and made him say "I" (for example, "I loooove my Liv-A Snaps"). It was amazing how his character changed precisely at the moment he was given a voice. This, in a word, is the magic of the trope *prosopopoeia*, or "throwing a voice." It's what the ventriloquist does when he throws his voice to the dummy, who then seems to speak autonomously from a wooden mouth. And prosopopoeia is a great friend of lyric poetry.

In his *Handlist of Rhetorical Terms*, Richard Lanham defines prosopopoeia like this: "An animal or an inanimate object is represented as having human attributes and addressed or made to speak as if it were human" (123). What I want to emphasize here is the second part of Lanham's definition: both the "animal or inanimate object" and the "*made to speak* as if." The nonhuman, "inanimate," or "animal" quality of prosopopoeia—in Lanham's terms—is what distinguishes it from dramatic monologue, which "throws a voice" to another person or character who speaks in the first person.

But *address* of the object—the first part of his definition—is for me actually the province of apostrophe, another rhetorical figure; and to my thinking, these two tropes are not at all the same thing. In a sense, prosopopoeia is the flip side of apostrophe's coin: you can call to the Western wind in your apostrophe, but is there any guarantee that it will answer?

Prosopopoeia is what makes that answer happen, if the poet ordains it. In that sense, prosopopoeia—or the "made to speak as if"—is the wish fulfillment of apostrophe.

For a poet, prosopopoeia can and probably should be thrilling: talking urns and cats are privileges that are usually denied the realist novel, after all. Prosopopoeia can alert us to the uncanniness in our everyday environments: what exceeds or flummoxes the limitations of human senses and rationality. It can provide a cloak for our own too-personal or over-emotional speech. It can give voice to personified ideas such as Love or Patience, as we hear in the poems of George Herbert and John Milton. And perhaps in the ultimate version of wish fulfillment, prosopopoeia makes the dead speak again, as we hear in some of the recent poems of Jean Valentine. Conversely, prosopopoeia can also alert us to the ethical and political dangers of speaking *for* another entity—concerns that critics such as W. J. T. Mitchell have convincingly outlined (*Picture Theory* 157).

But prosopopoeia can be most striking, even lacerating, when its speech is monologic. By this, I'm referring to cases in which the poet posits no reciprocity or dialogue involving the prosopopoeic figure. The animal, thing, or entity becomes a voice crying out in the wilderness, condemned to monologue. This situation is perhaps particularly poignant because the animal or object's personification is by definition incomplete: that is, it often seems to lack the defenses and rationality—let's say, the *armor*—of the fully human subject. And this is the conundrum of Louise Glück's *The Wild Iris*, in which flowers are made to speak to humans who never hear them. Here is "The Red Poppy," from that book:

The great thing
is not having
a mind. Feelings:
oh, I have those; they
govern me. I have
a lord in heaven
called the sun, and open
for him, showing him
the fire of my own heart, fire
like his presence.
What could such glory be

if not a heart? Oh my brothers and sisters,
were you like me once, long ago,
before you were human? Did you
permit yourselves
to open once, who would never
open again? Because in truth
I am speaking now
the way you do. I speak
because I am shattered. (29)

In this poem-length prosopopoeia, the flower speaks in the first person. Glück endows it with a voice of terrible appeal—and of paradoxically plangent vulnerability. The unanswerable nature of the poppy's questions is deeply connected to the flower's final "shattering." In that single word, we can envision fragile, torn poppy petals past their blooming peak: a material ruin that silvers the flower's voice. While Sylvia Plath also famously addressed these flowers in "Poppies in July," Glück chooses prosopopoeia instead—fairly announcing the trope when the flower says, "I am speaking now / the way you do," thus implying that the flower is "impersonating" humanness. In this way, Glück also points to one of prosopopoeia's most powerful assets: throwing a voice to the nonhuman is a way to intensify what is sometimes most painfully human in feeling, if not thought, as the poppy does very explicitly here when it contends that it lacks "a mind."

Despite my fondness for *The Wild Iris* and for the uncanniness of prosopopoeia in poems more generally, I struggled a bit when I was asked to discuss my own poems' relationship to this trope. I had never combed through my own work with the goal of finding prosopopoeia before—but when I recently tried to do this, I found no talking dogs, flowers, or vases. I've realized that my own approach to prosopopoeia is more layered, more diffuse, and probably more intertextual than the definitions I've provided here. But "The Voice, Midsummer," from my book *Grains of the Voice*, does provide a commentary on the trope and on the questions it may provoke us to ask as readers, especially contemporary readers. For example, where does a prosopopeic voice generate? Where and how is it received by a reader? Here is the poem:

If light falls orthogonally, sheering stipples on a dress—
if it irradiates the swelling of that slenderness, torch
slow-lit amid the banks of leafless forest evening,
how could the voice come silent in such groomed
space, plash and reverberant?—but it does, if you clasp
your hands behind you, lean against the nothing of the wind. (Grains 73)

Instead of speaking for a flower or an urn, this poem describes a voice that has emerged nearly anchorless, or without explicable origins, from a summer landscape. The voice is also, paradoxically, silent. Add to all this that the poem was inspired by a painting, and you'll get a sense of the variegated vocal textures I've tried to work with in this book, and how complicated prosopopoeia—even the edges of prosopopoeia—can become in it. In "The Voice, Midsummer," the speaker has a momentary crisis of belief in the prosopopoeic voice, which is really a crisis of imagination. She then resolves this by answering her own question: "how could the voice come silent in such groomed / space, plash and reverberant?—but it does, if you clasp / your hands behind you, lean against the nothing of the wind" (73). Ultimately the poem posits, and then knows, that the "thrown" voice of landscape only lives within a listener or receptor. Perhaps the poem is a miniphilosophy of prosopopoeia.

Thus it is only through the reader's participation and imagination—or leaning against the wind's "nothing"—that the voice of prosopopoeia can be heard. Though the wind is "nothing" to see, it is everything in the history of lyric poetry—or "the nothing that is," in Stevens's terms, from "Western Wind" to Shelley and after (Stevens, *Collected Poems* 9). This is a history we can lean not "in"—to, in Sheryl Sandberg's terms, but "against"—in the sense of a nearly bodily support that shores up our contemporaneity. Perhaps this nothing-wind is even a prosthetic with which we can reconstitute a lyric body. Though we may continually question and redraw its contours, prosopopoeia remains a living and imagined link to our literary past.

"Velvety Velour" and Other Sonnet Textures in Gwendolyn Brooks's "the children of the poor" (2017)

> *What shall I give my children? who are poor,*
> *Who are adjudged the leastwise of the land,*
> *Who are my sweetest lepers, who demand*
> *No velvet and no velvety velour;*
> *But who have begged me for a brisk contour,*
> *Crying that they are quasi, contraband*
> *Because unfinished, graven by a hand*
> *Less than angelic, admirable or sure. (Brooks, Selected Poems 53)*

"Poetry is not a luxury," Audre Lorde famously wrote (*Sister Outsider* 36). It is certainly no luxury for the "children of the poor" described in Gwendolyn Brooks's sonnet sequence that opens "The Womanhood" in *Annie Allen* (1949). First, the sonnet form itself is an exercise in parsimony. In contrast to heroic couplets or other poetic forms featuring the potential of infinitely extendable lines, the sonnet is restricted to just fourteen of them. For the Brooks of *Annie Allen*, such limitation creates a circumscribed poetic theater in which to critique racial discrimination and economic inequality in the first half of twentieth-century America.

This critique, however, is far from simple: Brooks's sequence shows what the sonnet form can accomplish in its more oblique guises. Within what Joyce Ann Joyce calls her "mastery of indirection," Brooks shows the many registers obliquity can inhabit—and that, in the right hands, obliquity can be the voice of urgency (Joyce, "Poetry" 251). Writing of Brooks's early work, Henry Taylor also notes "the Dickinsonian way in which sophistication sometimes becomes a shield, from behind which almost invisible darts fly often and accurately" ("Gwendolyn Brooks" 256). Though this metaphor implies a subterfuge in the work that I don't necessarily see, Taylor's coupling of darts and sophistication is very well suited to Brooks's project.

For Brooks at this time, the sonnet provided a serious platform from which to dramatize Black experience, often by creating characters or personae. She had already done this in "gay chaps at the bar," the sonnet sequence from *A Street in Bronzeville* (1945), which featured Black veterans of the Second World War. But in "The Womanhood," the sonnet's contraction is deeply connected to mothering. "I have contracted," Brooks had written in "the mother" (from *Bronzeville*), thereby suggesting both the contractions of labor and the legal contract of the birth certificate (*Selected Poems* 4). In the "children of the poor" sonnets, however, contraction is formal rather than thematic: it resides in the sonnet form itself, much as Paul Fussell described the Petrarchan sonnet structure as mimetic of "contraction and release in the muscular system" (*Poetic Meter* 116). As we'll see, Brooks took exactly what she needed from the Petrarchan rhyming template. But she also combines sonnets' formal contraction with linguistic luxuriousness and tautology—thereby creating a sinuous, multilayered protest against the inequities that her speakers suffer.

In 1948, William Carlos Williams called the sonnet a form that "does not admit of the slightest structural change in its composition" ("Poem" 57). Both *Bronzeville* and *Annie Allen*—the latter published one year after Williams's statement—showed how misguided this opinion was in both fact and spirit. For the virtuoso Brooks, the sonnet not only changes, but becomes an agent of greater cultural change; she shows it to be neither a stodgily British form, as it was for Williams, nor a narrowly patriarchal one. But by choosing the sonnet form at this moment in her collection, she also chooses circuitous, sometimes periphrastic poetic argument rather than a documentarian or even narrative approach to motherhood, race, and poverty. In other words, despite the swift pathos of the opening question, "What shall I give my children?," the voice of these sonnets is prolix, capacious, and erudite, featuring multifaceted and grandly detoured clauses.

In no way, however, does complexity minimize the immediacy with which Brooks dramatizes the pain and disenfranchisement caused by racial discrimination in 1940s America. In these poems, Brooks balances ratiocination with tenderness and regret; she tempers legalese with the language of child's play. In the sonnet I quoted above, for example, the mother says her children have asked her for "no velvet and no velvety velour." On the one hand, this line illustrates Brooks's own term "least-wise," or the children's internalization of how little they are valued by the dominant white culture: not only do they not demand the elegance and expense of authentically velvet clothing, but they don't even ask for "velvety velour," or the less-expensive fabric that would look like velvet and suffice in its stead.

The line's brilliance is also manifold. While the repeated "no" emphasizes the children's negation in the eyes of a racist culture, an unmistakable verbal pleasure unfolds if you actually speak the phrase "No velvet and no velvety velour." What it conveys is serious and even heartbreaking, but how can the line itself not make you smile? For me, the phrase is like frosting on a red velvet cake—sweets for the sweet(est lepers), if you will. "Velvet" combines with the almost kidlike "velvety" to concoct a verbal treat. Even as she negates the two fabrics' gradations of luxury, Brooks makes sure that we conspicuously consume their alliterative verbal material—showcasing the rare and wonderful letter *v*, no less!—much as "the mother," in the previous poem I referenced, suffers both from a "gobbling mother-eye" (4) and the inability to feed her aborted babies.

Verbal excess both surges and is tempered throughout the sequence. Brooks's first sonnet describes children whose "unridiculous / Lost softness softly makes a trap for us," creating a *los* sound that pulls across the enjambment, only to reveal itself assonant with the "softness" that then transforms to the adverb "softly" (*Selected Poems* 52). This is a veritable succulence of sound—in a poem about financially strapped, depleted parents. And appropriately, their children emit not just a whimper or a whine, but a double-barreled "Whimper-whine."

These intentionally tautological phrases allow Brooks to depict a poor mother's relationship both to her children and to the material items she cannot give them (and to the ratification or racially intelligible "contour" that she also cannot provide in the eyes of white America). But they also signify formally. For me, these moments signal Brooks's enormous agility and even relaxation within the strictness of the sonnet form—her willingness to let diction bask and wink within poems that are fundamentally serious. Her idiosyncratic ease unexpectedly serves her urgency.

These phrases also suggest an irresistible excess and gentleness associated with motherhood even in its direst imagined conditions. Surely Brooks's own experience as a mother was not identical to her speakers' in this sequence. But her son Henry Jr. was born in 1940, and her own parenting may play a role in these sonnets' linguistic and musical luxuriousness. As we've seen, her seeming tautologies allow childlike echolalia to ruffle the "graven" textures of time-honored sonnet forms. To mix metaphors a bit: she creates little fault lines, or rills, in what has been seen since Shakespeare as a sculptural or marmoreal tradition.

In this particular sonnet, Brooks's use of rhyme schemes from two classical sonnet forms, the Petrarchan and the Shakespearean, also provides an element of surplus. The sonnet embeds the Petrarchan octet's envelope rhymes before exploiting the repeated resonance of the Shakespearean form's closing couplet. Here Brooks is in the company of Donne, Milton, and others who mobilized similar strategies to reconstruct for the sonnet's hoary foot "Sandals more interwoven and complete," in Keats's terms ("If by dull rhymes," *John Keats* 237); as Stephanie Burt and David Mikics note, a poet cannot write a sonnet without participating in a long line of literary tradition (*Art* 21). But it is the very saturation of this tradition, even in the mid-twentieth century, that attracts the Brooks who writes "No velvet and no velvety velour." While excess will never derail these poems, she also whets our appetites for it.

She later comments on these strategies. In the fourth sonnet of "the children of the poor," Brooks juxtaposes violin playing and "bloody" rebellion, promoting the internal rhyme between "armor" and "harmony" (*Selected Poems* 54). Here the mother instructs her children to "Devote / The bow to silks and honey," rather than to "salt" (54). Silks and honey—again, extra-soft fabric and syrupy sweetness—perform a rhetorical function as metaphors for public performance.

This fourth sonnet creates both an alliterative juxtaposition and a small chronology. "First fight. Then fiddle" counsels a strict separation between militarism and the music to be played after war (54). While ostensibly independent, these activities are also defined by what each one is not, Brooks suggests; single-minded soldiers must "Be deaf to music and to beauty blind" (54). And yet "the music that they wrote / Bewitch, bewilder" suggests that a violinist must work sinuously, and strenuously, against the structural (and assuredly white) "they" who had the privilege of authoring mainstream music—even including "Bewitched, Bothered and Bewildered," with lyrics by Lorenz Hart of Rodgers and Hart, and first performed in 1940 (54).

It is here that the sonnet structure builds a bridge between the hyperbolic honey of pure music and the blood of war or protest, even as its letter insists on their separateness. In this way, it builds an allegory of poetic engagement. Not only does Brooks return thematically to "gay chaps at the bar" and its depiction of Black war veterans, but she also considers Black poetry more historically: looking back to the Harlem Renaissance and its accommodations of white patrons, and proleptically forward to the Black Arts movement that would profoundly affect her own racial consciousness. This sonnet suggests the power of poetry by allegorizing it as "music" and protest as "arms," but it does so with the "veiled civility" that Angela Jackson sees (in perhaps DuBoisian fashion) throughout Brooks's early work ("In Memoriam" 279).

On a more local level, like "gay chaps at the bar," this sonnet suggests that a person often has more than one identity. A musician becomes a soldier when he takes up arms. A woman is a mother and also Black. Perhaps this is part of the "bewitchment" Brooks describes—and yet such role-playing can be an ordinary aspect of daily life. In Brooks's hands, the sonnet form highlights such entwinements and circulations of the speaking self, especially in the complex syntax encouraged by its interlaced rhyme schemes.

The biographical Brooks also plays a complicated role with respect to her own sonnets, a role that is clarified by the free-verse poem ("Life for my child is simple, and is good") immediately following the "children of the poor" sequence. As the next movement in the larger symphony of "The Womanhood," the poem is a considerable switch: first, in its straightforward syntax and end-stopped lines; but also, even more startlingly, in its description of a curious and happy child for whom "reaching is his rule"; who, unlike the children of the poor, "begs" for nothing—because, unlike them, he feels "joy of undeep and unabiding things" (*Selected Poems* 55).

If anything, this poem seems in line with Brooks's delight in raising her own children. "At Christmas compare him to the Christmas tree," she wrote of Henry Jr. in *Report from Part I* (61)—a line that would be at home in "Life for my child," whose syntactic and linguistic directness foils the sonnets' high pitch of drama and hypotaxis. This very contrast becomes an interpoem version of contraction and release within "The Woman-hood," as well as a nod to the elaborate persona-scaffolding in Brooks's sonnet sequence. As Louise Glück wrote of John Berryman, personae may probe emotional truths (*Proofs* 44), and these truths are yet more complex for Black poets in the mid-twentieth century. One thing is certain, though: Brooks refuses to collapse the experience of Black motherhood into one monolithic way of speaking. Through her mastery of disparate poetic forms, including but not limited to the sonnet, she shows such experience to be—again, in her word—"legion" (55). This richness of formal variety, as well as her genius of juxtaposition, spotlights difference among and *within* Black women—even in 1949, before "difference" was a touchstone. Such variety may be the greatest wealth of all.

"Cinnamon. Eyeshadow. Dove"

Considering Jean Valentine, 1934–2020 (2021)

Jean Valentine taught me that the word "eyeshadow" could belong in a poem. Before I read her work, I had only seen that word in advertisements and fashion magazines. But far from describing surface femininity or sexiness, "eyeshadow" is the spiritual bedrock of Valentine's ars poetica called "Yield Everything, Force Nothing," from *The River at Wolf* (1992). Astonishingly, Valentine understood eyeshadow as a proper name, an allegorical figure, and an incantation:

The contest is over:
I turned away,
and I am beautiful: Job's last daughters,
Cinnamon, Eyeshadow, Dove.

The contest is over:
I let my hands fall,
and here is your garden:
Cinnamon. Eyeshadow. Dove. *(Door 213)*

"Cinnamon. Eyeshadow. Dove." This is a garden of spice, cosmetics, and the symbol of peace. Or does "Dove" refer to the soap brand instead? In its latticing of wit and enigma, Valentine's list reflects her own literary struggle and accomplishment over more than half a century. Though the speaker of the poem has dropped her hands in a gesture of abandonment, her offered garden is, in twenty-first-century parlance, a "win." She shows us that relinquishment can be a vanquishing.

Valentine, who died in December 2020, called herself "a well-kept secret" in New York, where she lived in the same Upper West Side apartment for over half her life (Newman, "Jean Valentine" 189). She always wore this modesty well—but her bountiful awards included the Yale Younger Poets prize, a Guggenheim fellowship, the Shelley Award from the Poetry Society of America, and the National Book Award. Though "Yield Everything, Force Nothing" dramatizes the gesture of turning away, her work succeeded and thrived without the buffering of public literary life.

"Yield Everything, Force Nothing" is, of course, much more than a meditation on literary competition. It is also about the untranslatable materiality of the list itself. "Cinnamon. Eyeshadow. Dove.": Valentine repeats the list without the italics that accompany its first iteration, then ends the poem without explanation. Like any proper name, the list resists translation or paraphrase. In this way, it brings to mind onomatopoetic aspects of early Stevens, whose birdcalls of "ki-ki-ri-ki / Brings no rou-cou, / No rou-cou-cou" are usually not analyzed much beyond their sounds' evocations (*Collected Poems* 63). At the same time, Valentine's list does very specific work: it renders the poet a transformer who, by renaming Job's three daughters (called Jemima, Kezia, and Keren-happuch in the biblical story), offers the reader a contemporary Garden of Eden. In the Old Testament, Job's daughters are praised for their beauty, but they are introduced at the end of their father's narrative and don't play a central role in it—in a sense, they constitute Job's "happily-ever-after." Here, Valentine revivifies them in her renaming, offering an odd new mythology of poetic creation. This creation is feminine and even quietist, but also authoritative—even as the poem's title counsels acquiescence.

Writing about "Yield Everything, Force Nothing" in *The Art of Description*, Mark Doty accurately notes that Valentine's poem is "not much interested in the textures and particulars of the outside world" (136). His comment also suggests why the large body of her work resists arrangement in a clear progression. Certainly, her poetry doesn't follow the formal turning points that we see in such poets as Yeats and Roethke. But in a deeper sense, though perennially fresh, it feels as if it were created by an old soul from the beginning. Changes in the outside world, or in the life of the poet, are not exactly extraneous to the work, but they don't feel essential to it either. Though Valentine often appeared to be governed by feelings, much like Louise Glück's "Red Poppy" in *The Wild Iris* ("Feelings: / oh, I have those; they / govern me," the flower says), Valentine's poems never feel predictably determined by life events like her divorces, the birth of her children, or the death of her friends (*Wild Iris* 29). Her poetic geography seemed broader than the experience of a single person without reaching for the scope of a universalizing "Everyman." Valentine was never limited to the perspective on life that her biological age might have conferred. Instead, she experienced the unconscious as a state of simultaneity in which young and old coexist. Not coincidentally, this is often where the lyric poem is most at home.

Despite her almost constitutional aversion to chronological development, Valentine took her place within a greater lyric lineage. Stevens's influence, though perhaps surprising at first, is unmistakable—for example, his famous definition of modern poetry as "The poem of the mind in the act of finding / What will suffice" (*Collected Poems* 239). Over the long haul of her poetry across time, Valentine shared a similar commitment to the *sufficient*. We can see it in her brevity, in her judicious use of the sentence fragment, and in the longevity, across books, of certain favored symbols (the poet-speaker as horse, for example—though a homier one than the superannuated gold horses in Stevens's "The Noble Rider and the Sound of Words"). Although Valentine went on to mine new subjects like the Ethiopian skeleton "Lucy," she never simply grasped at "the new." On the contrary, she valued the excavated, the durable, and the worn: "I keep the scraped-down leak marks from the rain / on the wall from two years ago / layers blue and tan" (*Break the Glass* 43). Here, the wall is a fossil or palimpsest created by benign neglect; in this way, ramshackle "found art" suggests an abiding commitment to craft. It is what the poet chooses to keep.

For Valentine, then, both durability and longevity are coordinates for the Stevensian "sufficient." But what are these durable things sufficient for, or what are they in service to? In Valentine's work, the answer may well be trauma. She hails from the historical age in which poets were, in Auden's words about Yeats, "hurt . . . into poetry" (*Selected Poems* 81). In this respect, Valentine was in good company alongside Sylvia Plath, Anne Sexton, and Adrienne Rich. The most visible poets of her generation struggled with depression, alcoholism, and family trauma, bringing the force of these troubles into their poems' content.

In her own life and work, Valentine was no stranger to any of these trials. Her childhood was turbulent. After returning from the Second World War when Valentine was ten, her father suffered from what we would now call post-traumatic stress disorder. Years later, she called this period "a very sad and awful time . . . for all of us" (Newman, "Jean Valentine" 190). As an adult, she battled drinking and depression and underwent two divorces. But the decade she spent in therapy was productive and helped legitimize her commitment to writing poetry. As Valentine told it, her therapist Dr. Shea helped her separate the vocation from its associations with the suicides of her peers like Plath and Sexton, emphasizing to his patient that "the force of poetry is a positive force, and probably kept those people alive longer than they would have been otherwise" (Newman, "Jean Valentine" 191).

To be sure, Valentine shared this conviction with Rich. Both of their careers stand as a protest against, and a triumph over, the Confessional mythology that dovetailed poetry with suicide—particularly women's suicide—in mid-twentieth-century America. "We have had enough suicidal women poets, enough suicidal women, enough of self-destructiveness as the sole form of violence permitted to women," Rich declared in a talk on Sexton in 1974 (*On Lies* 122). Still, both poets seem to have spent decades grappling with these suicides and their legacies.

Valentine's "To Plath, to Sexton" from *The River at Wolf* is a regretful yet admiring paean to the two poets, years after their deaths:

And when your tree
crashed through your house,

what use then
was all your power?

It was the use of you.
It was the flower. (Door 216)

In its retrospective view of Plath's and Sexton's work, this poem turns simply and movingly on a doubled definition of "use": it rotates from the futility of the second couplet's half-mocking, half-sorrowful rhetorical question ("what use then / was all your power?"), to an almost sacred valuation of "use" in the manner of a tool fulfilling, through work, what it was manually designed to accomplish.

Valentine's "It was the use of you" suggests that poetic power, born of dysfunction and illness, "used up" the lives of Plath and Sexton prematurely, but it also enabled them to be themselves, in an almost organic sense. Valentine saw them "flower" unquestioningly and instinctually as poets (regardless of how complicated their careers really were). Yet Valentine herself has taken "use" as a value, even a triumphal one, for her own work's longevity. So I can't help reading the unsaid in this poem: through her own survival, driven by writing, Valentine won the battle of "use," much as she won the contest described in "Yield Everything, Force Nothing." Any such euphoric interpretation, however, would run the risk of ignoring the unspoken loss and remorse in "To Plath, to Sexton." While "survivor's guilt" may be too strong a term for Valentine's feelings, she also confronted an irreconcilable dilemma: though she may have identified with Plath and Sexton both intellectually and emotionally, she also had to separate from them—not only as a poet, but also as a woman committed to living her life to its natural end.

Valentine often, and generously, acknowledged the gifts of her contemporaries. Yet she always had her own approach to representing trauma. She chose not to aggrandize it (as, arguably, Plath and Sexton did at times), nor to transform it into more didactic narratives of gender identity and the conversions involved in Second Wave or separatist feminism (as, arguably, Rich did at times). Instead, Valentine continually rebuilt the *stanza*—or *room*, in Italian—as a chamber scrubbed clean of both ornament and distraction. A Valentine stanza is a shelter and a refuge, but also a crucible and a watchtower. In her later work, it was a prison cell. Sometimes it excludes the elegance of protracted syntax, as in *Little Boat*'s "Hospital: Scraps":

Scraps of hard feelings
left on the floor
winter material

But out the window
sun on the snow

Dressmaker's pins
—somebody's soul
a feminine glint in the trees (Little Boat 37)

This is a later version of the Valentine stanza-room, but it remains an illustrative one. Syntactical connections, and much punctuation, have been "scraped" from these short lines, much as we saw earlier in Valentine's wall-fossil; and the dearth of verbs creates a sense of weightlessness or even disembodiment. As a result of these subtractions, the poem feels "fast"; it reads as a sketch or perhaps as notes jotted from a hospital bed. And the "Scraps of hard feelings" are never rendered concrete. They are softened, however, by the disconsolately musical "winter material," which suggests what lies beyond the window: "sun on the snow." In this way, the pain in the hospital room remains more elided than suggested. This elision functions like the figure of *syncope*—in which syllable, but not sense, is glided over. The poem becomes a stark, Dickinsonian "dwell[ing] in Possibility" (*Poems* 215), in which the inside meets what exists outside the room (in both its architectural and poetic senses). It is also the habitation of the soul, which pricks like pins but also lights as the gratifying internal slant rhyme in the phrase "feminine glint," coming as an aural relief—like "winter material"—after the hard consonants earlier.

The poem is a quick anatomy of an everyday observation. In the second stanza, the visual "sun on the snow" becomes metaphysical ("somebody's soul"), then unexpectedly gendered ("feminine glint"). Yet the last phrase is both dense and oblique. Since the noun for "soul" is feminine in French, Italian, and Spanish, a female body may underwrite this scene—but only as a flash of grammatical association. The "feminine glint," then, points to what the poem doesn't say and to what its title only suggests: there is a hurt or ill woman in this hospital room, and it may be Valentine herself. The body's trauma is deflected, not itemized.

At other times, Valentine turned a steelier eye on trauma. In the 1974 collection *Ordinary Days*, she described a different hospital room—a birthing room in which "huge tall masks / of women's faces" enter:

. . . not-women they were suicides, trees, soft,
pale, freckled branches bending over her—
I knew them as my own, their cries

took on the family whiskey voice, refusal,
need,—their human need peeled down, tore,
scratched for her life—
I hacked and hacked them apart— (Door 106)

Here Valentine nearly echoes Rich's *Of Woman Born*: the birthing room as a place of hostility and violence, the re-entrenchment of childhood trauma ("the family whiskey voice," perhaps recalling her troubled father), the equation of women and despair—even the unsettling parataxis in which women become "suicides, trees, soft / pale, freckled branches," in a ghostly return of Plath or Sexton. This poem also bristles with the verbs "scratched" and the repeated "hacked"; here, birth is a feral fight for the mother's and daughter's very lives. Valentine had two daughters, Sarah and Rebecca, in 1958 and 1960, respectively; while birthing conditions have changed considerably since then, and even since the poem's publication in 1974, the poem's emotional resonance reaches far into the present. Valentine refused to idealize childbirth; on the contrary, she portrayed it as a nightmare that some women would rather forget. In this and other poems in the volume, particularly one that laments the "mirrors closing in" on a doubled identity as daughter and mother (*Door* 118), Valentine seemed poised to define herself as a feminist writer in Rich's vein.

Over the course of her work, however, Valentine complicated her own status as a "women's writer," perhaps because she kept listening so intently to the atonal music made by the unconscious. Her poems derived substantially from dreams, one of Valentine's most powerful modalities since *Dream Barker* (1965). This fidelity to dream life may disallow the more programmatic, didactic moments that inevitably enter a poetry like Rich's. For Valentine, the dream was not so much a voyage into the interior of the self, nor even an enactment of Freudian displacement and condensation, but often something else entirely: the resistance to human limitation writ large, especially the traps of narcissism, greed, and narrowness of mind. Her poems enacted this struggle gently and insidiously over the decades. Valentine's poems are not self-help; neither are they essays. Yet they make a strong case for the benefits of self-knowledge in both the Freudian and Platonic senses.

Valentine often seemed to suggest that human transformation and enlargement is accomplished via the dream-emblem, by which she meant "image." And she understood the power of dreams' acuity. The image, then, becomes a thing that "feels real," in Plath's words (*Collected Poems* 245). Take, for example, "Sick, Away from Home," from *Growing Darkness, Growing Light* (1997):

My head
the Jenny Lind's head,
the painted tall ship's figurehead:
full, staring eyes,
beautiful:
but instead of the prow's wood at her back,
at my back a Monarch wing,

and the head and the wing
held up not by her wooden neck
and breasts of wood
but by an upright, silent thumb:
dream thumb
        —me dreaming
over the wet electric New York streets. (Door 219)

Here we are not in the realm of metaphor, but instead in dream-cinema: the poet transforms into the wooden effigy on a tall ship's prow. When Valentine states, without connectives, "My head / the Jenny Lind's head," she has become the legendary Swedish opera singer, her voice now departed; the "Swedish Nightingale" unable to sing. In contrast to this implicit silencing, however, Valentine's syntax is fluid over these short lines: a single sentence fragment, precisely punctuated, reaches across two seven-line stanzas. This lengthy fragment directs the reader's "eye," showing us the effigy's own head and eyes, wing, neck, breasts, and thumb; Valentine often places these items at the ends of lines to suggest a list or blazon. The repeated "thumb" becomes a fulcrum: in fact, the "dream thumb" is what supports the entire image, though the poem does not explain its significance. Instead, we can take pleasure in the imme-diacy of the strange description itself. (We are also told that the head is "beautiful." While it's risky to depend too much on this word in poems,

Valentine's moderate use of it is, for me, part and parcel of her plainspo-kenness. She understands "beautiful" as diction that reflects the conver-sational everyday.)

Freud would call this Lind-wing-thumb the "composite structure" of dreams: "The possibility of creating composite structures stands foremost among the characteristics which so often lend dreams a fantastic appear-ance, for it introduces . . . elements which could never have been objects of actual perception" (*Interpretation* 359). In the wooden head supported by the wing and thumb, then, Valentine has created a conglomerate, or a hybrid rebus that Freud discusses elsewhere. Less fantastical versions of the Jenny Lind head circulate patiently throughout Valentine's books; in addition to the glass-bottomed boat in "Dream Barker," the proem of *Little Boat* finds the speaker adrift in a whimsically painted *chalupa*: "the blue boat painted with roses, / white lilies," reminiscent of a children's toy, that she recalls from her early adulthood (*Little Boat* 1). For Valentine, the boat is both vehicle and aesthetic object. It is the instrument of both stasis and progress.

Valentine was not content to stop with the transformational emblem, however, because she realized that the dream has even more at stake. Could dreaming enable a different way of being with others in waking life? Valentine often suggested that it might. To do this, she combined the dream-emblem with shifting pronouns—the pronominal "musical chairs" that we also associate with Ashbery, to very different ends—in order to show psychic boundaries loosening during the dreaming state. This, she suggested, is how a dream might be shared among persons. But first, the speaking "I" must be dissolved. And at times, Valentine suggests the "I" is hypothetical or even imaginary: "left my soul not 'mine' / 'my' clothes   off / I left the edges of 'my' face / 'my' hands" (*Door* 23).

When Rich, in her blurb for *Door in the Mountain,* wrote that Valen-tine's work "lets us into spaces and meanings we couldn't approach in any other way," she may well have had the lines above, or others like them, in mind. There, the quotation marks around "mine" and "my" act as subtle disqualifiers of a unitary—and possessive—first person. The smallest lin-guistic marks, then, open the boundaries of a known personal identity. In this case, the identity belongs to Matthew Shepard, the young gay man beaten and left naked to die on a fence in Laramie, Wyoming, in 1998. The quoted pronouns search and hesitate almost palpably, perhaps out of respect for Shepard's life and the circumstances of his murder; after all, Valentine is reconstructing the aftermath of a violent hate crime. While Shepard was victimized due to his identity as a gay man, Valentine here hypothesizes the outer limits of personal identity in the most global of senses, when "my soul" is "not 'mine.'" The quoted pronouns bring Shepard's loss into a different kind of discourse than any media coverage ever could. They distribute his body and spirit among a readership, even as they visibly hesitate to speak "for" him.

Valentine had dissolved the "I" even more fully, in "March 21st" from *The Messenger* (1979):

And you, my sister, writing,
the hidden way of each of us, buried

To drift   allowing

forgetting my name   my life
the salt of our hands
touching

changing:

over and over: following

you   who I don't know
listening: changing

the play of the breath of the world

they   he   she   you   (Door 162–63)

In an epigraph for her later collection *Growing Darkness, Growing Light* (1997), Valentine quoted Native American poet Lance Henson, who says that he "like[s] to deal with the relationship between growing darkness and growing light, the dusk and the dawn, those times when there is a chance to see transition. . . . The dream is a connection, another transitional time" (*Door* 217). The entirety of "March 21st" captures such transitional moments. Who are we, the poem asks, in our first moments of waking? Its answer is the infinitive "To drift," which Valentine develops in participles ("forgetting," "allowing," "touching" "following," and "changing") rather than completed actions, suggesting the fugal period of liminal consciousness after sleep. Over a stanza break, the poem tumbles from "touching" to "changing," its single-word lines sweeping the reader up in their wake; we feel the tentative tenaciousness of an "I" fording fluid and unknown territory. And in the final line of suspended pronouns, "I" could be legion: the poet has even "for[gotten] [her] name." But though the poem never reassembles this dissolved "I"—its final list of pronouns excludes the first person—Valentine is also never alone in it. She begins by addressing her sister, and in "the salt of our hands / touching," the two women maintain a delicate connection. Despite its elliptical progression and fragmentary appearance on the page, then, this poem is buttressed by—and even basks in—the indissolubility of familial bonds.

For Valentine, dreams had powerful social capacities. She often suggested that the dream, far from being an adventure in navel-gazing, can instead provide self-knowledge that should be transferred to waking life: "You know how in dreams you are everyone: / awake too you are everyone: / I am listening   breathing your ashy breath" (*Door* 25). The suspension of the dreaming "I," then, requires *listening* to others when one wakes. It is here, against all odds, that the slenderness of a Valentine poem intersects with the capaciousness of a Whitman. Though their poetics appear very different at first blush, both poets wanted to turn outward—to give the self over to the reader or to the loved other. Thus Valentine's avowal that "Everyone else may leave you, I will never leave you, fugitive" (*Door* 203) is akin to Whitman's "I have loved many women and men, but I love none better than you" (*Leaves of Grass* 206). In both cases, the rush of plainspoken intimacy disarms us: we are gratified to have been "chosen" by both of these poets who have professed their devotion to us. Later in her work, in *Break the Glass*, Valentine echoes Whitman even more closely. In "On a Passenger Ferry," she writes of Grace Paley, "Nobody else saw her, but I saw her," invoking the shade of Whitman in "Crossing Brooklyn Ferry" and elsewhere (*Break* 15).

In *Poetry's Touch: On Lyric Address*, William Waters considers Whitman's care for, and power over, his readers:

Whitman inspires, or wants to inspire, trust. Although he is not there, he comes close to you, pulling off layer after layer of your disbelief. What characterizes his explicitly epitaphic poems is the relentless attempt to "meet" his reader—to stop her in her tracks—but for her sake, not . . . for his own. This investment in the needs of the reader, his care for her, is fundamental. . . . (122)

Valentine's project differs from Whitman's in many ways, yet she resembles him in wanting to create, as Waters says, "the unprotected moment of reading"—the combination of "trust" and abashment that an extraordinary poem can incite in a reader. In her introduction to an issue of *Ploughshares* that she guest-edited, Valentine implied that she herself demands a similar experience when reading, or selecting, poems: "What I was looking for was the chill shiver of poetry. I was biting a coin to see if it was real" ("Introduction" 7).

Chill shivers: this statement recalls, of course, Dickinson's famous pronouncement: "If I read a book [and] it makes my whole body so cold no fire ever can warm me I know *that* is poetry. If I feel physically as if the top of my head were taken off, I know *that* is poetry" (*Letters* 342a). In Valentine's case, however, this bodily response is not a self-indulgent aesthetic calculated to produce a narrowly personal *frisson*. Instead, it is imbued with a caring for someone else—a feeling that sometimes lacerates, much as Stanley Plumly described Kunitz's gardening hand as "torn with caring" ("Kunitz" 8). This is an important way that Valentine's work differs from other poetry that may be oblique, reliant on the unconscious, or based in dreams. As Christine Garren shows in her poem "The Analyst," there may be an inherent risk in writing such poems. When a therapist takes Garren's speaker to a small pond, the speaker first sees nothing—until she realizes that her own reflection has obstructed the view: "I stared into the flat glaze and saw a few gnats, a slight current. / And then I understood—/ my form covered the pool" (*Monarchs* 9).

As Garren eloquently suggests, dream poems often court the risk of narcissism. For Valentine, however, a vigilant "I" finally loosens its strictures and creates a salutary porosity that generates personal and even social transformation: "*everything / must be turned to love that is not love*" (*Door* 198). Such lyric moments hearken back to the prose writings of Shelley and Wordsworth, who argued for poetry's ability to create and promote an almost preternaturally enlarged "sympathy" in the reader.

Valentine does so by considering how the unconscious might open an individual toward others in the world. This may happen in erotic love or via fellow feeling. It's a notion that's condensed in the following lines that occupy, on their own, a full page in *Little Boat*: "Blessed are those / who break off from separateness // theirs is wild / heaven" (49).

These lines, with their biblical tone echoing "Yield Everything, Force Nothing," constitute a wish to be a "speech act": the words want to cause a change in the world. Here, the act is a blessing. The "break[ing] off" of these isolated words—what looks very much like "separateness" on the page itself—is also, paradoxically, what opens the boundaries between persons. The spatial isolation of these lines paradoxically *wants* to heal individuals' isolation. This is a complement to Valentine's belief in symbol—and a sensibility that becomes, finally, religious in nature.

This "breaking off" may have less to do with erotic merging and more to do with what lies on the other side of self-loss in trauma: a tenor of kindness, much in the manner of New Testament teachings. For Valentine, this kindness has potentially radical implications, as she describes ekphrastically in "Dufy Postcard":

Every day you move farther outside
the outlines, kinder, more dangerous.
Where will you be going.
Who will the others be. (Door 130)

Here, the flat questions-as-statements ("Where will you be going. / Who will the others be.") deftly undercut the poem's import: The desire to live "outside / the outlines" of the painting is a hunger to bypass human limitation. In this way, it is similar to the emptying or askesis that happens in sainthood. The saint must empty out her personhood in order to receive the deity: an act that may well be "dangerous," in Valentine's sense, as well as "kind." Such proximity of kindness and danger is key to the emotional geography of Valentine's poems. She understands that self-loss is a terrifying aspect of trauma, but that it also allows us to see and to hear others differently. Valentine affirms this joyously: "I was made for this: listening" (*Door* 243).

Valentine also listened to the voices of the dead, and her voice is movingly acute when she addresses them:

—*But to go away!*
And I wanted to be sure to reach you!

And the charge still in us   ankle waist & wrist
& eyes   —Not see you! (Little 42)

Both mournful and exclamatory, this one-sided colloquy echoes O'Hara's "To the Harbor Master" in depicting how the soul grasps at another life that has inexplicably flickered out (*Collected Poems* 217). The anatomical junctures of ankle, waist, and wrist light, after a line break, on the "eyes" that will never see the loved one again.

From its outset in *Dream Barker*, Valentine's work was always suited to the elegy—and to an elegiac positioning of the poet in a Venn diagram that intersects the circles of life and death. A Valentine elegy, however, refuses the closure that Peter Sacks and others have seen as endemic to the genre. If I could coin a phrase to describe what Valentine's elegies do, that phrase might be the "conversational uncanny":

You ask,

Could we have coffee?   —No, my truth,
I'm still on this side.
*   I saw you last night, again,*

at the bar on 57th,
O faceless dancer,
and I put down my mask

I wanted you to touch me
You stood there neither man nor woman,
beautiful edge   by the water (Break 45)

This agile poem captures grief in many ways. First, there's the humor: "Could we have coffee?" The dead friend's casual invitation can only be refused, since "I'm still on this side." Then the role of the locale: the dead friend is witnessed at the "bar at 57th" in New York City, a setting for poets from Whitman to O'Hara. Here, however, the city is less a place than a scrim, or a backdrop for mourning—and mourning is what happens when one is "just walking dully along," in Auden's terms, on city streets (*Selected Poems* 79). Valentine's elegies often don't commemorate, in any usual way. In them, grief becomes a wider way of seeing. And this must be done, paradoxically, by limitation—of stanzas and of sentence structure.

Here, though, something incalculable has happened in Valentine's lovely description of the dead person as "neither man nor woman" but an entity that has approached an inhuman and picturesque "beautiful edge by the water." The imprecision of this "edge" is intentional: "edge   by the water," is, in my reading, periphrastic for "shore." This rhetorical figure for linguistic circumlocution enables "edge" to perform many things that "shore" could not. It has the echoes of a knife's edge, as well as the imprecision of plural picturable "edges." In this way, "edge" is multiplied, then emptied out imagistically, which allows it to move in concert with the "faceless" dancing of the apparition that is "neither man nor woman." Now we confront the importance of *linguistic* locale: the blunting of one word ("edge") is what sediments the dead person into the environment—perhaps beautifully, but also facelessly.

The dead friend, then, is both the friendly conversationalist of *Could we have coffee?* and the voiceless fade of the "edge   by the water." In a Valentine elegy, few words exist in the space between these states. The poem does not explain itself, nor its lightning-quick associative leaps. Some readers would call it "difficult" poetry. Nonetheless, anyone who has lost a loved one will know exactly what Valentine is talking about. Mourning is not always identical to melancholia. It has room for the offhand aside and even the occasional laugh, as well as for the "faceless" and the devastating. The dead become, in her words, "this-world company" (*Door* 216).

Valentine's "this-world company" is populous, and it includes the unborn as well as the dead. In *The Cradle of the Real Life* (2000), she depicts an intelligent "listening" fetus who shares the poet's powerfully receptive nature. Valentine's poems also return periodically to the theme of an abortion or miscarriage, though her investment in this theme appears to be more emotional than political. Many of these poems show prebirth as a realm to which poetry may only point. In contrast, "My Mother's Body, My Professor, My Bower," from *The River at Wolf*, offers a rich and melodious list to reconstruct—or to imagine—Valentine's own experience as a newborn:

Who died? My mother's body,
my professor, my bower,
my giant clam.
Serene water, professor
of copious clay,
of spiraling finger-holes in the clay,
of blue breast-milk,
first pulse, all thought:
there is nothing to get. You can't eat money,
dear throat, dear longing,
dear belly, dear fatness,
dear silky fastness: ecstatic lungs' breath,
you can't protect yourself,
there is nothing to get. (Door 209)

Valentine suffered a traumatic childhood and perhaps an almost equally traumatic entry into motherhood. But this poem reaches beyond the poet's biographical experience into something much harder to grasp. In a mollusk-like spiraling of metaphor, the mother's body generates both viscosity and rationality: she's a "professor" not of any discipline, but of earthly material. What she teaches is the marvelously viscous "copious clay" in which the baby punches "finger-holes." By enjambing the fourth and fifth lines, Valentine further emphasizes the surprise of this juxtaposition. She creates a loop of sound-play that commingles cerebral striving and the instinctual burrow: mother become bower (in an ironically Spenserian Bower of Bliss), finally become professor. In the dreamlike rebus, the "giant clam" is also a professor of "blue breast-milk." The pulse is the thought, the expertise is in suction and secretion, and the poem's overall notion is that the mother must teach and nourish the infant who "can't eat money" or even use it, who "can't protect [herself]." Like every infant, she is born before she can provide for herself biologically.

For this reason, she is subject to both the ecstasy ("ecstatic lungs' breath") and abjectness of being her mother's neonatal student and erstwhile literal "pulse." In the anaphoric repetitions of "my" and "dear," we can hear both satiation and frustration: though the insistence is musical, it chafes against a dependence that is hard to bear. Yet embedded in this poem, I suspect, is the occluded origin of every Valentine poem: the trauma of birth itself.

This is a concern that is increasingly difficult for our capitalist, schismatic world to assimilate. Psychoanalysis has long fallen out of fashion here in the States. But women—and some men—are still wearing eye shadow. Precisely in that spirit. I'd like to return to another appearance of "eyeshadow" in *The River at Wolf*:

This is
true desire, it lets you be.
It says, "No money here."

What does it taste like?
True desire. Eye-
shadow, cinnamon. (Door 190)

Eye shadow returns us again, and counterintuitively, to Stevens. When he said that a poem must "resist the intelligence / Almost successfully," he might as well have been referring to the work of Jean Valentine, whose desire was to write "almost / unknowingly," as she once described Eurydice in "Orpheus," her translation of the Dutch poet Huub Oosterhuis (*Door* 143). Her poems move dialectically between striving and abiding, between "scratching" at the world and burrowing into it, always in plainspoken yet unpredictable language. From the compressed lines of "My Mother's Body, My Professor, My Bower" to the cloudlike white spaces in *Little Boat*, Valentine's work unearthed layers of thought and feeling without the aid of any philosophical apparatus. Her awareness also radiated to the social world: by listening to herself, and to the dream life, Valentine listened to others. For her, these were the lineaments of desire in its many guises. Eyeshadow and cinnamon—without their dove—can reliably transport both poet and reader beyond the limits of a too-deterministic currency ("'No money here'"). What does true desire taste like? It probably tastes like a Valentine poem.

On Ghosts and the Overplus (2016)

Tonight I saw myself in the dark window as
the image of my father, whose life
was spent like this,
thinking of death, to the exclusion
of other sensual matters,
so in the end that life
was easy to give up, since
it contained nothing. . . .

    —FROM *MIRROR IMAGE*, BY LOUISE GLÜCK

You can spend your whole life thinking of death. Or soaring from it. My father was the opposite of Glück's—steeped instead in the earthly, the decimal point, and the profit margin. Eight years into leukemia and he still had no time for death—no truck with it, as people used to say. He was a retired businessman still chairing company committees. He was a master gardener, devising ever-new systems for labeling squash and trellising tomatoes. He was industrious, in the best sense. Frost might have said that his vocation and avocation had successfully united, as two eyes do in sight. Hospice was the roadblock. His own mortality was the real shock.

Hospice broke his heart.

This is the story I'm telling right now. I believe it to be true. Or might there have been another, different truth—some truth beyond a living person's need to understand? I'd like to imagine a veiled waterway, hidden even from himself, that led him to a place beyond his conscious will and power. Could some internal stream have soothed the pain of his body's betrayal? I'm guaranteed never to know. But I can still wish.

Can poetry reside in the recess of that mystery?

· · ·

> There used to be no house, hardly a room, in which someone had not once died.
>
> —FROM *ILLUMINATIONS*, BY WALTER BENJAMIN

Some years ago, a friend was talking to an owl at an artists' colony near the Bighorns. Every morning before sunrise, she went out to greet the owl, and the owl spoke back. I understood that some profound content had been exchanged between the two of them—though it was also, perhaps predictably, hard to pin down in English. So I didn't press her too hard for details.

What stayed with me instead was the euphoria of *address*—what Roman Jakobson called the conative function in language, or "orientation toward the addressee" (*Norton* 1149). I like to think of it this way: the conversation's subject isn't really so important; the thrill is that the conversation happens at all. The linguistic rush of *face to face*. Or in French, conversation is *tête à tête*: literally "head to head," or putting two heads together.

This is what it feels like to fall in love.

Still, wouldn't you be skeptical about the owl story?

A few years later, during my own stay at a colony, I myself became the surprised target of a "visitation"—a ghost. It was said that a person, or persons, had died in the house where I was staying. One of them followed me up the staircase and spoke in my dark bedroom. Tripped the electrical circuit's "light fantastic." And made my keyboarding fingers type the initials "BS"—in a succinct (and, yes, hilarious) pan of everything I'd written that day.

The other residents there didn't find my experience unusual. They had similar stories. One of them told me not to worry.

To me, it had felt terrifying and then a little silly. A good agnostic, and a good empiricist, is not supposed to be visited like this, even if she's also a poet. I couldn't square that ghost—but I couldn't deny its existence, either. It had all really happened. So I tried to redefine it as a local artifact. Or put it in the zoo. I told myself, *Ghosts are part of the discourse here.*

That sentence is a paradox: *discourse* sparks the intellect while *ghost* flouts its every rule. The sentence is also a diplomat—it brings reason and inexplicability to the same table. Most of all, though, it muzzles the ghost. *Discourse* routs the uncontainable. The uncountable. I fenced that ghost in language.

Since poetry is made of words—as Mallarmé told Degas—it's capable of doing this, too. But a poem is also something else. Poetry is what lets the ghost reply, *Don't fence me in.*

• • •

> You have told me you gave it all away
> then, sold the house, keeping only the confirmation
> cross she wore, her name in cursive chased
> on the gold underside, your ring in the same
>
> box, those photographs you still avoid,
> and the quilt you spread on your borrowed bed—
> small things. Months after we met, you told me she had
> made it, after we had slept already beneath its loft
> and thinning, raveled pattern, as though beneath
> her shadow, moving with us, that dark, that soft.
> —FROM *ARTIFACT*, BY CLAUDIA EMERSON

Look at the smallest, most ephemeral things around you. How many fingers have touched them? Do you know whose?

In Claudia Emerson's sequence "Late Wife: Letters to Kent," a newly remarried woman encounters her husband's first wife, dead of cancer, in precisely those sorts of things. There is the quilt the late wife made, and one stray "driving glove" in the car. The late wife also made a video of her then-husband Kent coming home to their adorably excitable dog.

When she watches this home video, Emerson realizes that its erstwhile camerawoman and "director" is now, impossibly, directing *her*: "as though she directs / me to notice the motion of her chest / in the rise and fall of the frame" (*Late Wife* 48). Kent—the "you" in this passage from "Homecoming"—is unwittingly complicit in the strategy:

Then, at last, you come home
to look into the camera she holds,
and past her into me—invisible, unimagined
other who joins her in seeing through our
transience the lasting of desire. (48)

The "you," the "me," and the "she." Three pronouns that don't always go well together. But this particular triangle is full of generosity. Emerson becomes the late wife's coconspirator, confidante, receptor, continuation. Kent is the natural bridge: love for him has brought two strangers together, one posthumously, in these poems' "unimagined" scenes. A single wife is not enough; two marriages combine in time to serve an idea, or "the lasting of desire."

I don't know how "true" these poems are, nor do I need to know. In other words, I don't know whether, or to what degree, Emerson actually experienced the late wife as I did the ghost at the colony. Regardless, I see her poems as an act of radical empathy and eros—one that reimagined and loosened the outlines of a single self, or of a couple. It was an act that redefined triangulation not as tension or obstacle—the way it has been since time immemorial, or at least since *Jane Eyre*—but as the perfecting of each couple's love, moving forward and backward in time.

I didn't know Claudia Emerson. She died in 2014, also from cancer, at the young age of fifty-seven. When I read the news, my mind flew to *Late Wife*. It was all I could think about. At first, I felt it all had to be a mistake: that *Late Wife* made Emerson's early death impossible. As if the book itself should have been a prophylactic. Then I wondered if the opposite were true.

I wondered, that is, if the poems were talismanic. They didn't foretell Emerson's death, but they narrated what had, in a sense, already happened: she herself was in the process of becoming the "late wife" that the poems so lovingly inhabited.

In a sense, every poem becomes a site of askesis, or self-evacuation—since we don't write literally with blood, but with black marks on paper, or their electronic equivalents. As we learn in our first workshops, our bodies (and explanations, and justifications) can't follow our poems around in the world. But Emerson's askesis seems different, as if she exchanged her very life for a rapt concentration on the dead. The danger of that statement, of course, is that it sounds a lot like magical thinking. It sounds like an aesthetic justification for a death that occurred too soon.

And maybe it is. But consider this: elsewhere in the poem I just quoted, Emerson calls the late wife's video "scripted" (48). In the course of writing these poems, had Emerson tapped into something more powerful than poetry, or even than her life? In this case, the rhetorical term is *prolepsis*—meaning that, in some sense, we are always living with a future that has already happened.

What role can poetry play in such a life-script? Here are the first wife's X-rays, as her doctors described them to Kent:

> By the time they saw what they were looking at
> it was already risen into the bones
> of her chest. They could show you then the lungs
> were white with it; they said it was like salt
> in water—that hard to see as separate—
> and would be that hard to remove. Like moonlight
> dissolved in fog, in the dense web
> of vessels. (46)

Like the disease in the lungs, metaphor is everywhere. It's ineluctable, even in the doctors' diagnosis. The first wife's illness becomes beautiful as an ocean or as moonlight dissolved in fog. It seems to me there is always a risk in lyricizing pathology, but I also sense that this is the perfect accommodation—the hand-in-driving-glove, if you will—between the ghost of the late wife and the poet who will become her successor. Like salt in water, the two of them had already grown so very hard to see as separate.

Maybe metaphor incites such eerie inevitability, which became the achievement of Emerson's Pulitzer Prize–winning book. Yet the poet's biography shows that the poems themselves are not the end. It calls us beyond the poems, into the script.

This is what made Emerson's death the hardest-hitting for me, despite our recent and staggering losses of giants like Seamus Heaney, Philip Levine, and Mark Strand—Strand who, in one of his last talks at the Poetry Foundation, discussed "the inevitability of surprise" in poems. He said that current poetry fashion had lost the taste for it.

Though she was alive when he spoke it, Strand's phrase also describes Emerson's demise.

· · ·

> All I know is a door into the dark.
> —FROM *THE FORGE*, BY SEAMUS HEANEY

The history of the novel has a discrete historical place for the Gothic and its revenants. In poetry, though, the ghost can't be confined to a single era. Claudia Emerson had so many ancestors. There was Coleridge and "Christabel." Hardy's final ghost poems. Rilke "transcribing" the sonnets to Orpheus, inspired by the dead Vera Knoop. Yeats writing *A Vision*. Merrill and his Ouija board. And so on.

Why do so many of these ghosts seep into the lives and deaths of poets? All I know is that the more I write poetry, the surer and less sure I become. The more deeply I listen to both the inflections and innuendos of language, to paraphrase Wallace Stevens, the more astute and also superstitious I seem to be. The more densely I describe the textures of the world around me, the more of it I realize I am missing. The negatives of

Matthew Brady's Civil War photographs, built into greenhouse glass and described by Linda Bierds in *The Profile Makers*, make lovely analogues for this. Of course, it's a short journey from photographic negatives to Keatsian negative capability, or the valuation of doubt and mystery that animates so many poets.

For me, poetry proliferates and flourishes in the intellect's blind spot. But you have to have the intellect first; you can't skip that step. I find intelligence to be most interesting when it's tested—not when it's challenged, but when we restrain it from being the default mode by which we apprehend the phenomena around us. Can strategies in the martial arts speak to this?

By the same token, the way of mind that attends the supernatural or numinous is hardly compelling without a formidable and even mutually exclusive foil. Ratiocination. This is where poetry inserts itself, again with Stevens, as what "must resist the intelligence / Almost successfully" (*Collected Poems* 350).

• • •

> *My Ben!*
> *Or come again,*
> *Or send to us*
> *Thy wit's great overplus. . . .*
>   —FROM *AN ODE FOR HIM*, BY ROBERT HERRICK

> *The dead have no ears, no answering machines*
> *that we know of, still we call.*
>   —FROM *LEAVE A MESSAGE*, BY BOB HICOK

The "O" of apostrophe. The vocative, in Latin—and for Jakobson, too. For the critic Barbara Johnson, apostrophe was what made lyric poetry itself; its long history could have been distilled into a single cry. Robert Herrick's apostrophe transformed his dead friend, the bon vivant Ben Jonson, into "Saint Ben." We cry to the dead, and we imagine that they answer us. The weirdness in me wants to say they sometimes even do.

Herrick was right, too, about the dead's "overplus." This is the uncanny excess that can't be contained by empirical limits—even if it's sheathed in Jonson's wit or my own ghost's "BS." If Herrick's term sounds mathematical, so much the better. Think of the late wife's doctors and their metaphors.

Can we greet the overplus without relinquishing our skepticism? Poetry keeps asking the impossible.

My father died two years ago today, in my childhood home that had become, for six short and endless hours, Hospice. His pain ripped him, even with morphine. To the end, I think, he was battling death, his legs still muscled enough to fight.

When it was over, the funeral home attendants zipped up his body and wheeled it away, leaving a silk rose behind.

Later that night, I startled awake and sat up. He was lying next to me, as if still in his hospital bed. But his eyes were peacefully closed, the way they weren't in death. His face and body were calm—as if conflict and even muscularity had flown or floated down a river. I leaned over and reached for his hand. Then realized I was clawing my own bedsheet.

He was there. Or not. How would I ever know?

In poetry, perhaps more than anywhere else, we can try.

The answers won't be there. Still we call.

Works Cited

Abrams, M. H. *A Glossary of Literary Terms*. 6th ed. New York: Harcourt, 1993.

Alter, Robert. *The Pleasures of Reading in an Ideological Age*. New York: Norton, 1996.

Ammons, A. R. *Tape for the Turn of the Year*. New York: Norton, 1965.

Ashbery, John. *Selected Poems*. New York: Penguin, 1986.

Ashbery, John. *Selected Prose*. Ann Arbor: University of Michigan Press, 2005.

Ashton, Jennifer. "Our Bodies, Our Poems." *American Literary History* 19.1 (Spring 2007): 211–31.

Attridge, Derek. *The Rhythms of English Poetry*. London: Routledge, 1982.

Auden, W. H. *Selected Poems*. New York: Vintage International, 1989.

Auerbach, Erich. "From *Mimesis*." *Norton Anthology of Theory and Criticism*. 2nd ed. Ed. Vincent B. Leitch. New York: Norton, 2010. 1030–46.

Barber, David. *Wonder Cabinet*. Evanston, IL: Northwestern University Press, 2006.

Barthes, Roland. *Camera Lucida*. Trans. Richard Howard. New York: Hill and Wang, 1982.

Barthes, Roland. "The Death of the Author." *Image Music Text*. Trans. Stephen Heath. New York: Hill and Wang, 1977. 142–48.

Barthes, Roland. "The Grain of the Voice." *Image Music Text*. 179–89.

Barthes, Roland. *The Pleasure of the Text*. Reprint ed. Trans. Richard Miller. New York: Hill and Wang, 1975.

Beauvoir, Simone de. *The Second Sex*. Ed. and trans. H. M. Parshley. New York: Vintage, 1989.

Beckett, Samuel. *Watt*. New York: Grove Press, 1953.

Benjamin, Walter. *Illuminations*. Ed. Hannah Arendt. Trans. Harry Zohn. New York: Schocken Books, 1968.

Bentley, Toni. *Winter Season*. New York: Random House, 1982.

Bergson, Henri. *Laughter: An Essay on the Meaning of the Comic*. Trans. Cloudesley Brereton and Fred Rothwell. Los Angeles: Green Integer, 1999.

Bierds, Linda. *The Profile Makers*. New York: Henry Holt, 1997.

Birkerts, Sven. *The Gutenberg Elegies*. New York: Ballantine, 1994.

Bishop, Elizabeth. *Complete Poems, 1927–1979*. New York: Farrar Straus, 1980.

Bishop, Elizabeth. *Edgar Allan Poe and the Juke-Box: Uncollected Poems, Drafts, and Fragments*. Ed. Alice Quinn. New York: Farrar Straus, 2006.

Bishop, Elizabeth. *One Art: Letters*. Ed. Robert Giroux. New York: Farrar Straus, 1994.

Bishop, Elizabeth and Robert Lowell. *Words in Air: The Complete Correspondence between Elizabeth Bishop and Robert Lowell*. Ed. Thomas Travisano and Saskia Hamilton. New York: Farrar Straus, 2008.

Blasing, Mutlu Konuk. *Lyric Poetry: The Pain and the Pleasure of Words*. Princeton: Princeton University Press, 2007.

Bogan, Louise. *The Blue Estuaries*. New York: Farrar Straus, 1968.

Bolker, Joan, ed. *The Writer's Home Companion*. New York: Holt, 1997.

Brock-Broido, Lucie and Wayne Koestenbaum. "A Conversation between Lucie Brock-Broido and Wayne Koestenbaum." *Parnassus: Poetry in Review* 23.1–2 (1998): 143–65.

Brontë, Charlotte. *Villette*. New York: Penguin, 1979.

Brooks, Gwendolyn. *Report from Part One*. Detroit: Broadside Press, 1972.

Brooks, Gwendolyn. *Selected Poems*. New York: Harper & Row, 1963.

Bryson, Norman. *Vision and Painting*. New Haven: Yale University Press, 1986.

Burt, Stephanie. Rev. of *Smokes*, by Susan Wheeler. *Boston Review* 23.3 (September 1998): 58.

Bushell, Sally. *Text as Process: Creative Composition in Wordsworth, Tennyson, and Dickinson*. Charlottesville: University of Virginia Press, 2009.

Calvino, Italo. *If on a winter's night a traveler*. Trans. William Weaver. New York: Harcourt, 1982.

Cameron, Sharon. *Choosing Not Choosing*. Chicago: University of Chicago Press, 1993.

Cameron, Sharon. *Impersonality*. Chicago: University of Chicago Press, 2007.

Cameron, Sharon. *Lyric Time*. Baltimore: Johns Hopkins University Press, 1979.

Chapman, Danielle. "Bad Habits." *Poetry* 185.4 (January 2005): 320–24.

Cixous, Hélène. *Coming to Writing and Other Essays*. Ed. Deborah Jenson. Trans. Sarah Cornell et al. Cambridge: Harvard University Press, 1992.

Cole, Teju. *Blind Spot*. New York: Random House, 2017.

Collins, Billy. *Picnic, Lightning*. Pittsburgh: University of Pittsburgh Press, 1998.

Culler, Jonathan. *Structuralist Poetics*. Ithaca, NY: Cornell University Press, 1975.

Delbanco, Nicholas. *The Sincerest Form*. Boston: McGraw Hill, 2004.

de Man, Paul. *Blindness and Insight.* Minneapolis: University of Minnesota Press, 1983.

D'Erasmo, Stacey. "The Uses of Doubt." *Ploughshares* 28.4 (Winter 2002–3): 24–35.

Derrida, Jacques. *Archive Fever.* Trans. Eric Prenowitz. Chicago: University of Chicago Press, 1996.

Derrida, Jacques. *Paper Machine.* Trans. Rachel Bowlby. Stanford: Stanford University Press, 2005.

Dickinson Electronic Archives. Ed. Martha Nell Smith. "About the Archives." Web. 2 December 2022.

Dickinson, Emily. *The Manuscript Books of Emily Dickinson.* Ed. R. W. Franklin. Cambridge: Belknap-Harvard University Press, 1981.

Dickinson, Emily. *The Poems of Emily Dickinson.* Reading ed. Ed. R. W. Franklin. Cambridge: Belknap-Harvard University Press, 1999.

Dickinson, Emily. *Selected Letters.* Ed. Thomas H. Johnson. Cambridge, MA: Belknap-Harvard University Press, 1986.

Doty, Mark. *The Art of Description.* St. Paul: Graywolf, 2010.

Edelman, Lee. "The Geography of Gender: Elizabeth Bishop's 'In the Waiting Room.'" *Elizabeth Bishop: The Geography of Gender.* Ed. Marilyn May Lombardi. Charlottesville: University Press of Virginia, 1993. 91–110.

Eliot, T. S. "Reflections on *Vers Libre*." *To Criticize the Critic.* New York: Farrar Straus, 1965. 183–89.

Eliot, T. S. *Selected Poems.* New York: Harcourt, 1958.

Eliot, T. S. "Tradition and the Individual Talent." *Critical Theory since Plato.* Ed. Hazard Adams. New York: Harcourt, 1971. 784–87.

Emerson, Claudia. *Late Wife.* Baton Rouge: Louisiana State University Press, 2005.

Erkkila, Betsy. "The Emily Dickinson Wars." *The Cambridge Companion to Emily Dickinson.* Ed. Wendy Martin. Cambridge: Cambridge University Press, 2002. 11–27.

Fineman, Joel. *Shakespeare's Perjured Eye.* Berkeley: University of California Press, 1986.

Forrest-Thomson, Veronica. *Poetic Artifice.* Manchester: Manchester University Press, 1978.

Foster, Susan. *Reading Dancing.* Berkeley: University of California Press, 1986.

Freud, Sigmund. *The Interpretation of Dreams.* Trans. A. A. Brill. New York: Avon Books, 1965.

Friedan, Betty. *The Feminine Mystique.* Reprint ed. New York: Norton, 2001.

Frost, Robert. *Collected Poems, Prose, & Plays.* New York: Library of America, 1995.

Fulton, Alice. *Feeling as a Foreign Language*. St. Paul: Graywolf, 1999.

Fussell, Paul. *Poetic Meter and Poetic Form*. New ed. New York: Random House, 1979.

Gaddis, William. *Agape Agape*. New York: Viking, 2002.

Garren, Christine. *Among the Monarchs*. Chicago: University of Chicago Press, 2000.

Gibbons, Reginald. "On Russian Meta-realist Poetry: A Conversation with Ilya Kutik." *American Poetry Review* 36.2 (March–April 2007): 19–25.

Gilbert, Sandra M. and Susan Gubar. *The Madwoman in the Attic: The Woman Writer and the Nineteenth-Century Literary Imagination*. New Haven: Yale University Press, 1979.

Gioia, Dana. *Disappearing Ink: Poetry at the End of Print Culture*. St. Paul: Graywolf, 2004.

Glück, Louise. *Ararat*. New York: Ecco, 1990.

Glück, Louise. *Proofs and Theories*. New York: Ecco, 1994.

Glück, Louise. *Vita Nova*. New York: Ecco, 1999.

Glück, Louise. *The Wild Iris*. New York: Ecco, 1992.

Graham, Jorie. *The End of Beauty*. New York: Ecco, 1987.

Graham, Jorie. *Hybrids of Plants and of Ghosts*. Princeton: Princeton University Press, 1980.

Graham, Jorie. *Materialism*. New York: Ecco, 1995.

Gregory, Tobias. "Murmur and Reply: Rereading Milton's Sonnet 19." *Milton Studies* 51 (2010): 21–43.

Grennan, Eamon. *The Quick of It*. St. Paul: Graywolf, 2005.

Grossman, Allen with Mark Halliday. *The Sighted Singer: Two Works on Poetry for Readers and Writers*. Baltimore: Johns Hopkins University Press, 1992.

Gunn, Thom. *The Man with Night Sweats*. New York: Farrar Straus, 1992.

Heaney, Seamus. "Above the Brim." *Homage to Robert Frost*, by Joseph Brodsky, Seamus Heaney, and Derek Walcott. New York: Farrar Straus, 1996. 61–92.

Heaney, Seamus. "The Makings of a Music." *Preoccupations: Selected Prose, 1968–1978*. New York: Farrar Straus, 1980. 61–78.

Heaney, Seamus. *Opened Ground: Selected Poems, 1966–1996*. New York: Farrar Straus, 1999.

Hejinian, Lyn. *The Language of Inquiry*. Berkeley: University of California Press, 2000.

Herrick, Robert. "Delight in Disorder." *Seventeenth-Century Prose and Poetry*. Ed. Alexander M. Witherspoon and Frank J. Warnke. 2nd ed. New York: Harcourt, 1982. 811.

Herrick, Robert. "An Ode for Him." *Seventeenth-Century Prose and Poetry.* 823–24.

Hicok, Bob. *Elegy Owed.* Port Townsend, WA: Copper Canyon, 2013.

Hoagland, Tony. "Fear of Narrative and the Skittery Poem of Our Moment." *Poetry* 187.6 (March 2006): 508–19.

Hofmann, Michael. "The Linebacker and the Dervish" (review of *Words in Air*). *Poetry* 193.4 (January 2009): 357–67.

Hollander, John. "Breaking into Song: Some Notes on Refrain." *Lyric Poetry: Beyond New Criticism.* Ed. Chaviva Hošek and Patricia Parker. Ithaca, NY: Cornell University Press, 1985. 73–89.

Hopkins, Gerard Manley. "[No Worst, There Is None. Pitched Past Pitch of Grief.]" *Norton Anthology of Poetry.* 4th ed. Ed. Margaret Ferguson, Mary Jo Salter, and Jon Stallworthy. New York: Norton, 1996. 1065.

Howe, Susan. *The Birth-Mark: Unsettling the Wilderness in American Literary History.* Middletown, CT: Wesleyan University Press, 1993.

Hughes, Frieda. Foreword. *Ariel: The Restored Edition.* By Sylvia Plath. New York: Harper Collins, 2004.

Hunter, J. Paul. "Poetry on the Page: Anglophone Couplets and Historical Practices of 'Silent' Reading." Newberry Library, Chicago. 26 March 2010. Lecture.

Irigaray, Luce. *This Sex Which Is Not One.* Trans. Catherine Porter and Carolyn Burke. Ithaca, NY: Cornell University Press, 1985.

Jackson, Angela. "In Memoriam: Gwendolyn Brooks." *On Gwendolyn Brooks: Reliant Contemplation.* Ed. Stephen Caldwell Wright. Ann Arbor: University of Michigan Press, 1996. 277–84.

Jackson, Virginia. *Dickinson's Misery.* Princeton: Princeton University Press, 2005.

Jakobson, Roman. "From Linguistics and Poetics." *Norton Anthology of Theory and Criticism.* 2nd ed. Ed. Vincent B. Leitch. New York: Norton, 2010. 1144–52.

James, Henry. "The Art of Fiction." *Critical Theory Since Plato.* 660–70.

Jarman, Mark and David Mason, eds. *Rebel Angels: 25 Poets of the New Formalism.* Ashland, Oregon: Story Line, 1996.

Johnson, Barbara. *A World of Difference.* Baltimore: Johns Hopkins University Press, 1987.

Johnson, W. R. *The Idea of Lyric.* Berkeley: University of California Press, 1982.

Joyce, Joyce Ann. "The Poetry of Gwendolyn Brooks: An Afrocentric Exploration." *On Gwendolyn Brooks: Reliant Contemplation.* 246–53.

Karagueuzian, Catherine Sona. *"No Image There and the Gaze Remains": The Visual in the Work of Jorie Graham.* New York: Routledge, 2005.

Keats, John. *John Keats: A Longman Cultural Edition*. Ed. Susan J. Wolfson. New York: Pearson, 2007.

Keats, John. "Negative Capability." *The Modern Tradition: Backgrounds of Modern Literature*. Ed. Richard Ellmann and Charles Feidelson Jr. New York: Oxford University Press, 1965. 70–71.

Kennedy, X. J. "Famous Poems Abbreviated." *Poetry* 188.4 (July–August 2006): 284.

Kinzie, Mary. *A Poet's Guide to Poetry*. Chicago: University of Chicago Press, 1999.

Kinzie, Mary. "The Rhapsodic Fallacy." *The Cure of Poetry in an Age of Prose*. Chicago: University of Chicago Press, 1993. 1–26.

Kirsch, Adam. *The Wounded Surgeon*. New York: Norton, 2005.

Knapp, Steven. *Personification and the Sublime: Milton to Coleridge*. Cambridge: Harvard University Press, 1985.

Koch, Kenneth. *Collected Poems*. New York: Knopf, 2007.

Komunyakaa, Yusef. "Facing It." *The Handbook of Heartbreak*. Ed. Robert Pinsky. New York: William Morrow, 1998. 107.

Kristeva, Julia. *Revolution in Poetic Language*. New York: Columbia University Press, 1984.

Lacan, Jacques. *Écrits: A Selection*. Trans. Alan Sheridan. New York: Norton, 1977.

Langer, Susanne K. *Feeling and Form*. New York: Scribner, 1953.

Lanham, Richard. *A Handlist of Rhetorical Terms*. 2nd ed. Berkeley: University of California Press, 1991.

Levine, Philip. Cover endorsement. Petrie, Paul, *The Runners*. Amherst, NY: Slow Loris Press, 1988.

Lewis, C. Day. *The Lyric Impulse*. Cambridge: Harvard University Press, 1965.

Lispector, Clarice. *The Hour of the Star*. Trans. Giovanni Pontiero. New York: New Directions, 1986.

Logan, William. "'I Write Entirely for You'" (review of *Words in Air*). *New York Times*, 31 October 2008.

Lombardi, Marilyn May. *The Body and the Song: Elizabeth Bishop's Poetics*. Carbondale, IL: Southern Illinois University Press, 1995.

Longenbach, James. *The Art of the Poetic Line*. Minneapolis: Graywolf, 2008.

Longenbach, James. *The Resistance to Poetry*. Chicago: University of Chicago Press, 2004.

Lorde, Audre. *Sister Outsider*. Berkeley: Crossing Press, 2007.

Lowell, Robert. *Imitations*. New York: Farrar Straus, 1990.

Marvell, Andrew. "The Gallery." *Seventeenth Century Prose and Poetry*. Ed.

Alexander M. Witherspoon and Frank J. Warnke. New York: Harcourt, 1982. 966.

Marvell, Andrew. "To His Coy Mistress." *Seventeenth Century Prose and Poetry.* 966.

McCarthy, Catherine. *Flower Arranging.* 2011. Show of visual art. Miller Gallery, Boston.

McCarthy, Catherine. *We Walk on Jewels.* 2003. Show of visual art. Howard Yezerski Gallery, Boston.

Mead, Jane. *The Usable Field.* Farmington, ME: Alice James Books, 2008.

Merrill, James. *Recitative.* Ed. J. D. McClatchy. San Francisco: North Point Press, 1986.

Merrill, James. *Selected Poems, 1946–1985.* New York: Knopf, 2001.

Michaels, Walter Benn. *The Shape of the Signifier.* Princeton: Princeton University Press, 2004.

Mikics, David and Stephanie Burt, eds. *The Art of the Sonnet.* Cambridge: Harvard University Press, 2010.

Mill, John Stuart. "What Is Poetry?" *Critical Theory Since Plato.* Ed. Hazard Adams. New York: Harcourt, 1971. 537–43.

Miller, Cristanne. *Emily Dickinson: A Poet's Grammar.* Cambridge: Harvard University Press, 1987.

Miller, Paul Allen. *Lyric Texts and Lyric Consciousness.* New York: Routledge, 1994.

Milosz, Czeslaw, ed. *A Book of Luminous Things.* New York: Harcourt, 1997.

Milosz, Czeslaw. *Collected Poems.* New York: Ecco, 1990.

Milton, John. *The Poetical Works of John Milton.* Ed. Rev. H. C. Beeching. London: Humphrey Milford / Oxford University Press, 1922.

Mitchell, Joni. "Little Green." *Blue.* Reprise Records, 1971. LP.

Mitchell, W. J. T. *Picture Theory.* Chicago: University of Chicago Press, 1994.

Nelson, Marilyn. *The Fields of Praise: New and Selected Poems.* Baton Rouge: Louisiana State University Press, 1997.

Newman, Amy. "About Jean Valentine." *Ploughshares* v. 34: no. 4 (Winter 2008–9): 188–92.

O'Hara, Frank. *Collected Poems.* Berkeley: University of California Press, 1996.

O'Hara, Frank. *Lunch Poems.* San Francisco: City Lights, 1964.

O'Hara, Frank. "Personism: A Manifesto." *Twentieth Century American Poetics.* Ed. Dana Gioia, David Mason, and Meg Schoerke. Boston: McGraw Hill, 2004. 282–83.

Orr, David. "Rough Gems" (review of *Edgar Allan Poe and the Juke-Box*). *New York Times* 2 April 2006. Web. 6 December 2022.

Petrie, Paul. *The Collected Poems*. Simsbury CT: Antrim House, 2014.

Phelan, Peggy. *Mourning Sex*. New York: Routledge, 1997.

Phillips, Carl. *The Coin of the Realm*. St. Paul: Graywolf, 2004.

Plath, Sylvia. *Collected Poems*. New York: Harper Perennial, 1981.

Plath, Sylvia. *The Unabridged Journals*. New York: Anchor, 2000.

Plumly, Stanley. "Kunitz Tending Roses." *To Stanley Kunitz with Love, from Poet Friends*. New York: Sheep Meadow Press, 2002. 7–8.

Preminger, Alex and T. V. F. Brogan, eds. *The New Princeton Encyclopedia of Poetry and Poetics*. Princeton: Princeton University Press, 1993.

Pucci, Joseph. *The Full-Knowing Reader*. New Haven: Yale University Press, 1998.

Pugh, Christina. "Ghosts of Meter: Dickinson, after Long Silence." *Emily Dickinson Journal* 16.2 (2007): 1–24.

Pugh, Christina. *Grains of the Voice*. Evanston, IL: Northwestern University Press, 2013.

Pugh, Christina. "No Experience Necessary." *Poetry* 186.3 (June 2005): 243–47.

Pugh, Christina. *Restoration*. Evanston, IL: Northwestern University Press, 2008.

Rector, Liam. *The Sorrow of Architecture*. Port Townsend, WA: Dragon Gate Press, 1984.

Rich, Adrienne. Cover endorsement. Jean Valentine, *Door in the Mountain*. Middletown, CT: Wesleyan University Press, 2004.

Rich, Adrienne. *The Dream of a Common Language*. New York: Norton, 1978.

Rich, Adrienne. *On Lies, Secrets, and Silence*. New York: Norton, 1979.

Rich, Adrienne. "Vesuvius at Home: The Power of Emily Dickinson." *By Herself: Women Reclaim Poetry*. Ed. Molly McQuade. St. Paul: Graywolf, 2000. 33–60.

Rich, Motoko. "New Elizabeth Bishop Book Sparks a Controversy." *New York Times*, 1 April 2006. Web. 6 December 2022.

Ricks, Christopher. *Allusion to the Poets*. Oxford: Oxford University Press, 2002.

Rilke, Rainer Maria. *Sonnets to Orpheus*. Trans. Stephen Mitchell. New York: Simon & Schuster, 1985.

Rimbaud, Arthur. "Le Bateau ivre." Institut de France. Web. 26 November 2022.

Roberson, Ed. *City Eclogue*. Berkeley, CA: Atelos, 2006.

Roberson, Ed. *Voices Cast Out to Talk Us In*. Iowa City: University of Iowa Press, 1995.

Ronell, Avital. *Stupidity*. Urbana: University of Illinois Press, 2003.

Rose, Jacqueline. *The Haunting of Sylvia Plath*. Cambridge: Harvard University Press, 1991.

Rubin, James H. *Manet's Silence and the Poetics of Bouquets*. Cambridge: Harvard University Press, 1994.

Ryan, Judith. *Rilke, Modernism and Poetic Tradition*. Cambridge: Cambridge University Press, 1999.

Ryan, Kay. "Notes on the Danger of Notebooks." *Parnassus* 23.1–2 (1998): 323–32.

Ryan, Michael. *New and Selected Poems*. Boston: Houghton Mifflin, 2004.

Ryan, Michael. "Poetry and the Audience." *Poets Teaching Poets*. Ed. Gregory Orr and Ellen Bryant Voigt. Ann Arbor: University of Michigan Press, 1996. 159–84.

Sacks, Peter. *The English Elegy: Studies in the Genre from Spenser to Yeats*. Baltimore: Johns Hopkins University Press, 1987.

Sandberg, Sheryl. *Lean In*. New York: Knopf, 2013.

Shakespeare, William. *The Complete Works*. Ed. Alfred Harbage. New York: Viking, 1969.

Stevens, Wallace. *Collected Poems*. New York: Vintage, 1982.

Stevens, Wallace. *The Necessary Angel*. New York: Vintage, 1951.

Stevens, Wallace. *Opus Posthumous: Poems, Plays, Prose*. Ed. Samuel French Morse. New York: Knopf, 1972.

Stewart, Susan. *Columbarium*. Chicago: University of Chicago Press, 2003.

Stewart, Susan. *Poetry and the Fate of the Senses*. Chicago: University of Chicago Press, 2002.

Strand, Mark and Lenny Emmanuel. "Mark Strand and Lenny Emmanuel at the Trestle" (interview with Mark Strand). *Antioch Review* 67.1 (Winter 2009): 44–66.

Suckling, Sir John. "Out upon it! I have loved." *Ben Jonson and the Cavalier Poets*. Ed. Hugh Maclean. New York: Norton, 1974. 271.

Taylor, Henry. "Gwendolyn Brooks: An Essential Sanity." *On Gwendolyn Brooks: Reliant Contemplation*. 254–75.

Teare, Brian. *The Room Where I Was Born*. Madison: University of Wisconsin Press, 2003.

Thoreau, Henry David. *Walden*. New York: New American Library, 1960.

Travisano, Thomas. "The Elizabeth Bishop Phenomenon." *New Literary History* 26.4 (1995): 903–30.

Trio A. Chor. Yvonne Rainer. Perf. Yvonne Rainer. 1978. Museum of Modern Art. Film.

Valentine, Jean. *Break the Glass*. Port Townsend, WA: Copper Canyon Press 2010.

Valentine, Jean. Cover endorsement. Teare, *The Room Where I Was Born.*

Valentine, Jean. *Door in the Mountain: New and Collected Poems, 1965–2003.* Middletown, CT: Wesleyan University Press, 2004.

Valentine, Jean. "Introduction." *Ploughshares* 34.4 (Winter 2008–9): 7–8.

Valentine, Jean. *Little Boat.* Middletown, CT: Wesleyan University Press, 2007.

Valentine, Jean. *Lucy: A Poem.* Louisville: Sarabande Books, 2009.

Valentine, Jean. *The River at Wolf.* Farmington, ME: Alice James Books, 1992.

Vendler, Helen. "The Art of Losing" (review of *Edgar Allan Poe and the Juke-Box*). *New Republic Online,* 6 April 2006. Web. 6 December 2022.

Vendler, Helen. *The Art of Shakespeare's Sonnets.* Cambridge: Belknap-Harvard University Press, 1999.

Vendler, Helen. *The Breaking of Style: Hopkins, Heaney, Graham.* Cambridge: Harvard University Press, 1995.

Vendler, Helen. *Poets Thinking.* Cambridge: Harvard University Press, 2006.

Volkman, Karen. *Nomina.* Rochester, NY: BOA Editions, 2008.

Warren, Rosanna. *Fables of the Self.* New York: Norton, 2008.

Waters, William. *Poetry's Touch: On Lyric Address.* Ithaca, NY: Cornell University Press, 2003.

Werner, Marta. "Flights of A821: Dearchiving the Proceedings of a Birdsong." *ebr* 6 (1997). Web. 6 December 2022.

Werner, Marta. "'A Woe of Ecstasy': On the Electronic Editing of Emily Dickinson's Late Fragments." *Emily Dickinson Journal* 16.2 (2007): 25–52.

Werner, Marta and Jen Bervin, eds. *The Gorgeous Nothings: Emily Dickinson's Envelope Poems.* New York: New Directions, 2013.

Whitman, Walt. *Leaves of Grass and Selected Prose.* London: Everyman, 1993.

Williams, William Carlos. "The Poem as a Field of Action." *Twentieth-Century American Poetics.* Ed. Dana Gioia, David Mason, and Meg Schoerke. New York: McGraw Hill, 2004. 51–57.

Willis, Elizabeth. *The Human Abstract.* New York: Penguin, 1995.

Winters, Anne. *The Displaced of Capital.* Chicago: University of Chicago Press, 2004.

Wollheim, Richard. "What the Spectator Sees." *Visual Theory: Painting & Interpretation.* Ed. Norman Bryson, Michael Ann Holly, and Keith Moxey. New York: HarperCollins, 1991. 101–50.

Wordsworth, William. *The Oxford Authors: William Wordsworth.* Ed. Stephen Gill. Oxford: Oxford University Press, 1984.

Wordsworth, William. "Preface to the Second Edition of *Lyrical Ballads*." *Critical Theory since Plato.* 433–43.

Wright, C. D. *Deepstep Come Shining*. Port Townsend, WA: Copper Canyon, 1998.

Wright, Charles. *Black Zodiac*. New York: Noonday, 1997.

Wright, Charles. *Negative Blue*. New York: Farrar Straus, 2000.

Yakich, Mark. Letter. *Poetry* 186.5 (September 2005): 470.

Yeats, W. B. *The Collected Poems*. New ed. Ed. Richard J. Finneran. New York: Macmillan, 1989.

The

WAR

against

WORRY

A thirty-one-day strategy

The

WAR

against

WORRY

A thirty-one-day strategy

Simon J. Robinson

LS20170425

ISBN: 978-0-9965168-3-9

Published by www.greatwriting.org

Dedicated to my grandchildren:
Benjamin, Addison, and Ethan

Table of Contents

Foreword 11

1 The Big Picture 14

2 God's Property 18

3 The Unshakable Kingdom 20

4 The Good Shepherd 24

5 Look at What God Has Given Us!................................... 28

6 God has not finished with me yet! 32

7 Kosher Cares... 36

8 Stop the Rot 40

9 Little Faith... 44

10 Worry Exposed 48

11 Pre-empting Panic 53

12 The Pursuit of Peace 57

13 Medication Matters... 61

14 Watch out: There's a Lion about! 65

15 Checking out Trust.. 70

16 Who is in control? 74

17 The Fear Factor 79

18 Unearthing Our Uniqueness 83

19 I Think, Therefore I am 88

20 Tomorrow's World 92

21 Early Morning Anxiety 96

22 The Path to Peace 101

23 "Leave it with me" 104

24 Submit to God 108

25 Challenge Your Thoughts 112

26 Living with Uncertainty 117

27 Think Outside the Box 121

28 The Ultimate Focus 125

29 The Power of God's Purpose 129

30 How to Keep Going When the Going Gets Tough 133

31 Join the Fight! 137

More Tactical Gear 143

About the Author 144

Appreciation

Worry is a universal wound. Almost nothing saps the joy out of our lives the way worry does. Simon Robinson has done good work in showing us the loving salve of our Savior that will begin healing this deepest of wounds.

Terry Esau, Writer and Speaker, Long Lake, Minneapolis, MN

It is easy to say, "Don't worry," but hard to achieve. In these reflections, Simon Robinson shares very honestly from his experience, bringing practical insights and drawing on a range of Bible passages. A helpful book for any Christian who struggles with anxiety.

Dr Debbie Hawker, PhD DClinPsy CPsychol AFBPsS, Clinical Psychologist, Nottingham, England

I have known Simon for a number of years and have observed his pastoral and compassionate heart for people. His years in the ministry have taught him how to apply God's Word to the issue of fear, anxiety and worry. These are emotional states experienced by everyone from time to time, so we can all benefit from this book.

Debra Green, OBE, Founder and National Director, REDEEMING OUR COMMUNITIES, Manchester, England

Acknowledgements

In December 2014, I had the privilege of bringing daily Bible teaching for a New Year event at Otford Manor in the UK. One of my talks was about dealing with worry, and a few weeks later I found out that there had been a number of emails from people who found the talk very helpful.

When I was talking about this with Jim Holmes, Director of Great Writing, he suggested expanding on the biblical principles I had been teaching and providing a day-by-day approach to tackling worry.

I am very grateful to my wife, Hazel, for her proof-reading skills and her unstinting support. To Jim Holmes, Director of Great Writing who—as always—has been a delight to work with, and to Pastor Doug McMasters for contributing an excellent foreword.

I would also like to thank my friends at Church in the Peak, Chesterfield, for their support and encouragement in writing this book.

Foreword

A lady prone to worry received some excellent advice. Her friend told her that every time she was tempted to worry, to write down her cares on a card and place them in a box. Then, after collecting her cares throughout the week, she could open the box and worry about them on Worry Wednesdays.

The oft-anxious woman took the advice, and dutifully wrote down all her cares and tucked the cards away. To her surprise, she found her week was delightfully worry free. But a better discovery came on the first Worry Wednesday. As she readied herself for a day of anxiety and thumbed through her cards of cares, she realized that nearly all of her concerns had already been resolved. There was very little left unresolved that needed any attention!

There's certainly something to the advice to allow circumstances to unfold before succumbing to worry. But there is a much better way to confront worrying situations!

And that is precisely what you will find from Simon's practical handbook. He offers biblical advice to equip us to meet any present or coming situation that will tempt us to worry.

The format is accessible. There are brief entries for each day of the month, each containing a carefully selected passage from God's Word, a short, yet significant, explanation and related anecdote, a challenge to put the truth into action, and a concluding prayer. This elixir provides just the right preventative medicine or corrective for the anxiety-riddled.

The best counselors are those who have a deep understanding of the human condition and of God's revelation. This book demonstrates that Simon is a keen student of both. It is evident that he understands Scripture deeply and masterfully reveals the meaning of several passages, selecting just the right phrases to convey truth briefly, yet effectively.

But Simon also shows he knows how temptation unchecked by biblical thinking blossoms into worry. He's realized that there is no temptation we face that isn't common to us all. Many of his examples are auto-biographical, yet remain perfectly suitable to everyone. Placing himself under a microscope equipped with a biblical lens, Simon uses his knowledge of the Scriptures to address his—and our—temptations and tragic unwillingness to trust the Lord for everything. This quote stands out as a perfect example:

"When I look at a verse like this one [Romans 8:32], I realize that I have become incredibly short-sighted. I cannot see what God has done for me so I do not trust him to take me through difficulties and this results in paralyzing worry. I often have to remind myself that God is not reluctant to help me in the problems I face or to provide for my needs."

Our Lord Jesus calls us to place ourselves under the care of our loving, heavenly Father. The contents will help you to do just that and to discover in the Lord's hands "the peace of God, which transcends all understanding, [that will] will guard your hearts and your minds in Christ Jesus" (Philippians 4:7).

Doug McMasters
Senior Pastor
New Hyde Park Baptist Church
New Hyde Park, New York, USA

Day 1

The Big Picture

*For he chose us in him before the creation of the world
to be holy and blameless in his sight. In love he predestined us to be adopted as his sons through Jesus Christ,
in accordance with his pleasure and will—to the praise
of his glorious grace, which he has freely given us in the
One he loves.*
(*Ephesians 1:4–6*)

Blurred Vision

I stared until my eyes went blurry but the painting hanging on the wall of a prestigious London gallery looked like a mass of paint strokes in different shades of blue. "It's no good," I said to my cultured friend, "I can't see anything in this." He gently put his hand on my shoulder and ushered me a few feet back. "Now look at it," he said, with an air of sophistication. I sighed, blinked my tired eyes, and reluctantly took another look. To my surprise, what had first appeared to be a collection of delicate brush strokes in pretty colors now formed themselves into a beautiful picture; I had been standing too near to understand what the artist was doing.

Worry has a way of getting us fixated on a problem and searching for possible solutions so that we cannot think of anything else. The first victory I scored against it was when I stood back and thought about God's overarching plan. I began to see the big picture and understand what was going on in my life in that context.

Stand Back and See Things Differently

Paul wrote to a group of Christians who lived in a very difficult place. Ephesus was a pagan city and home to the Temple of Diana; every day they would face opposition and struggles. He began his letter by gently putting his hand on their shoulder so they

[15]

could stand back and see the big picture, and what a masterpiece it is! His letter is bursting with great facts about God, facts that will help us fire the first shot in our war against worry. Everything God does is fashioned by love which stretches from eternity to eternity. Paul tells us that God "chose us before the creation of the world" and that he "predestined us." And he has a purpose in mind—to make us "holy and blameless in his sight." This has been made possible through Jesus' death and resurrection. When we trust in Christ, God makes us right with him, and the Holy Spirit makes us holy (that is, he sets us apart) so that we become more like Jesus. One day we will meet God face to face and be welcomed into heaven.

Join the Fight!

Enlist in the war against worry by thinking about these wonderful truths from the Bible: God chose us before the world was created, and one day he will welcome us into his presence. In the meantime, the Holy Spirit is at work in us to make us more like Jesus. What will the things we worry about now look like when we get to heaven?

Food for Thought

- Consider how different today's problems appear in the light of God's eternal purpose.

Prayer

Praise be to the God and Father of our Lord Jesus Christ, who has blessed us in the heavenly realms with every spiritual blessing in Christ.
(Ephesians 1:3)

Loving God, I praise you that you loved me before the world was created and that you will love me for eternity. It is so amazing, I can hardly begin to get my mind around it. Thank you that you want to make me holy and blameless in your sight, and have made this possible through Jesus. Sometimes I can get so consumed by the cares of everyday life that I forget these truths. Please help me to stand back and look at the great work you are doing in Christ. When my mind turns to worry, may the Holy Spirit help me to redirect my thoughts to your great purposes and to trust you with the needs of this day.

Day 2

God's Property

And you also were included in Christ when you heard the word of truth, the gospel of your salvation. Having believed, you were marked in him with a seal, the promised Holy Spirit.
(Ephesians 1:13)

There were three short raps on my door; I opened it to be greeted by our local police officer. He asked me if I would like to be part of a new scheme to reduce crime in the local area. It involved putting a code on items such as TVs and laptops so that stolen property could be traced back to the rightful owner. Ownership is an important matter.

Yesterday, we thought about the importance of standing back to look at God's great plan. God has not only made us part of his eternal purpose, but he has also put his seal of ownership on us. This was an everyday picture for the Christians in Ephesus. They would use a stamp and press it onto a surface so that it created a unique mark showing whom the object belonged to. This "seal" is none other than the person of the Holy Spirit who gives us new life and who dwells within us.

Jesus spoke of the Spirit as "The Comforter"— someone who strengthens and helps us. When we get caught in the grip of worry, we start to imagine the different scenarios that may occur and wonder how we will cope with them. It is natural to think about such things and consider what we can do about them but a lot of the time we leave God out of the equation. We belong to God, and the Spirit within us is his mark of ownership. God will never abandon his possession and—through the Spirit—he will enable us to face any situation that may come into our life.

Food for Thought

- Think about a possible scenario you have imagined concerning something that is worrying you. How does it play out?
- Now consider it in the light of the fact that you belong to God and the Spirit is within you to help you. How different does the outcome look now?

Prayer

I will ask the Father, and he will give you another Counselor to be with you forever. (John 14:16)

Heavenly Father, I praise you that I am your child because of Jesus' death and resurrection. Thank you for the way in which you have sent the person of the Holy Spirit to give me new life and put your mark of ownership upon me. When I get caught up in my worries, I imagine all sorts of possible outcomes but I rarely think about the way in which you will take care of me because I belong to you. Help me to correct my thinking and to face the challenges of this day in the power of your Holy Spirit.

Day 3

The Unshakable Kingdom

Therefore, since we are receiving a kingdom that cannot be shaken, let us be thankful, and so worship God acceptably with reverence and awe.
(Hebrews 12:28)

We had explored the Swiss mountains and enjoyed one another's company for the week. Sadly our trip had come to an end and we were asked to get out of our vehicle to show our passports before boarding the Channel Tunnel from France to England. There were two places to form a line: below a sign that said "European Union Citizens" and one that said "All Others." A bleary-eyed group of overnight travelers stood under the first sign but two people could not stand with us because they held citizenship of a different country.

I tend to worry about short-term issues such as whether I can pay the mortgage or how much the latest problem with my car is going cost. All of these issues are important but as I have got stuck into my counter-attack, I have realized the importance of seeing them in the context of my new citizenship. When I gave my life to Christ, I placed myself under his rule and became part of his kingdom. And what a kingdom it is! Jesus rules over it and will bring it to completion when he returns, and whatever may be going on around me, it "cannot be shaken." So I have total security in Christ. Of course it does not mean that everything will go smoothly; in fact, in context, the verse quoted from Hebrews shows that God *is* shaking all things, and when he does so our mortgages and jobs will not be exempt. However, our future is certain and God has promised to provide all our needs—no matter what happens. When the tendrils of worry begin to wrap themselves around my mind, I try to stop myself in my tracks and remind myself that I am part of God's unshakable kingdom.

Jesus said, "Seek first [God's] Kingdom and his righteousness and all these things will be given to you as well" (Matthew 6:33). In other words, channel the energy used for worry into concern about serving God and extending his kingdom. This came home to me one meal time when my wife asked me why I was so quiet. "I'm worried about how long the car is going to last," I said. She smiled sweetly, shook her head in disbelief and said, "How about worrying about the decorating instead!"

Food for Thought

- Think about the fact that you are part of God's unshakable kingdom.
- How does this change the way you perceive worry?

Prayer

Sovereign God, I praise you that while there is chaos around me, you never change. Thank you that you have made me a citizen of your unshakable kingdom. I am the one who changes, especially when I panic and act as if you are not there. Help me to remember where I belong and to live as a child of the King, especially when circumstances threaten to make me anxious.

Day 4

The Good Shepherd

I am the good shepherd. The good shepherd lays down
his life for the sheep.
(John 10:11)

Silly Animals

They bleat endlessly and wander in front of cars with no regard for their own safety. They are a familiar feature of the countryside. If there's one thing I have learned in the twelve years I've lived in the Peak District—a beautiful part of England—it is that sheep are rather silly and reckless animals. It is no wonder that this is the image Jesus uses to describe us; it certainly depicts me when I am in the grip of worry.

Deep Roots

The Shepherd caring for his sheep is an image that has deep roots in the Old Testament. In one of the best-known passages in the Bible, David describes the Lord as his Shepherd and goes on to speak about the way in which God tends and cares for him, making him "lie down in green pastures" and leading him to "still waters."

With his dying breath, Jacob said that God had been his shepherd throughout his life (Genesis 48:15). The prophet Ezekiel thundered a message from God against the leaders of the day describing them as shepherds who had neglected and abused their "sheep." He said that God was going to take this role upon himself, gather them together, bind their wounds, and care for them (Ezekiel 34:14-16). Jesus is the ultimate fulfillment of this promise: he is the "good shepherd who lays down [his] life for the sheep."

A Personal Picture

We have been gathering some heavy artillery for our war against worry by thinking about how we are part of the big picture of God's plan and that we are citizens of his unshakable kingdom. Here we have a personal picture which will bring Jesus right into the midst of the situations we worry about. In Psalm 23, David affirms that the Lord "makes [him] lie down in green pastures."

I once watched a shepherd lead his sheep in the Judean desert and wondered why he took them through such barren terrain. But my guide told me that there were clumps of grass scattered across this wasteland and the shepherd would know exactly where to take them. It made me realize that Jesus leads us through problems to take us to a place of rest.

Food for Thought

- Think about ways in which the Lord has been in the midst of your problems.
- How can you be more attentive to his guidance, help and provision?

Prayer

He leads me beside quiet waters, he refreshes my soul. (Psalm 23:3-4)

Lord Jesus, I praise you for the way in which you fulfill all of the promises about God being a shepherd to his people. You are the "Good Shepherd who has laid down his life for the sheep"; you have risen from the dead to lead and care for us. Thank you that, through your death and resurrection, the Father has sent the Holy Spirit who brings you right into the midst of our problems. Not only do you watch over us—you are right here with us. Help me to remember this when worry starts to creep into my mind so that I can rest in the tender care of the Shepherd.

Day 5

Look at What God Has Given Us!

He who did not spare his own Son, but gave him up for us all—how will he not also, along with him, graciously give us all things?
(Romans 8:32)

Bartering with Dad

It was drawing to the end of an eventful few weeks of mission. Along with all the ups and downs of such a trip, there had been some unexpected expenses and one of the team members had almost run out of money. He got straight on the phone, spoke to his father, and asked him for a cash transfer. When he returned, the team leader asked him if his father had given him what he asked for. "Not exactly," he said with a mischievous smile, "but I got what I wanted." When the leader shot him a bemused look, he explained what he meant: he had asked for more than he wanted, knowing that his father would never give him the full amount requested.

A Generous God

That father may have had very good reasons to be sparing with his son but his attitude was totally different from the way God provides for us. He is overwhelmingly generous; in fact he gives "more than all we could ask or even imagine" (Ephesians 3:20). This is proved by what he has already given us—his Son. I love the way today's verse from Romans says that God did not spare his own Son. The word *own* is translated from a Greek word that describes someone's personal possession. Jesus was one with the Father and the Holy Spirit, yet the Father did not withhold him from us. If he was willing to give someone

[30]

SO precious to make us his children, he will also give us everything we need to live for him and serve him. Some people give resentfully but God gives "all things ... graciously."

A Shortsighted Son

When I look at a verse like this one, I realize that I have become incredibly shortsighted. I cannot see what God has done for me so I do not trust him to take me through difficulties and this results in paralyzing worry. I often have to remind myself that God is not reluctant to help me in the problems I face or to provide for my needs. He has already given the greatest gift of all and anything else is small fry in comparison.

Food for Thought

- Spend time throughout the day thinking about how much it cost the Father to send his Son.
- What does this say about his concern for the problems you worry about?

Prayer

Loving God, you have shown me overwhelming kindness and love by not withholding your Son from me. This is such an amazing gift. Forgive me for the way I take this for granted. Everything else I need is small in comparison. Thank you that you are extravagantly generous. May this truth help to worry-proof my mind.

Day 6

God Has Not Finished with Me Yet!

Being confident of this, that he who began a good work in you will carry it on to completion until the day of Christ Jesus.
(Philippians 1:6)

An Expert at Work

Whether it be painting and decorating, woodwork or building work, Steve could put his hand to anything practical, and he always did a fantastic job. His knew what he wanted to do and would not stop until he was completely satisfied with his work. This could be a bit frustrating if you wanted something done by a particular time because he would never be rushed, but you would not be disappointed by the end result.

Worries about Paul

The Christians in Philippi are worried about Paul. They have heard that he is in prison and are so concerned about his welfare that they have sent someone to bring a financial gift to help him and to find out how he is. Paul sends a letter back assuring them that God has a purpose for his imprisonment and urges them to focus on spreading the gospel. As he begins his letter, he realizes that he probably will not see them again but draws confidence from the fact that God will finish the work he began. Literally he is saying, "God will keep on putting the finishing touches on his work."

God Never Gives Up on Us

God began this work when he chose us before the world was created. He has put his seal of ownership on us (see Day 2), he is continuing this work, and he will bring it to completion. I have been a pastor for over twenty-six years and during that time I have often found myself worrying about people's spiritual welfare. Of course, it is right to be concerned about people in my care but there have been times when I have moved into worry. This is because I consider that it all hinges on me instead of God. There are two huge flaws in my thinking: pride (I think it is all about *me*) and idolatry (I regard it as my work instead of God's). It is such a relief to come back to the fact that God is the one who starts and finishes a job, and that I am just his servant.

A double-edged sword

This verse equips me to fight worry on two fronts. First, it helps when I worry about people who are not following the Lord as they once did. After encouraging or warning them, I rest in the fact that God will not quit on his work. Secondly, when I get anxious about a mistake or a mess I have made of something, I take heart from the fact that God has not given up on me. He knows what he wants to do with me and will do whatever is necessary to get me to that place!

Food for Thought
- How confident are you that God will finish the work he began in you?

- Do you think this level of confidence is linked to the things you worry about?

Prayer

Creator God, I praise you for the way in which you have begun a work in me. Thank you that it is still a work in progress, to be completed when I see you face to face. Help me to have confidence in the work you are doing and not worry about the times I think I have failed or let you down.

Day 7

Kosher Cares

If anyone does not provide for his relatives, and especially for his immediate family, he has denied the faith and is worse than an unbeliever.
(1 Timothy 5:8)

Hakuna Matata

We had a friend who did not seem to have a care in the world. She loved to roller-blade and jog, and she was always cheerful. After the Disney Film "The Lion King" was released, she made "Hakuna Matata" her theme song. The title is taken from a Swahili phrase meaning "No problems" or "Don't worry—Be happy." Although worry is an activity to defeat, we need to steer clear of a completely carefree attitude, expressed in that song, which does not take everyday responsibilities very seriously.

Bible Balance

God's Word gives us the balance between not being dominated by the cares of this life and working to provide for our needs. Here are some things we should care about:

Family It is right to keep a caring eye over our loved ones. This involves looking out for health issues that need to be brought to the doctors, taking an interest in our children's education, and watching out for signs that they are being bullied or pressured to conform to their peer group in ways that are harmful to them. As our parents grow older, we take an interest in their well-being and help them to plan for the future.

Finances It is good to plan our finances and set a realistic budget.

Practical issues It would be foolish to ignore a warning light in the car or a leaky roof in one's home. We need to find out what is wrong and how much it will cost to repair.

Work We live out the Christian life in our jobs so we should care about the quality of our work and deal with problems as best we can. If there are rumors of redundancies, there is nothing wrong with taking action and looking for other work.

The Challenge

The challenge is to get these things into perspective. I have always taken genuine issues like these very seriously. However, instead of taking sensible steps to plan ahead, act on existing and potential problems and then leave them with the Lord, my concern has often intensified into worry.

My first step toward getting the right balance has been to make sure that I place all of these responsibilities under Jesus' lordship. At the end of the day, my job, family, house, car, health—and everything else in my life—belong to him. I want to address the cares of life in a way that honors him, and entrust to him the cares I cannot do anything about. We will be thinking about how to do this in the next few days as we look at Matthew 6.

Food for Thought

- Think about the practical issues presently on your mind.
- Make two lists. The first should be of the things you can do something about; the second should be of what is beyond your control. Take action on the first, and commit the second list to the Lord.

Prayer

Heavenly Father, you have given me responsibilities in this life (mention these to him as you pray this prayer). Help me to put them under the lordship of Jesus. Help me to do what I need to do and to leave the rest with you.

Day 8

Stop the Rot

Therefore I tell you, do not worry about your life, what
you will eat or drink; or about your body, what you will
wear. Is not life more important than food, and the body
more important than clothes?
(Matthew 6:25)

Over and Over

Anxiety, for me, usually begins when I pick up issues of concern, run them through my mind, and then repeat the process again and again. I never intend to worry but as I continually process these concerns, I find myself in the grip of my old enemy again.

A Sense of Perspective

After Jesus tells us not to worry about life and what we will eat and drink, he asks a striking question: "Is not life more important than food, and the body more important than clothes?" The word he uses for life is "psyche," which means our essence. In other words, God is not just concerned about the things we need to keep us alive, but he cares about every part of our lives—about our very essence. If God has given us a life—a body and soul—he will give us everything we need to go on living.

A Lesson from the Birds

Jesus gives us two lessons from the world around us to get his point home. First, there is a lesson from the birds. "They do not sow or reap or store away in barns, and yet your heavenly Father feeds them." (Matthew 6:26). I have never seen a sparrow begging in the street with a sign saying, "Wife and two chicks to support." The rain falls down, the worms pop up, and the birds gobble them up—that is how God has designed it. And if God has thought so carefully about providing for our feathered friends, it is logical that he will take much more care of us. "Are you not much more valuable than they?" asks Jesus. There's a lovely old poem based on this verse:

> Said the robin to the sparrow,
> "I should really like to know,
> Why these anxious human beings
> Rush about and worry so."
>
> Said the sparrow to the robin,
> "Friend I think that it must be,
> That they have no Heavenly Father,
> Such as cares for you and me."

A Lesson from the Lilies

The second lesson is taken from the flowers, which surpassed the splendor of Solomon in his royal robes. "Why do you worry about clothes?" he asks. "See how the lilies of the field grow" (Matthew 6:28). They grew naturally, flowered majestically, and died gracefully, after which they were cut with the grass and used to fuel people's ovens. So if God took so much care in "clothing" these flowers that are here today and gone tomorrow, surely he will provide the clothes on our back.

A Truth to Grasp

It is right to be concerned about feeding and clothing my family but this must be underpinned by a realization that God is the one who provides for my needs, whether that be through the wage that is paid to me, or the children's clothes given to us just when they had gone up a size and we were too short of money to buy any more. However I need to acknowledge the fact that I am going over my concerns again and again, when I should be leaving them with my heavenly Father who cares for me. Looking back over the forty years that I have been a Christian, I can affirm that he has never let me down.

Food for Thought

- How much do you think God cares for you?
- Are your worries consistent with the answer you have just given?

Prayer

Loving Father, I praise you that you care for me as a person, as your child, and so you care about the needs I have. Thank you for the way in which you have provided for me in the past. Please help me to stop worry setting in by enabling me to hold on to this truth.

Day 9

Little Faith

If that is how God clothes the grass of the field, which is here today and tomorrow is thrown into the fire, will he not much more clothe you, O you of little faith?
(Matthew 6:30)

Sometimes film producers make alternative endings for their films. I would like to recount a story that has alternative beginnings.

Version 1

After a great few days with our friends in Minneapolis, we were ready to head off to Louisville, Kentucky, for a conference. As the last item was put into the case, I checked our itinerary and noticed that we only had twenty minutes to spare between flight connections in Cincinnati. I calmly told my wife and we committed it to God and went to the airport with a huge sense of peace.

Version 2

The case was packed for the next stage in our journey. It was time to say goodbye to our friends in Minneapolis and to commence our journey Louisville. My heart seemed to double its speed as I looked at the details on the travel documents: we had only twenty minutes between flight connections. I began to panic, packed extra clothes in my hand luggage in anticipation of missing our connection, and set off for the airport with a horrible feeling that we may not get to Louisville in time for the conference.

I would love to tell you that the first version is the most accurate, but I am ashamed to say that the second version is the true one! However, this is how it ends:

A Happy Ending!

I nervously approached the check-in desk. The woman processing our booking acted as if everything was in order and let our bags go through. "Are those turnaround times correct?" I asked. She looked at my booking again, frowned and shouted to a baggage handler, "Take those bags back, Joe." My heart sank and I prepared myself for an extra night in Minneapolis and a late arrival at the conference. But then something surprising happened. The woman then made a phone call which finished with her saying, "That's great, thanks!" My sprits began to rise and for a good reason: the airline we were flying with had just merged with another which had a direct flight to Louisville, and there were just two seats available on the next flight. As I breathed a deep sigh of relief and thanked the Lord for his provision, five words spoken by Jesus gently stung me: "O you of little faith."

When Jesus describes us this way, he is making an observation rather than a condemnation. As C.H. Spurgeon says, "Little faith believes in God for eternal life but it cannot trust him with the needs of the day." Sometimes I think that my little worries are too insignificant for God, but I could not be more wrong. Jesus says, "Are not five sparrows sold for two pennies? Yet not one of them is forgotten by God. Indeed, the very hairs of your head are all numbered. Don't be afraid; you are worth more than many sparrows"

(Luke 12:6–7). Big faith is not just about "moving mountains." It is also about trusting the Lord to care for the details of my life.

Food for Thought
- Write down the things about the week ahead which worry you.
- Then write these words at the bottom: "God cares about *all* of this."

Prayer

Father God, you are the Creator of the universe, and yet you care about the details of my life. This is truly a mark of your greatness. Help me to have big faith, the kind that can trust my everyday life to you, as well as to move mountains.

Day 10

Worry Exposed

Who of you by worrying can add a single hour to his life?
(Matthew 6:27)

Thursday morning would see me jump out of bed with unusual energy and enthusiasm. It was the day my favorite comic called "Whizzer and Chips" would be delivered. I particularly loved a character called Willy Worry who, as his name suggests, seemed to spend all of his waking hours worrying. In one of the stories, someone asked him if he was "building castles in the air," a phrase meaning was he daydreaming, or making plans that would never become reality. Willy took this statement literally and became very bothered about the possibility of the castles falling out of the sky and landing on top of him.

I could identify with Willy Worry because I seemed to spend so much time thinking about what might happen to me. While my sister lived a carefree existence, I would often be churning potential problems over in my mind. Once I was so concerned about how our family would cope if my dad lost his job that I even asked my grandparents whether they would help to pay the bills; I was six at the time! Unfortunately that seems to be the way I am wired. However, part of my counterattack has been to look at this verse and see worry for the waste of time that it is.

In all of the years I have been on this planet, worry has never helped me. Not only has it been completely unproductive, it has actually done me a lot of harm because it has sapped my energy and demanded my attention so that I am not focused on the Lord and his kingdom.

There have been times in my life when worry has become a tyrant—a tyrant that is never satisfied. For example, I get worried about how long my car is going to last so I look at my cash reserves to see whether I can buy a new one when it becomes necessary. Then I think, "What if they don't have the right kind of car for me?", "What if I have to use this money to pay for repairs on my house?" and "What if the price of secondhand cars goes up?" There are always many more questions for each answer I provide. At the risk of people thinking I am slightly unhinged, I have found the best way to deal with this little voice is to tell it to shut up and remind myself that it is not going to give me any help at all.

Food for Thought

- Your friend is anxious about something she thinks may happen. She is so caught up with this that she cannot think about anything else. It seems to be affecting every area of her life. What would you say to her?
- Remember this advice so that you can implement it the next time you are in the grip of your own anxious thoughts.

Prayer

Be self-controlled and alert. Your enemy the devil prowls around like a roaring lion looking for someone to devour. (1 Peter 5:8)

I praise you, Lord Jesus, that you are the Victor. Help me to enter into your victory and face down this tyrant who tries to dominate me. You, Lord, are the only one with the right to rule my life and I submit to you.

Day 11

Pre-empting Panic

My heart is not proud, O Lord, my eyes are not haughty; I do not concern myself with great matters or things too wonderful for me.
(Psalm 131:1)

recently received a letter inviting me to come to my doctors' office for a free health checkup. I have to admit that I have not yet taken up the invitation. I know it is a good idea, but I just feel a bit uncomfortable with the thought of being poked and prodded and told that I may have an illness on the horizon. However, I will overcome these reservations and go because I know that prevention is better than cure. There have been times in my life when I have been gripped with panic, which throws me into "fight or flight" mode. However, Psalm 131 has helped me to develop a way of preventing it before it takes a hold of my life.

I Check Out My Heart

David said, "My heart is not proud, O Lord". This is the king speaking, the man who commanded one of the most powerful armies of the day and had hundreds of people around him waiting to do his bidding. However, when he comes into God's presence he realizes exactly who he is: a mortal man with many failings, a finite speck on God's infinite canvas. In another psalm, David says, "Search me, O God, and know my heart; test me and know my anxious thoughts. See if there is any offensive way in me, and lead me in the way everlasting" (Psalm 139:23-24). A proud heart is a massive obstacle to resting in God's presence and knowing his peace.

I Check Where My Sights Are Set

Having reminded himself of who he really is, David goes on to say, "My eyes are not haughty." Literally he is saying, "My eyes are not lifted high." This phrase—lifted up—is often used in the Old Testament to describe someone who is proud and arrogant (see Proverbs 21:4). However, David has jettisoned this attitude, realizing that his perspective on what is happening in his life is very limited.

I Change My Perspective

Checking out my attitude and my heart enables me to change my perspective. I can say, with David, "I do not consider myself with things too great, too marvelous for me." In other words, "I'm not going to try to fathom out things which are way beyond my comprehension."

It is hardwired into us to try to comprehend what is going on around us, and our fallen nature imparts a desire to know everything—which is impossible. So I stop trying to work out what is happening and rest in the One who knows all things and who rules the universe.

I Switch Off the Commentary

We live in a 24-hour news culture where everything is put under scrutiny. Events are looked at from every angle imaginable. My mind is often like this, providing endless commentary on what is happening in my life. I have to make a conscious decision not to listen. Instead I turn my mind to a verse of Scripture.

These simple steps have helped me preempt panic and to experience God's peace

Food for Thought
- What right do we have to know everything we might like to know?
- How do you think this desire creates panic when things go wrong?

Prayer
Peace I leave with you; my peace I give you. I do not give to you as the world gives. Do not let your hearts be troubled and do not be afraid. (John 14:27)

God of peace, you rule the heavens; you know the end from the beginning. I realize that I am just a speck on the canvas of eternity but I know that I am your precious child. Please help me to have a humble and submissive heart, knowing that you are working all things according to your purposes. Help me to shut down the commentary that goes on in my head and to listen to you.

Day 12

The Pursuit of Peace

*"I have calmed and quieted myself, I am like a weaned
child with its mother,
Like a weaned child I am content."
(Psalm 131:2)*

On special occasions, our youth group was invited to Barry and Jean's home for a meal. I used to enjoy those evenings. Barry and Jean made us feel welcome and gave us more food than we could manage but the best part of it was watching their dog, Sally. After we had eaten, we would sink into our chairs and listen to Barry give us great teaching about how to live the Christian life. As he spoke, Sally continually paced up and down the room until Barry looked up from his Bible to say, "Sally, be still."

I dare not add up the hours I have wasted by being churned up by worry. In Psalm 131, David tells us how he has taken a very different route. He talks about the way he has "stilled" his mind. The word he uses has the idea of bringing something back to its equilibrium, rather like a boat that has been rocking and has now moved into calm waters. And quietened means "to silence" or "to wait." Put them together and we see that David has made a conscious effort to stop and come before God, and as he does so he silences the nagging fears, doubts and worries that might drive one to distraction. "I am not listening to those questions racing around in my mind anymore," says David. "I am silent and still before God." He likens his state of mind to that of a child in her mother's arms. This is a beautiful picture of contentment and safety which is one of only two maternal references to

God in the Old Testament (the other is in Isaiah 49:15). Although I have battled with worry all of my life, there have been times when I have known the reality of what Paul describes as a sense of "peace that passes all understanding" (Philippians 4:7) and an overwhelming realization that I am safe in God's hands. I realize that I do not need to try to work things out or keep bringing the situation to him.

How do we get there?

To get to this place I have had to make a conscious decision not to be ruled by my worry, and then take several simple steps.

- I recognize the turmoil that is going on in my heart and mind. There is little point in being in denial about it; I have to square up in order to get to a place of peace.
- I stop what I am doing and sit quietly before God. Worry and panic have released adrenaline into my system but sitting still puts me in a different frame of mind.
- I take a few deep breaths; this slows my system down and helps me to think more clearly.
- I remind myself that God is my Father and is in complete control. Martyn Lloyd-Jones calls this "talking to yourself in the Lord." It is something we see David doing in another psalm when he says, "Why, my soul are you downcast? Why so

disturbed within me? Put your hope in God, for I will yet again praise him, my Savior and my God" (Psalm 42:5).

- I meditate on a verse of Scripture. I have memorized some ready for such an occasion. Here are some verses I would recommend.

Isaiah 26:3 You will keep in perfect peace him whose mind is steadfast, because he trusts in you.

Psalm 91:1 He who dwells in the shelter of the Most High will rest in the shadow of the Almighty.

Psalm 46:1 God is our refuge and strength, an ever-present help in trouble.

Food for Thought

- Set out the steps you will take to get to a place of peace.

Prayer

Heavenly Father, you show me such tender mercy and care through the Lord Jesus. When I worry, I turn my back on your care and try to take matters into my own hands. Thank you that you graciously call me back to a place of peace and safety. Help me to take the step not to run around in panic, but to rest in your eternal arms.

Day 13

Medication Matters

Yet for us there is but one God, the Father, from whom all things came and for whom we live; and there is but one Lord, Jesus Christ, through whom all things came and through whom we live.

(1 Corinthians 8:6)

just had endured eighteen stressful months of guerrilla warfare from a group determined to force me out of my pastorate. After countless hostile meetings and abusive emails, I had reached breaking point and sat in the doctor's office in a crumpled heap. The doctor asked me a series of questions and we talked about what had been going on and how it had affected me. Dr. Smith sat back, looked at me reassuringly, and said, "Simon, you are showing symptoms of clinical depression and you need some medication." I frowned and slowly shook my head; this had always been an anathema to me. "I'd rather not," I said, trying to muster the limited spirit left in me. Dr. Smith, a Christian, smiled and said, "I know that you want to depend on God, which is good, but don't forget that he gave people the ability to make these pills." I trusted this counsel, took the prescription, and remained on the medication for the next year.

Common Grace

Although medication was not the answer to the extreme problems I was experiencing, it is a product of God's common grace and has helped me get through such an excruciatingly difficult period in my life. Theologian Wayne Grudem says, "Common Grace is the grace of God by which he gives people immeasurable blessings that are not part of salvation. They are common to all and not restricted to Christians. Using the earth's resources and skills in productive work". (*Systematic Theology* 1994 edition, page 657)

What Does Medication Do?

The anxiety and depression I experienced was different from anything I had known before. My face felt constantly hot, my heart was racing, and my sleep patterns were interrupted. I woke up every morning with an overwhelming sense anxiety and hopelessness. I knew that I needed help.

After a period of time in which I took the tablets, I began to feel better. The medication did not stop the problem or make my worries disappear. However, it acted as a safety net which stopped me falling further into despair and gave me space to think more clearly so that I could prayerfully decide what I should do. God has created humanity with skills to produce medication.

There are times, in extreme circumstances—such as my own—when it is sensible to use this to help deal with the symptoms of stress and anxiety so that one may tackle the underlying causes.

Food for Thought

- How do you know when you have moved from everyday worry into intense anxiety and/or depression?

- What steps would you take in these circumstances, and who could help you?

Prayer

Creator God, I praise you that you have made everything good. You have given people the ability to invent and develop medicines. Help me to discern whether I need to use such a mark of your grace as I continue to look to you and as I depend on your help.

Day 14

Watch out: There's a Lion About!

Cast all your anxiety on him because he cares for you.
Be self-controlled and alert. Your enemy the devil
prowls around like a roaring lion looking for someone
to devour.
(1 Peter 5:7–8)

H is velvet-coated feet enabled him to pace the bush quietly. From the safety of our vehicle, we watched him identify his prey and prepare for the kill. But just as the lion was about to pounce, the impala he had set his sight on sped off into the distance and lived to see another day.

After my safari, Peter's description of Satan as a lion on the prowl has taken on a new dimension. Satan stalks us and waits for us to become vulnerable so that he can devour us. It's no wonder Peter tells us to be alert. Have you noticed that Peter puts this in the context of worry? That is not to say that worry is a work of the Devil but it certainly plays into his hands, giving him opportunity to pounce on us to attack our relationship with the Lord.

Peter says we must not to be ignorant of his schemes. And when we are in the grip of anxiety, Satan will tempt us to take refuge and get relief from things that are not pleasing to God. Here are some examples:

Drink can anaesthetize people from the effects of anxiety but this will only last for a time. The longer-term effect is that it makes them feel worse and can cause addiction. The Internet offers an array of images to tantalize people's eyes and provide distraction through pornography but this opens them up to all manner of darkness and sin. Over-indulgence on TV and computer games may numb the mind but it can take over people's lives. In effect, all of these activities become idols, because they will usurp God's rightful place as Lord over all of life.

Are we helpless in the face of such a powerful enemy who is out to tempt us in these ways? The Bible says that no temptation has seized us except what is common to man. And God is faithful; he will not let us be tempted beyond what we can bear. But when we are tempted, he will also provide a way out so that we can stand up under it (see 1 Corinthians 10:13).

Look for a Way Out
Here are some practical steps to find the "way out" that God provides.

Ask questions
Before giving yourself to something offering temporary relief, ask these questions:

"What will this do to me in the long run?" Imagine what would happen if your life became ruled by anything other than God.

What will this do to my relationship with God? It will quickly become clear that it can only have a negative effect.

Where does God figure in my thinking? Psalm 14:1 says, "The fool says in his heart there is no God." I used to quote this verse with atheists in mind but it is actually a reference to believers who try to push God out of their minds.

Re-orientate

When Satan first appears on the scene, he takes the form of a serpent, speaks to Eve, and questions whether God had really told her and Adam not to eat the fruit of the tree of the knowledge of good and evil. He bursts into the New Testament during Jesus' forty days in the wilderness, trying to divert him from his mission and to abuse his power. His tactics are simple: undermine God's Word, and displace him from our thinking. Our counterattack is to do as the psalmist says and "set the Lord always before me" (Psalm 16:1).

Draw strength

Jesus has defeated Satan and has given us the Holy Spirit so that we can overcome temptation.

Worry is not just a problem we struggle with; it takes us into the arena of a spiritual battle and we can be victorious through Christ.

Food for Thought

- What have I been tempted to turn to when I am overwhelmed with worry?
- How can I protect myself from Satan's tactics in the future?

Prayer

Lord Jesus, you were victorious over Satan in the wilderness, and conquered him in your death and resurrection. I know that he stalks me, like a lion, so that he can devour my faith. Help me to enter into your victory and to resist temptation when he tries to use anxiety to draw me away from you.

Day 15

Checking out Trust

"Trust in the Lord at all times, you people,
Pour out your hearts to him,
For God is our strength and refuge"
(Psalm 62:8)

J ohn had performed all the checks and fuelled up his plane. After making sure I was strapped in correctly, he was ready to rev up the engines and take off. I have taken many flights over the years but I have never sat next to a pilot in a small plane. I have to admit that I was slightly nervous. I reminded myself that the man in the control seat was an extremely experienced pilot. I exercised trust in him by sitting back and letting him fly the plane to our destination.

One of the biggest catalysts for worry in my life is a lack of trust in the Lord. I do not like the idea of letting him take control of my circumstances—I want to be in the driving seat! And this is an issue I have had to work through.

The English word for "trust" originates from an Anglo Saxon word which means "to rely on someone's integrity." In the Old Testament, the word is used to describe taking refuge in God. In the New Testament, the word is all about having faith in God.

Trust has not come easy to me; it is something I have had to work at. Here are three steps I take to develop my trust in God and thus stave off worry.

Step 1: Believe

The basic problem lies with my head and my heart. My head tells me that life is spinning out of control and I have to do something about it. I think about what I should do, but every time I identify a solution, another potential problem arises. Of course, if there is something that needs to be done (such as going to the doctor to get a health issue checked out or arranging my finances better) I will act on it. However, there are many issues that I am powerless to change. So I bring verses of Scripture to mind that speak of God's sovereignty and power. This is more than reciting a few favorite Bible verses; I need to affirm my belief in the truth about God that they reveal.

Step 2: Restrain

In Psalm 40:1, David tells us that he has waited on the Lord. A literal translation would be, "In waiting, I waited for the Lord." And it is worded in this way to show us how David restrained the urge to rush away and take matters into his own hands. He was going to stay in God's presence until he had heard from him. It takes a lot of effort to stop myself taking matters into my own hands rather than to trust God. I have to make a clear decision to wait on God. As I do so, I become conscious of the adrenaline rushing around in me but I make myself sit tight and trust in God. Often, if I get a bit of exercise—like going to the gym or taking a walk—that will help to channel the energy that has been building up in me.

Step 3: Rest

Finally, I rest in the Lord. This is a consciousness of

being totally dependent upon him and trusting him to work out his purposes. It is rooted in my relationship with God. I speak to him about what is going on; I express my sense of dependence upon him; and I ask for the Spirit's help and turn my heart, mind and voice to worship.

Trust does not come naturally to us because our human nature drives us to seek to control what is going on around us. However, as our relationship with Jesus develops, our trust will grow, and that will help us in the war against worry.

Food for Thought

- Think about the reasons why God is worthy of our trust.
- How can we develop a relationship of trust with him?

Prayer

Sovereign God, you created me. Through your Son and by your Spirit, you have given me new life. Thank you for this living relationship I enjoy with you. Help me to resist the urge to take matters into my own hands. My relationship with you began with trusting you in the work you had done in Christ to save me; so help me to deepen my relationship with you by trusting you fully.

Day 16

Who Is in Control?

Now listen, you who say, "Today or tomorrow we will go to this or that city, spend a year there, carry on business and make money." Why, you do not even know what will happen tomorrow. What is your life? You are a mist that appears for a little while and then vanishes. Instead, you ought to say, "If it is the Lord's will, we will live and do this or that." (James 4:13–15)

Moving On

After ten years of ministry on the south coast of England, I had responded to a call to be a pastor in the north of England. The "For Sale" sign had been put up outside our house, and we began the arduous process of buying and selling homes. Added to all this, we struggled to get our son into a school because the local one was full and we also discovered that houses in our new location were more expensive than we had first thought.

Change Can Be Hard

I have never found uncertainly easy. I like life being on an even keel, and I enjoy the security of routine and predictability. My tendency towards worrying intensified the stress induced by this life-change. One day I sat in a friend's house, feeling completely wrung out by the whole experience. Close to tears, I struggled to express the turmoil going on inside me. "I feel as if my life has gone into freefall," I said. "I don't have control over it anymore." One of the biggest lessons I learned during that time is that only God has his finger on the control panel.

The Illusion

Billions of people are living under the illusion that they are in control of their destinies. But it only takes an unexpected event or a brush with death to prove this is not so and that they are but a breath away from eternity.

Another Way

James has some strong words to say about making plans as if we had control of our lives. He reminds us of the uncertainty of life—"You do not even know what will happen tomorrow". While we can make projections and assumptions, life has a way of taking us by surprise and throwing us onto a different course. A friend of mine is a pastor in Myanmar. He leads a thriving network of churches and has to plan his time very carefully. At the beginning of another busy day in his life, a cyclone wreaked havoc on his city, turning his plans upside down. However, as his churches helped the victims of the disaster, they had countless opportunities to talk about Jesus, and led many people to him in repentance and faith.

So does this mean we should be fatalistic and let life happen around us? Of course not! We need to remember that God is in control and submit to his sovereign will: "Instead, you ought to say, 'If it is the Lord's will, we will live and do this or that'" (James 4:15).

Reminding Myself

When I find myself in an uncertain situation (which I have been in as I write this book), I remind myself that I have never been in control, I stop myself from imagining potential scenarios, and I thank God that he is sovereign and I submit to his will.

Food for Thought
- Think about an event that has shattered all of your carefully made plans.
- How did God guide you through it?

Prayer
Sovereign God, you created the universe, you put the stars in their places, and you made light and darkness. You have created me and you have a plan for me. Thank you that it is you, not I, who are in control. I gladly submit to your will and I put my trust in you.

Day 17

The Fear Factor

Be strong and courageous. Do not be afraid or terrified because of them, for the Lord your God goes with you; he will never leave you nor forsake you.
(Deuteronomy 31:6)

Release the Beast

My friends and family call me a "Trekkie," as I am a fan of that great TV program, "Star Trek." In an episode entitled "And the children shall lead them," the crew of the Starship Enterprise rescue a group of children. Unbeknown to them the children are influenced by a malevolent alien called Gargon who wants control of the ship. He tells the children to "release the beast" that is within the crew and gives them powers to identify the things people fear and make it seem as if their fears have become reality. This reminds me how fear can be a monster that will rule us, if we allow it.

Fear Is Not All Bad

Sometimes fear can be constructive. It is part of our defense mechanism. It warns of danger so that we can do something about it and prepares us to tackle difficulties. If I am crossing a busy road and hear the roar of an approaching car that is clearly going too fast, fear kicks in and I get out of the way quickly. However, I am a fallen human being and this means that fear can become destructive. It often gets out of proportion so that my life becomes dominated by a potential problem.

Fear in Full Throttle

I had just settled into my seat on a plane bound for

Alabama when I heard a lady behind me call the flight attendant. "Excuse me," she said with a tremor in her voice, "should that light be flashing?" The flight attendant reassured her and explained that it was all quite normal but throughout the flight the lady persistently asked about things that were making her anxious. It was obvious that she had a fear of crashing and could not stop thinking about it.

Facts vs. Fear

In Deuteronomy 31, the people of Israel are about to enter the Promised Land. The previous generation had failed to enter because they let fear mold their perception of the terrain they were called to possess. The people who had scouted it out said that the land was full of giants. Because of this, all but Caleb and a few other faithful people remained in the wilderness. Now their children were about to launch into the Promised Land, and it was vital that they were not overtaken by fear and consigned to more decades in the desert. Moses gave them two facts which—if they took them to heart—would dispel their fear:

The Lord your God goes with you.

He will never leave you or forsake you.

Just before Jesus ascended into heaven, he said he would always be with us (Matthew 28:20) and he promised that the Father would send the Holy Spirit to be the "Comforter"—the one who comes alongside us (John 14:26). If we hold on to these facts, we can keep fear locked in tight boundaries.

Time to Take Action

Fear does not magically disappear, so we need to take action against it. Here are some of my tactics:

I take time out to write down exactly what I fear. Recording it on paper serves to stop my imagination going into freefall. My circumstances never seem to look quite so bad when I see them in writing.

I ask myself what the worse-case scenario would be, and I write it down.

I speak to God about all that I have written. There is nothing like pouring one's heart out to the Lord to express heartache and fear. Many godly people in the Bible have done this, so if it is good enough for them, it is good enough for me!

We can never completely remove fear from our lives because we need it to steer us away from danger. However, we can act to stop it dominating our thinking and fuelling worry.

Food for Thought

- How do we discern between fear that alerts us to danger, and fear that dominates our thinking and destroys lives?

Prayer

God of peace, your Word tells me that "perfect love casts out all fear" (1 John 4:18) and you have given this to me through Jesus. Help me to hold on to the facts that you are with me wherever I go, and that you will never leave me.

Day 18

Unearthing Our Uniqueness

For you created my inmost being; you knit me together in my mother's womb. I praise you because I am fearfully and wonderfully made; your works are wonderful, I know that full well.
(Psalm 139:13–14)

Knowing Yourself

I have a friend who has faced many difficulties in his life but he has never been anxious about them. He just shrugs his shoulders and says, "Ah well, I'll just let it unfold and see what the Lord will do." I wish I were like him, but I am temperamentally prone to worry. I find uncertainty very difficult to handle, and I feel uneasy about doing something unfamiliar. And I often wake up feeling anxious. This does not mean that I am a weak Christian; it is all a product of my temperament, and once I have faced up to it I have been able to address my weaknesses more effectively.

Christian Extremists

Christians often go to extremes. Some of us may compare ourselves to people who never seem to have a care in the world (like my friend) and feel condemned because we are not like them. The root of this kind of thinking comes from our enemy who is described as "the accuser" (Revelation 12:10) and "Satan" which means "slanderer." On the other hand, others accept that anxiety is a byproduct of their disposition and spend a huge chunk of their time consumed by the cares of life and do not try to change this.

Another Way

I have found a better way.

I learn from people who are different from me. The person I wrote about has been a great inspiration to me. While I can never be exactly like him, I can learn from the way that he approaches problems and uncertainty. He never seems to expect to know what is going on; instead he stands back and looks for the way that God will work out his purposes.

I try to understand myself better. Sometimes I list the negative and positive traits that make me who I am. I have realized that I like to do everything in my power to control my environment and that I am impatient. However, I find it easy to get to know people and I can communicate with them easily.

I remind myself that I do not need to know every detail about the future. As I write, I am on a ministry trip in Europe. Tomorrow I head home and I can sense my mind demanding to know every detail about the journey: What will the traffic be like? Will I be delayed? How am I going to manage a long two days on the road? But I am going to sit still, check that I have done everything necessary to prepare for my journey, commit the rest of it to the Lord, and look for his hand upon all the details.

I was using a friend's cottage in a remote part of the countryside for a day of prayer a while ago. It is a lovely secluded spot but proved to be very difficult to find. I could feel the anxiety begin to surge in me but I overrode this and asked the Lord to help me. A young man came up to ask if I needed help, when I told him I was looking for "Rose Cottage" he broke into a smile and said, "That's Roger's house; it's not easy to find, so I'll take you there."

I see the times when anxiety begins to creep in as opportunities for "the renewal of [my] mind" (Romans 12:2). I may be more susceptible to worry than other people but God is in the process of changing me and each set of uncertainties is a prelude to the Spirit and Word transforming me.

The Bible tells us that we are "fearfully and wonderfully made" (Psalm 139:14). We do not need to feel condemned about our weaknesses that cause us to worry. However, we must square up to them and turn them into opportunities for growth.

Food for Thought

- Think about how your temperament makes you more likely to worry.
- How can you use this to grow to greater maturity?

Prayer

Creator God, I am "fearfully and wonderfully made." You know everything about me. Help me to understand myself so that I can turn the trials—the ones that make me worry—into opportunities to grow in grace and to trust you more.

Day 19

I Think, Therefore I Am

Therefore, I urge you, brothers, in view of God's mercy, to offer your bodies as living sacrifices, holy and pleasing to God—this is your spiritual act of worship. Do not conform any longer to the pattern of this world, but be transformed by the renewing of your mind. Then you will be able to test and approve what God's will is—his good, pleasing and perfect will. (Romans 12:1-2)

I'll Be Coming down the Mountain!

I had finally cracked it. After a day of slipping, sliding and crashing in the snow, I had learned to ski from the top to the bottom of a short slope. Mark, our instructor, was ready to take us all to the next level. He took us to a slightly steeper slope, stood in the middle of it and watched us ski down, one by one. I began to wonder whether I could manage it and when it got to be my turn, I nervously turned my skis downwards, made a few cautious turns, and then took a tumble. As I got up and brushed off the snow, Mark said, "I can tell you exactly what you were thinking." Sure enough, he was right; my mind had been telling me that I could not possibly get to the bottom without falling, and my body took the cue.

The Bible and the Brain

When the New Testament talks about the mind, it speaks of the way our mind-set has changed. We "should no longer walk as the rest of the Gentiles walk, in the futility of their mind," (Ephesians 4:17). Rather, we must be renewed in the spirit of our minds," (Ephesians 4:23), and be transformed by the renewing of our minds (Romans 12:2).

Worry is essentially a mental activity. All of the other things that go with it arise as a consequence of the brain telling the body to be ready to face danger.

So, to win the war against worry, it is essential to get our thought life in proper order.

Total Commitment

Today's verses from Romans tell us to "offer [our] bodies as living sacrifices, holy and acceptable to God." In Old Testament times, God's people were required to make sacrifices in the process of receiving his forgiveness and as they worshiped him. Jesus' death and resurrection have made the sacrificial system redundant once and for all. However, one sacrifice remains—the whole of our lives; our time, hobbies, jobs, family and, above all, our thoughts. When we put this into practice, we "test and approve" God's will. In other words, we bring our lives and thoughts into line with what he wants.

Toward Transformation

We will need to stop our mind-set from being "conformed to the pattern of this world" or as J.B. Phillips' paraphrase puts it this way: "Don't let the world around you squeeze you into its own mould." Our culture demands that we seek total financial security, enjoy life to the maximum—whatever the cost—and live free from difficulties. However, God's Word tells us that "with much tribulation we must enter the Kingdom of God" (Acts 14:22).

Belief, Adversity, Consequence

A friend has introduced me to the "belief, adversity, consequence" model. The idea is that what we *believe* about our *adversity* will have *consequences*. If we change what we believe, the consequences will be different. This does not mean that there will be a different outcome from what we fear but that we will be much better equipped to deal with the situation and find a way forward.

To put this into practice, I began to list my worries and the beliefs that lay behind them and then challenge them with God's Word. Here are some verses that have helped me:

> But I trust in you Lord; I say, "You are my God.
> My times are in your hands."
> Psalm 31:14-15

That is why I began this book by looking at truths about God. You may want to spend some time reviewing them in order to bring your thinking into line with God's Word.

Food for Thought

- What are the beliefs that lie behind what you are worrying about?
- Challenge them with verses from the Bible.

Prayer

God of renewal, I surrender my whole life to you and ask that you would help me to bring my thoughts into line with your Word. Transform my mind so that it is molded by your truth rather than by the world around me.

Day 20

Tomorrow's World

*Therefore do not worry about tomorrow, for tomorrow
will worry about itself. Each day has enough trouble of
its own.*
(Matthew 6:34)

Partial Predictions

I t predicted online banking and the mobile phone, but the British TV program "Tomorrow's World" also made some fanciful forecasts. The very first episode pondered the feasibility of intelligent life on Mars. And when Steve Davis won the World Snooker Championship in 1981, the presenters confidently looked forward to the day when he would be able to face a mechanical opponent.

While we may be able to have a general idea about the future, no-one—except God—knows exactly what it holds. Worry occupies our thoughts with what may or may not happen tomorrow but Jesus tells us that today's challenges are sufficient.

A Helpful Commentary

I have found that these verses from Ecclesiastes provide a great commentary on what Jesus is saying.
"If clouds are full of water, they pour rain upon the earth. Whether a tree falls to the south or to the north, in the place where it falls, there will it lie. Whoever watches the wind will not plant; whoever looks at the clouds will not reap. As you do not know the path of the wind, or how the body is formed in a mother's womb, so you cannot understand the work of God, the Maker of all things, for you do not know which will succeed, whether this or that, or whether both will do equally well." (Ecclesiastes 11:3-5)

The writer is telling us to stop sitting around and fretting about what might be, and rather to get on with what God has given us to do here and now: "Sow your seed in the morning, and at evening let not your hands be idle" (verse 6). That is the principle Jesus gives us—"sufficient is today." The Puritan Bible commentator, Matthew Henry, said, "Let us not pull upon ourselves all together at once which providence has wisely ordered together to be bound in daily parcels." God has divided our lives into 24-hour segments, and this is the secret to handling worry.

One Day at a Time

I have found this principle to be one of the most powerful weapons in my war against worry. God has given me this day and I will use it to its full potential. "Tomorrow," said Jesus, "will worry about itself." In other words, it can be left to its own devices while, with God's help, I tackle today's challenges.

Food for Thought

- What are the joys and challenges I can anticipate today?
- How can I focus them and leave tomorrow to its own devices?

Prayer

Jesus, you are Lord of my life. Thank you for the joys and challenges of this day. Help me to rejoice in the gifts you have given me and to tackle difficulties in your strength and with "the wisdom that comes from above" (James 3:17). May this be a pattern for each day throughout my life.

Day 21

Early Morning Anxiety

O Lord, be gracious to us; we long for you. Be our strength every morning, our salvation in time of distress.
(Isaiah 33:2)

Morning Blues

It is said that the world is divided into "larks" and "night owls." The former wake up ready to face the challenges of the day and jump out of bed at the first opportunity, while the latter often struggle to emerge from the fog of sleep. I have been an irrepressible morning person for most of my life but at times I have struggled with early-morning anxiety.

Some Strategies

Here are some strategies that I have developed to fight this.

Focus

Before going to bed, I choose my focus for the morning. For example, my waking thought today was writing this chapter, and although there were some feelings of anxiety lurking in my system, I eagerly got out of bed to get on with my task!

Scripture at the ready

I select Bible verses to turn my mind to when I wake up with anxious feelings. Here are some examples:

In the morning, O Lord, you hear my voice; in the morning I lay my requests before you and wait in expectation. (Psalm 5:3)

My eyes stay open through the watches of the night that I may meditate on your promises. Let the morning bring me word of your unfailing love, for I have put my trust in you. Show me the way I should go, for to you I lift up my soul. (Psalm 143:8)

This is the day the Lord has made; let us rejoice and be glad in it. (Psalm 118:24)

The Lord is my strength and my shield; my heart trusts in him, and I am helped. My heart leaps for joy and I will give thanks to him in song. (Psalm 28:7)

Because of the Lord's great love we are not consumed, for his compassions never fail. They are new every morning; great is your faithfulness. (Lamentations 3:22–23)

Break the link
Morning anxiety becomes more potent if I attach issues that I have been worrying about to the anxious feelings I am experiencing. I have learned to avoid this by reminding myself that, to a certain extent, the feelings I experience originate from a chemical in my system. (The body produces a hormone called cortisol to enable us to deal with the challenges of the day, but this also creates feelings of anxiety.) This tactic

breaks the link between these feelings and the challenges I am currently facing.

The long-term

These are effective but short-term tactics in the fight. In the long term, it is important to change one's perception so that waking up is seen as a positive experience. The Lord has brought me safely through the night, he has provided sleep, and given another day in which to explore his goodness and mercy.

Food for Thought

- Put together your own strategy to get ready to attack morning anxiety before you sleep.
- How can you change your long-term perception about mornings?

Prayer

Loving God, I praise you that your mercies are new every morning (Lamentations 3:23). Some mornings I wake up feeling as if I cannot face the day, yet I thank you for your compassion and love. Please help me to rise above these moods and reach out to your eternal love.

Day 22

The Path to Peace

Do not be anxious about anything, but in everything, by prayer and petition, with thanksgiving, present your requests to God. And the peace of God, which transcends all understanding, will guard your hearts and your minds in Christ Jesus.
(Philippians 4:6–7)

During my war with worry, I have never discovered a weapon that gives me instant victory. Instead it has been a steady, step-by-step approach. Today's verses provide six firm steps which have helped me tread the path to peace.

Step one: Stop!

When a situation arises that has the potential to make me anxious, I stop. In the original language Paul literally says, "Stop worrying" and the word he uses has to do with carrying tomorrow's burdens. I have lost count of the times when my cares about tomorrow have robbed me of the joys of today.

Step two: Turn to God

I change direction and orient myself toward God. The word used for "prayer" is a general one that describes coming to God, praising him for who he is, and speaking with him. This is the very thing that anxiety stops us doing. Martyn Lloyd-Jones describes it in this way:

> Come into the presence of God and for the time being forget your problems. Do not start with them. Just realize that you are face to face with God. The idea of being face to face is inherent in the very word "prayer".

Step three: Ask for help!

I ask God for his help. I still do not bring my specific requests to him. "Supplication" or "petition" describes a sense of our helplessness which is a contrast with God's greatness. It would be used to speak of the way an ordinary person would approach a king to plead for help.

Step four: Give thanks

Paul says that all of this must be done "with thanksgiving." So I thank him for who he is, what he has done through Christ, and what he has promised in the Bible. I also look back over the way he has shown his care for me in the past and I channel this into thanksgiving.

Step five: Ask

At this stage I am ready to "present [my] requests to God." I tell him about my problem and I ask him to provide for my needs.

Step six: Receive

When I take these steps, I invariably receive "the peace of God, which transcends all understanding." It is poignant that Paul describes this as the peace *of* God rather than peace *from* him. This is because it is part of God's being; he cannot be anxious because he is sovereign. He is always at peace because he is in complete control. Paul tells us that this peace will "guard our hearts and minds in Christ Jesus." The word that translates "guard"—meaning "garrison"—would have been very pertinent to the Christians in Philippi because their town was a Roman colony. They would have known how secure the local garrison was and thus rejoiced in the way that God's peace had the same effect on their hearts.

Food for Thought
- Memorize today's verse.
- Make a note of the six steps so that you are ready to put them into action.

Prayer
Heavenly Father, you are the God of peace. You know all things, and you rule over this universe. You are never troubled or uncertain about the future. Help me to turn away from anxious thoughts and to seek your presence. Help me in my time of need and keep me in your perfect peace.

Day 23

"Leave It with Me"

Cast all your anxiety on him because he cares for you.
(1 Peter 5:7)

A Trustworthy Tradesman

No job is too much for him. Ted Glenn can fix your leaky roof and repair your blocked sink. His catchphrase is "Leave it with me." Sadly, Ted is a fictional character from a children's TV program. I have sometimes wished that I knew someone like him! However I can bring my problems to God and leave them with him.

Throw It Off

Peter tells us to "cast" our anxieties upon God. The Greek word means that you throw an object to someone or something so that it is no longer with you. It's like throwing a blanket on a horse. And we are to "throw" our worries onto God because he cares for us. Literally, he has a constant care and concern for us.

Make Up Your Mind!

I have to make a conscious decision to throw my concerns onto the Lord. When a big house move was on the horizon, I felt as if I was sinking in a quicksand of worry. I pondered everything that could go wrong with the inspector's quality report and how that may impact the sale. It was necessary to take on a bigger mortgage so I spent hours raking over figures for our finances again and again. Eventually, I realized that this was not what God wanted for me, so I decided to give my cares to him and leave them there. I made a decision to commit myself to a different course by bringing my worries to God and leaving them with him. When I am tempted to try to take things back, I remind myself that these issues are in better hands than mine.

Food for Thought
- Think of your worries as an object that is pulling you down.
- Develop a mental picture of throwing it onto the Lord.

Prayer
God, you are compassionate and caring. Thank you that the things that bother me matter to you and can be safely left with you. Help me to make a conscious decision to cast them onto you so that I may live free from worry.

Day 24

Submit to God

Submit yourselves, then, to God. Resist the devil, and he will flee from you.
(James 4:7)

My heart sank the moment I saw her march purposefully down to the front of the church to talk to a church leader. Sabrina was a formidable woman at the best of times but something about the look in her eyes and the angry expression on her face sent shivers down my spine. When I asked the leader she had spoken to what the discussion was about, he said that she registered her "concerns." These he had asked her to put in writing. It was the starting pistol for one of the darkest periods of my life, eventually resulting in my departure from the church I had served as pastor for eleven years.

The turmoil lasted for a year. Each Sunday I could see Sabrina talking to different members of the small group who had been opposing me for some years. She was animated and energized, holding an open Bible in front of her as if it were a weapon. Because of her influence on others, I had to endure agonizing meetings with Sabrina, her husband, and the leadership, during which they attacked me about my preaching and leveled unfounded accusations against me.

Every day I would open my email program with a sense of dread about what abusive message the couple or members of their group would be sending next. I later discovered that three church members were gathering names to arrange a meeting to call for my suspension. When I asked them what their issue was, they told me that I did not handle conflict very well.

During those turbulent days, I fought the urge to leave my pastoral charge. I was determined not to be beaten; my thinking had always been to remain in service to the church until it was time to retire. However, the situation became impossible and my health was rapidly deteriorating, to the extent that my doctor put me on sick leave. This provided the space I needed to reassess the situation. It was impossible to carry on: opponents were well-organized and entrenched and most of the leadership team were unwilling to face them down. However, my worries about how I could live without an income and what I would do in the future prevented me from being more decisive.

The Point of Submission

After many anxious weeks of prayer and seeking counsel from pastors and doctors, I finally accepted that I had to resign. I remembered something that had always struck me in the story of Esther. Her people were at risk and Mordecai pleaded with her to speak to the king of Persia. In fear of her life, Esther resisted until she realized that it was the only course of action. "I will go to the King even though it is against the law," she said. "And if I perish, I perish" (Esther 4:16). Like Esther, I had to set my fear aside and come to a point of complete submission to God's will. It was at this point I knew his peace and had to learn to trust him for my day-to-day needs. He has never let me down!

Sometimes defeating worry involves surrendering to God's will and accepting that the worst case scenario that we fear may actually be part of his plan. When I came to this position, I began a thrilling adventure of new ministry that I could never have imagined.

Food for Thought

- Ask yourself whether the situation you are presently worrying about revolves around something you do not actually want to face.
- Come to a position of complete submission to the Lord.

Prayer

Gracious God, I know that you are good and your way is perfect. Show me when I am fighting something that is inevitable, and help me to take refuge in your arms and to submit to your will.

Day 25

Challenge Your Thoughts

*We demolish arguments and every pretension that sets
itself up against the knowledge of God, and we take
captive every thought to make it obedient to Christ.
(2 Corinthians 10:5)*

Battling with Bleakness

There have been many people who have supported me during my years in pastoral ministry, but Mike stands head and shoulders above them all. Mike had served with me in leadership at the church for some years and was someone I always depended upon for honest advice and loyal support. Although I was at peace during the weeks that followed my decision to leave the church of which I had been the pastor, for much of the time I felt shell-shocked. "I can't believe this has happened," I stammered, during an emotional phone conversation with Mike. "Whatever will become of me?"

Countering the Lies

In the following weeks I had many similar thoughts. I worried whether I was finished in ministry and about what kind of future I would face. During that time, I was under the care of a Christian psychologist. It was helpful to talk to someone who understood how the mind works and who applied biblical principles to help her patients recover. She showed me a method to challenge these thoughts with the Bible. So when I despaired that my life and ministry were irrevocably damaged, I would bring these verses to mind:

"Being confident of this, that he who began a good work in you will carry it on to completion until the day of Christ Jesus" (Philippians 1:6).

"And we know that in all things God works for the good of those who love him, who have been called according to his purpose" (Romans 8:28).

"'For I know the plans I have for you,' declares the LORD , 'plans to prosper you and not to harm you, plans to give you hope and a future.'" (Jeremiah 29:11).

Sometimes—as part of "taking every thought captive"—I write down my negative and fearful thoughts in my journal and put questions below each of them such as:

- Where is the evidence?
- Is this based on emotion or fact?
- If it is emotion, why am I feeling this way?
- Why would God cast me off?
- What would I say to someone in the same position?

This has required effort and discipline. In many ways, it is easier to let anxious, fearful and gloomy thoughts take hold of me but it has paid dividends. I know that "I can do all things through him who gives me strength" (Philippians 4:13). As time has gone, on it has become less difficult and I have noticed a change in my patterns of thinking. Perhaps you are like me, and the fight continues, so I would encourage you, with God's enabling, to join me in it.

Food for Thought
- List the five most common anxious thoughts that you struggle with.
- What Scriptures can you challenge them with?

Prayer
Lord, you are "compassionate, slow to anger and abounding in steadfast love" (Exodus 34:6). There are times when my mind becomes full of thoughts that contradict this truth. Give me the strength I need to challenge these thoughts and live the life of faith.

Day 26

Living with Uncertainty

Trust in the Lord with all your heart and lean not on your own understanding; in all your ways acknowledge him, and he will make your paths straight.
(Proverbs 3:5–6)

The Waiting Game

Try as I might, I found it impossible to concentrate. I must have walked the length of my kitchen a hundred times to shed my nervous energy. However, I knew that by four o'clock, when my exam results were to be announced, it would all be over.

I had worked hard throughout the year and revised as much as I could but I struggled with the uncertainty that hung over me, especially as I would not be able to continue the course if I failed. When the results were posted on the wall (these were pre-Internet days!) my mood changed from anxiety to elation because I had passed!

Give Me Certainty!

I have always found uncertainty difficult to live with, and this has been a major catalyst for anxiety. I am sure that others are the same. We like to know our jobs are secure, and there is nothing more unsettling than rumors of redundancies at work. If we get struck by an illness, we invariably ask the doctor if we will recover. We have aspirations for our children, and we plan our finances carefully. All of these things are good but there is no getting away from the fact that life can be very uncertain. In an instant, events can sweep away all that was familiar to us.

A Dream Delayed

A young man had been given the most amazing glimpses of what was going to happen to him. He dreamed that he and his brothers were working in the fields during the harvest when his sheaf stood upright and his brothers' sheaves bowed down to his. And in another dream, the sun and the moon and the eleven stars were bowing down to him (Genesis 37:5-9). Joseph looked forward to a bright future where he would enjoy some kind of elevated position over his family. However, his brothers' jealousy led to his being thrown into a pit and sold into slavery. For many years, life was full of uncertainty: he was falsely accused of molesting his master's wife, and he languished in prison for years. Finally, the future God had revealed became reality. He was appointed as Pharaoh's prime minister and his brothers unknowingly bowed down before him in their desperate search for food during a famine.

Coping with Uncertainty

No-one enjoys uncertainty but I have found that it is possible to live with it by following these principles.

Face the facts—life is uncertain: James says, "You do not know what tomorrow will bring" (James 4:17). Only God knows the end from the beginning; it is not for us to know.

Focus on certainties: There are many certainties, given to us in the Bible, that we can focus on. Here are some examples

- God has loved us from eternity (Ephesians 1:4).
- Jesus has made us right with God (2 Corinthians 5:21).
- God will finish the work he began in us (Philippians 1:6).
- God will provide all of our needs (Philippians 4:19).
- God will bring us safely to heaven (Jude 24-25) .

Have an eternal perspective: God has revealed our final destination, and although we cannot yet see it, we know it is where we belong. The things we are not sure about—health, jobs and money—are all temporal. However, the New Testament calls us to "Fix our eyes not on what is seen, but on what is unseen. For what is seen is temporary, but what is unseen is eternal" (2 Corinthians 4:18).

Food for Thought
- List the things you are uncertain about.
- Compare these things to the certainties we have thought about today.

Prayer

Sovereign God, I praise you that you have begun a work in me which you will bring to completion on that great day when I see you face to face. I humble myself before you in awe of your majesty. I recognize my own limitations and gladly leave uncertainties in your eternal hands. Help me to focus on the certainties revealed in your Word so that I may have an eternal perspective.

Day 27

Think Outside the Box

And pray in the Spirit on all occasions with all kinds of prayers and requests. With this in mind, be alert and always keep on praying for all the saints.
(Ephesians 6:18)

My worries invariably revolve around myself. The more I let this churn around my head, the more self-indulgent I become. I need to break out of this box and I can do so by praying for other people.

In today's verse, Paul writes to Christians living in a very oppressive situation. Ephesus was the center for worship of the pagan goddess Diana, and the huge temple that was dedicated to her would have dominated the skyline. We have already looked at verses from Ephesians in which Paul directed our attention to God's great plan. Now, as he draws the letter to a close, he urges us to pray. We do this "in the Spirit"— enabled by God with his Spirit's leading. "At all times": this is not an activity to be confined to a morning or evening prayer-time but something that goes on throughout the day. And "for all the saints": this describes fellow Christians, people whom God has set apart for himself. In order to do so, we must be "alert." The Greek word means "to be awake and vigilant."

Being on the lookout for people to pray for and bringing them to the Lord has become a powerful weapon in my war against worry. It takes me right out of myself and puts the focus on another person's needs. It gets me interested in someone else's welfare, strengthens my relationship with that person, and puts my own situation into perspective. When I wake up in the night with anxiety, I turn this nervous energy into prayer until I return to sleep.

Just before I sat down to write this, I was battling negative, anxious thoughts which revolved around my circumstances. My Skype box suddenly came to life asking me to accept a call from a Christian friend in Pakistan. He is a young pastor living in a remote mountain village. We talked about the ministry he is involved in and I found myself astounded by his vision to help the young children suffering terrible treatment from ISIS sympathizers in the village. It made me realize how blessed I am and that I have no cause to complain. Here was a man who lived in a desperate situation yet who was determined to make a difference. This has turned my outlook inside out!

Food for Thought

- List seven needy people you know and pray for one each day. Each time your mind starts to drift toward worry, intercede for the person you have chosen.
- Look out for people you can pray for throughout the day.

Prayer

Heavenly Father, thank you that I am part of your worldwide family. Forgive me for the way that I am often so engrossed with my own problems that I do not see the needs of those around me. Help me to break out of the selfishness worry induces and to care for others. Make me alert, prayerful and supportive.

Day 28

The Ultimate Focus

Let us fix our eyes on Jesus, the author and perfecter of our faith, who for the joy set before him endured the cross, scorning its shame, and sat down at the right hand of the throne of God.
(Hebrews 12:2)

"Where You Look Is Where You'll Go"

I t was my third driving lesson and I was still nervous about driving the car. My instructor was an exuberant Londoner of Italian descent. "Just remember this," he said, frantically waving his arms around. "Where you look is where you'll go." However, at that point I was looking at a tree, which was a cue for him to grab the wheel from me!

Focusing on Jesus

When I have focused on my worries and allowed them to dominate my life, my relationship with God has invariably faltered. However, setting my sights on Jesus enables me to draw together the strategies I have written about in this book and get on with my walk with God.

When the writer to the Hebrews urges us to "fix our eyes on Jesus," he uses a word which means "to look attentively." This is like how an athlete focuses on the finishing line of a race or a musician is attentive to his or her conductor. We do this because Jesus is the "author and perfecter of our faith." In other words, he is the one who has done everything necessary for us to have a living relationship with God. He has paid the price for our sins and he will bring us safely to heaven.

Practicalities

When I was a young Christian, people used to say "just fix your eyes on Jesus." I really liked the principle but I was never too sure how to do it. If you are in the same position, let me give you some practical ways to put this exhortation into practice.

1. Put your faith in Christ alone. The verse goes on to speak of how Jesus endured a humiliating death on the cross and is now seated at God's right hand—the place of authority and power.

2. Love Christ. Christianity is not a religion but a living relationship with God. Peter says, "Though you have not seen him, you love him; and even though you do not see him now, you believe in him and are filled with an inexpressible and glorious joy" (1 Peter 1:8). The more I know Christ, the greater my love for him. It is a fact, not a feeling (although I can often get emotional about my relationship with Jesus). This love grows as I spend time with him in prayer and reading the Word of God.

3. Remind yourself that Jesus is king over your life. Everything you are and have belongs to Jesus.

4. Live for his kingdom. I have already said that my worries tend to revolve around my life. However, Je-

sus calls us to be concerned for his kingdom and has promised to care for our needs (see Matthew 6:33). Fixing our sights on Jesus is a spiritual discipline which will lift us out of worries and deepen our relationship with him.

Food for Thought

- How much do you need to exercise faith in Christ throughout each day?
- Think about how you can incorporate this into your daily routine.

Prayer

Lord Jesus, you are the author and completer of my faith. I praise you for the way in which you laid down your life, enduring that horrific death and taking the wrath of God upon yourself so that I can be saved. You have risen from the dead and now you sit at the Father's right hand. However, I often look at my worries instead of setting my sights on you. Help me to change this so that I can live by faith.

Day 29

The Power of God's Purpose

And we know that in all things God works for the good
of those who love him, who have been called according
to his purpose.
(Romans 8:28)

Mr. Mickawber

He bumbled from one disaster to another but Mr. Mickawber was never short of optimism. When the future was looked bleak, his watchword was, "Something will turn up; it usually does." Mickawber is one of my favorite characters created by Charles Dickens; I love his cheerful disposition. However, he rarely had reasons for his confidence; in fact, the odds were usually stacked against him.

There have been times when I have reduced Romans 8:28 to a platitude similar to Mickawber's maxim. However, this verse does not vaguely assure us that everything will turn out all right. It is saying that God will work out his purposes in our lives which will be for our ultimate good and his glory. And this is a key principle in the war against worry.

Know This!

Paul begins this magnificent statement with the words, "We know." He is not communicating a nice idea to cheer us up when things are difficult; rather, he is imparting a crucial truth that should underscore our whole approach to life. "You must keep these facts in your head," Paul is saying. "They are essential to living out the Christian life."

Vital Facts

There are two vital facts we must know. First, God is at work in the lives of people who love him. They are "called according to his purpose." Our relationship with God is rooted in love and our calling is to fulfill his purpose rather than pursue our own ambitions. The second fact is that he is working for our ultimate good—"to be conformed to the likeness of his Son." God is doing this now as he sets us apart, challenges and builds us up with his Word, and changes us by the power of the Holy Spirit. And he will complete the work when we have resurrection bodies.

A Different Perspective

Throughout this book, we have seen that worry puts the focus on ourselves. However, we can focus on God, secure in the knowledge that he is using everything that goes on around us to make us more like Jesus. When I make this my chief concern, worry fades into the background but when I am wrapped up with myself, it ties me up in knots.

Food for Thought

- Memorize Romans 8:28.
- Throughout this day, remind yourself of the two vital facts it contains.

Prayer

Heavenly Father, I want to express my love to you. You have created me, saved me from eternal punishment, and given me "every spiritual blessing in the heavenly places in Christ" (Ephesians 1:3). Help live my life according to your purposes and trust you to work all things together for your glory and for my ultimate good.

Day 30

How to Keep Going When the Going Gets Tough

Consider it pure joy, my brothers, whenever you face trials of many kinds, because you know that the testing of your faith develops perseverance. Perseverance must finish its work so that you may be mature and complete, not lacking anything.
(James 1:2–4)

[133]

From the very outset, I was adamant that I would not do it but somehow I allowed myself to be persuaded to "give it a go." I was standing at the pinnacle of the steepest ski slope in Europe, and there was no turning back. The run looked tough but I had to keep going.

A lot of my worries have been about whether I can cope with difficulties, such as poor health or loss of income. I have discovered that the most effective way of tackling this has been to change my mind-set. Today's verses have helped me to do so.

Face Reality

James presents us with two statements to face us up to the reality of trials. Like it or not, every one of us will have to endure hard times. That is why James says, "Count it all joy *whenever* you face trials." Trials will hit us and hurt us.

James tells us that we will face "various" trials. The same Greek word is used in Matthew 4.25 describing the way that Jesus healed "any and every kind of sicknesses." It is an inclusive term which covers big and small trials.

Change Our Thinking

James calls us to "consider it pure joy" when difficulties are unleashed into our lives. He says this in a way that describes something that we should do once and for all—in other words, "Get this mind-set and keep it." The word translated "consider" was used in the world of accounting. Some translations say "reckon" because it would be used when you were reckoning in a payment due to you. R.T. Kendall says, "Counting it all joy is to dignify God's providence because it shows that you can see God's hand in every area of your life."[1]

The Outcome

Trials become a source for joy when we realize their long-term potential. First, they prove the reality of our faith. James describes this process as "the testing of [our] faith". In the same way that the authenticity of a piece of gold can be proved in the refiner's fire, the credibility of our relationship with God is demonstrated to everyone around us, and to ourselves, as we continue to trust him and live for him when times are tough. Secondly they enable us to grow in our faith—"you know that the testing of your faith develops perseverance." The Greek word for "perseverance" is both active and passive: Actively it describes the persistence that enables us to keep going. And passively it talks about holding on patiently. We do this by trusting in God to work out his purpose and by refusing to give up living for Jesus. Thirdly, we

---

[1] From a sermon preached at Westminster Chapel

will be "complete, not lacking in anything," literally "perfected all over." Trials have a way of exposing our deficiencies and when we face up to them, asking for God's help, we are transformed by the Holy Spirit.

The philosopher Descartes coined the famous expression, "I think, therefore I am." Worry is the result of flawed thinking but when we allow our mind-set about difficulties to be changed by God's Word, we will score an essential victory in the war against worry.

Food for Thought

- Meditate on these verses during the next week, asking God to use them to change your mind-set.
- James 1:2-4

Prayer

Heavenly Father, I praise you that your hand is on every area of my life. I often see trials as hostile intrusions into my peaceful existence. I worry about when they will hit me and what shape they will take. Help me to see them as powerful tools in your loving hands and consider them to be "pure joy" because of the way they will transform me and draw me closer to you.

Day 31

Join the Fight!

For our struggle is not against flesh and blood, but against the rulers, against the authorities, against the powers of this dark world and against the spiritual forces of evil in the heavenly realms.
(Ephesians 6:12)

Enough Is Enough!

The year was 1914, war had been declared, and troops were being mustered to fight for their country. A picture of Lord Kitchener—the British Secretary of State for War—with his forefinger extended could be seen on posters all over Britain. The posters were emblazoned with the slogan, "Your country needs you!" Millions of men responded by attending recruitment centers up and down the country to enlist to join the war effort.

This book has been written as a recruitment drive for a war against worry. In my own case, I have expended a lot of time wrestling with anxious thoughts. My deepest desire is that you join me in this war against worry. Today we will establish the key steps that need to be taken in order to put into practice the biblical principles that have been set out in the last thirty days.

1. Enlist in the War

We have to make a decision not allow ourselves to be dominated by worry any longer.

2. Change Priorities

Paul told Timothy that, "No-one serving as a soldier gets involved in civilian affairs—he wants to please his commanding officer" (2 Timothy 2:4). During the last thirty days, we have seen that worry has the effect of getting us wrapped up with ourselves and our problems instead of focusing on God and extending his kingdom. In the early part of the book, we thought about the amazing things God has done for us which fly in the face of the issues that occupy our anxious thoughts.

- God chose us before he created the world (Ephesians 1:4-6).
- He has put his seal of ownership on us (Ephesians 1:13).
- We are citizens of the kingdom of God—an unshakable kingdom (Hebrews 12:28).
- Jesus is "the good shepherd" who cares and provides for us (John 10:11).
- We need to ensure that God's Kingdom is our priority.
- God will complete the work he began (Philippians 1:6).
- Since God did not spare his Son, he will graciously give us "all things with him" (Romans 8.32).

3. Identify the Enemy

Worry is not something we have to endure; it is an enemy we need to defeat. Jesus asked a powerful question: "Who of you by worrying can add a single hour to his life?" (Matthew 6:27). It is time to see worry for what it is—a destructive force that has no benefit whatsoever.

4. Get into Battle

Here are the core tactics given to us in the Bible:

(a) Commit:
We do not have to carry cares that weigh us down. Peter tells us to "cast" them onto the Lord (1 Peter 1:8), knowing that he cares for us. And he uses a word that speaks of tossing something away.

(b) Resist:
In the very next verse, Peter urges us to be "self-controlled and alert" because Satan is like a roaring lion, on the prowl for prey to devour. We must resist him by "standing firm in the faith" (1 Peter 1:9). Satan will try to use our tendency to worry to destroy us, and we must refuse to allow him to succeed.

(c) Reduce:
Worry usually has a long-term perspective: what will happen tomorrow, and the day after that, etc.? However Jesus says we must reduce the scope of our concern to the challenges of today—"Sufficient for the day is its own trouble" (Matthew 6:34, ESV).

(d) Surrender:
In my experience, the worst-case scenario I imagined did actually become reality. However, when I surrendered to God and said, "Not my will but yours be

done" (Luke 22:42), peace flooded my heart and soul, and I saw God work out his purposes in surprising and exciting ways. Surrender also involves the realization that we are not in control. As the old hymn says, "God holds the key of all unknown."

5. Stay in the Fight

Our thirty-one-day battle-briefing has come to an end. I hope this book has equipped you to get stuck into the fight. You are not on your own; God has sent the Holy Spirit to be within you and to strengthen you (John 14:15-17). Now it is for you to stay in the fight with dependence upon God, knowing that you are on the victory side.

Food for Thought

- Think about how these key tactics can become part of your everyday life.
- Commit yourself to a personal program in which you will reinforce all the principles you have learned in reading this book.

Prayer

Mighty God, you are victorious in battle and your Son has conquered death and sin. Help me to live in light of your victory. I choose to reject worry and "seek first your kingdom" (Matthew 6:33). I acknowledge that I need the power of the Holy Spirit to help me fight this war against worry. In faith, I ask for the Spirit's help, and I look forward to seeing you at work in my life.

More Tactical Gear

Bible References for When I Feel Worried

Memorize or look up and refer to the following Bible passages:

- Matthew 6:34
- 1 Peter 5:7
- Hebrews 13:6
- John 14:27
- Psalm 55:22
- Psalm 56:3-4
- Isaiah 26:3
- Philippians 4.6-7
- Matthew 6:25-27

Seven People for My Prayer List

Seven people I will pray for, and who may benefit from reading this book:

1 _____

2 _____

3 _____

4 _____

5 _____

6 _____

7 _____

About the Author

Simon Robinson has been in pastoral ministry since 1988. He is the author of eight books, including *Improving your Quiet Time* and *Growing for God*. He engages in an itinerant ministry teaching the Bible in Europe, Asia and the USA, as well as being a police chaplain and leader of the work of Redeeming our Communities in Chesterfield, England. He and his wife Hazel have two adult sons and three grandchildren.

Find out more about Simon (and his writing and speaking ministry) at www.simonjrobinson.org.

The Still Small Voice of Love

A journey into
a deeper relationship with Jesus

Leoma Gilley

Cover design: Howell Graphics
Artwork: Jo Davis

Library of Congress Control Number: 2020902484

ISBN 978-1-970037-34-0

Second Edition 2020
Printed in the United States of America

Introduction

In the spring of 2009, someone gave me the book *Nearer to Jesus* by Sarah Young. It had been very special to the person who gave it to me, and she wanted to share it in expectation that it would also be a blessing to me. I began to read the reflections, which seemed to come from Young's *lectio divina* or divine reading of the Scriptures. She was finding in her reading that she could speak to God about what was challenging her, and then she was listening and hearing God speak to her with some amazing and loving answers.

I read these reflections with a growing awe that God would talk to anyone in that manner, but after some months, I also began to notice a strong feeling of envy. Why did God talk to HER like this but not to ME!?! After all, doesn't God love us all the same? So, why is Sarah Young special?

Finally, I got around to asking God about this. I said, "Why don't You talk to me the way You talk to Sarah?"

His very simple reply in my mind was, "Why don't you listen?"

What else could I do? I started to listen, and He did talk to me. He had a lot to say. It has taken some practice to get the hang of this new kind of interaction, and I'm still learning. This is not a book to teach you how to do it. It is not just for you to hear what God said to me, though I hope you will be blessed by that. I hope to spark in you the same kind of envy I felt, so that you, too, will ask God, "Why don't You speak to ME like that?"

Having practiced this method of interacting with God for several more months, I went through a crisis. Actually, there were a number of factors that all conspired to flatten me emotionally, physically, psychologically. During this time of weakness, God began to whisper words of love to me, in that still, small voice of His.

After a few more months, I was asked how I was responding to His Love. "It is like my little, shriveled heart is caught in a tsunami of love and He is trying to pour this vast amount of love into my little, dry heart a drop at a time." My friend Jo Davis heard me describing this, and kindly produced the painting used on the cover of this book.

God has continued to grow my heart to receive His love. I hope you will also draw closer to the Lover as you learn to hear His voice.

Hearing God in the Scriptures
(Lectio Divina)

Lectio (Read)
Thoughtfully read a brief passage from the Word
of God, listening with the ears of your heart.
Note what word or phrase seems to call to you
What *sparkles*?*

Meditatio (Meditate)
Slowly reread the passage, and repeat the word
that has chosen you, asking God,
"What do you want me to learn from this today?"
Ask your heart, "Why this word, here and now?"*

Oratio (Pray)
As you read the passage a third time, savor it.
Let it move you to place yourself before the One
who has invited you into intimate dialogue.
Trust God enough to speak from your heart.*

Contemplatio (Contemplate)
Read the passage a last time and as you sit quietly,
let the Holy Spirit speak to your heart.
Let go of the text and simply rest in God.
As the fragrance of God's word fills the room,
enjoy the sweetness of your communion with the
God of the Scriptures.

*Allow a few minutes of silence before moving to
the next section.

How to use this book

At the beginning of each reflection is the reference and the verse[i] or verses with the part in **bold** that were 'my words' for that day. These are the words God used to speak to me.

Then there is a brief conversation between the Lover (God) and the Beloved (you or me) .

Finally, there is a short passage of Scripture that expands on the idea that the Lover is trying to get across.

You may wish to use a journal or the space in these pages to record your own reflections and prayers to help you hear what the Lover, the Shepherd, is saying to you.

1

Luke 22:15

Jesus said, "**I have been very eager to eat this Passover meal with you** before my suffering begins."

Lover: I am eager to spend time with you, My precious child. And I long for you to share that desire to spend time with Me. Relationships and trust are built over time as we share events and struggles together. As you learn to trust Me, we can do more exciting things together. Take each opportunity to listen and talk with Me.

[5]LORD, you alone are my inheritance, my cup of blessing. You guard all that is mine. [6]The land you have given me is a pleasant land. What a wonderful inheritance! [7]I will bless the LORD who guides me; even at night my heart instructs me. [8]I know the LORD is always with me. I will not be shaken, for he is right beside me. [9]No wonder my heart is glad, and I rejoice. My body rests in safety. [11]You will show me the way of life, granting me the joy of your presence and the pleasures of living with you forever. (Psalm 16:5-9, 11 NLT)[ii]

*   *   *   *   *   *   *   *

Read the verses above for a word or phrase that calls to you.

Write down the word or phrase.

Why does this word call to you?

Dialogue with God. Write out your thoughts and His response.

Read the verse(s) again. Rest in silence.

2

John 21:9

When they got there, they found breakfast waiting for them—fish cooking over a charcoal fire, and some bread.

Beloved: Shepherd, how often do You prepare and then wait for me to show up, and I never come or come in such a rush that I don't even notice what You have prepared for me? Forgive me and help me to break away from the life that seems so real but isn't the true reality You offer.

Lover: Come, My child, come and sit with Me awhile and enjoy the richness of all I have to offer you. Invite Me into your life and see how everything changes.

[8]Examine and see how good the LORD is. Happy is the person who trusts him. [9]You who belong to the LORD, fear him! Those who fear him will have everything they need. [10]Even lions may get weak and hungry, but those who look to the LORD will have every good thing. [11]Children, come and listen to me. I will teach you to worship the LORD.
(Psalm 34:8-11, NCV)[iii]

*   *   *   *   *   *   *   *

Read the verses above for a word or phrase that calls to you.

Write down the word or phrase.

Why does this word call to you?

Dialogue with God. Write out your thoughts and His response.

Read the verse(s) again. Rest in silence.

3

Luke 15:12, 21-22

[12]The younger son told his father, '**I want my share** of your estate now before you die.' [21]His son said to him, '**Father, I have sinned** against both heaven and you, and I am no longer worthy of being called your son.' [22]"But his father said to the servants, 'Quick! **Bring the finest robe** in the house and put it on him. Get a ring for his finger and sandals for his feet.'

Beloved: The younger son began his journey full of pride. His misfortunes taught him humility and lowered his self-image. Father, that's where I am. I'm glad to receive a lovely covering so that I appear acceptable to others, but in reality I feel unworthy, unlovable, and fearful that the truth will come out.

Lover: My dear, precious child, can you see that My heart is filled with love and compassion for you? I see and know the truth, and still I love you. And if you are so loved, you cannot be unlovable—for I love you. By being loved and accepting My Love, you will learn to love, and that is how it will be between us.

[18] So the LORD must wait for you to come to him so he can show you his love and compassion. For the LORD is a faithful God. Blessed are those who wait for his help. [19]O people of Zion, who live in Jerusalem, you will weep no more. He will be gracious if you ask for help. He will surely respond to the sound of your cries. [20]Though the Lord gave you

adversity for food and suffering for drink, he will still be with you to teach you. You will see your teacher with your own eyes. [21]Your own ears will hear him. Right behind you a voice will say, "This is the way you should go," whether to the right or to the left. (Isaiah 30:18-21, NLT)

*   *   *   *   *   *   *   *

Read the verses above for a word or phrase that
calls to you.

Write down the word or phrase.

Why does this word call to you?

Dialogue with God. Write out your thoughts and
His response.

Read the verse(s) again. Rest in silence.

4

Luke 24:38.
"Why are you frightened?" he asked. "Why are your hearts filled with doubt?"

Beloved: I was awakened in the night. It was so hard to breathe. Being out of control frightens me. The inability to bring about the changes I want in other parts of my life both angers and frightens me.

Lover: Little One, you don't have control over anything, really. Sometimes it appears that you do, but that is only an illusion. I, on the other hand, fully control EVERYTHING. So, the solution to this dilemma is to trust Me in all things. Can you do that?

20It will be like waking from a dream. Lord, when you rise up, they will disappear. 21When my heart was sad and I was angry, 22I was senseless and stupid. I acted like an animal toward you. 23But I am always with you; you have held my hand. 24You guide me with your advice, and later you will receive me in honor. 25I have no one in heaven but you; I want nothing on earth besides you. 26My body and my mind may become weak, but God is my strength. He is mine forever.
(Psalm 73:20-26 NCV)

*   *   *   *   *   *   *   *

Read the verses above for a word or phrase that calls to you.

Write down the word or phrase.

Why does this word call to you?

Dialogue with God. Write out your thoughts and His response.

Read the verse(s) again. Rest in silence.

5

I Corinthians 11:24

. . . Then he broke it in pieces and said, "This is my body, which is given for you. **Do this in remembrance of me."**

Beloved: I so need reminders to think of You. I wish it were automatic, but all too quickly Your reality fades as my reality takes over my thoughts.

Lover: Memories can be so short. How many things have you forgotten since last week, let alone things that happened years ago? Things that happened before you were born have even less hold on memory. So, repetition is good—to keep important things in your mind and not forgotten. Remember My broken body and shed blood, an act done for you. Review it often. Know how much I love you.

[32]Then Moses said, "This is what the LORD has commanded: Fill a two-quart container with manna to preserve it for your descendants. Then later generations will be able to see the food I gave you in the wilderness when I set you free from Egypt." [33]Moses said to Aaron, "Get a jar and fill it with two quarts of manna. Then put it in a sacred place before the LORD to preserve it for all future generations." (Exodus 16:32-33, NLT)

[19]He took some bread and gave thanks to God for it. Then he broke it in pieces and gave it to the

disciples, saying, "This is my body, which is given for you. Do this to remember me."
(Luke 22:19, NLT)

*   *   *   *   *   *   *   *

Read the verses above for a word or phrase that calls to you.

Write down the word or phrase.

Why does this word call to you?

Dialogue with God. Write out your thoughts and His response.

Read the verse(s) again. Rest in silence.

6

Luke 11:8
But I tell you this—though he won't do it for friendship's sake, if you keep knocking long enough, he will get up and give you whatever you need **because of your shameless persistence**.

Beloved: As I sit in my rocking chair looking out my window with the sunlight coming through the maple tree leaves, I enjoy knowing You are here with me. We sit in comfortable silence as I reflect on Your admonition to ask for things with "shameless persistence." That is not comfortable for me. I fear that being a pest will annoy You and end up working against me in the end. There, I've said it.

Lover: Dearest One, don't be afraid. We want the same things, though you do not always know what to want. Prayer and asking is our way of working together. It is a way to strengthen your faith and trust in Me as you see your requests answered. You fear to pray for some issues because they seem too overwhelming. I'm big enough to handle those. Some things seem too small and insignificant to bother Me with. If it touches you, it is significant to Me. Sometimes I may seem unresponsive to your prayers. That's when you need to exercise 'shameless persistence.' These times stretch your faith and help you grow. But in the end, you will receive all that I want to give you, if you keep asking. I promise.

[7]"Ask, and you will receive. Search, and you will find. Knock, and the door will be opened for you. [8]Everyone who asks will receive. The one who searches will find, and for the one who knocks, the door will be opened. [9]"If your child asks you for bread, would any of you give him a stone? [10]Or if your child asks for a fish, would you give him a snake? [11]Even though you're evil, you know how to give good gifts to your children. So how much more will your Father in heaven give good things to those who ask him?
(Matthew 7:7-11 *God's Word*)[iv]

"Do not bring before God small petitions and narrow desires, but remember as high as the heavens are above the earth, so high are His ways above your ways and His thoughts above your thoughts. Ask therefore, after a God-like fashion. Ask for great things because you are before a great throne."   —Charles Hadden Spurgeon[v]

*   *   *   *   *   *   *   *

Read the verses above for a word or phrase that calls to you.

Write down the word or phrase.

Why does this word call to you?

Dialogue with God. Write out your thoughts and His response.

Read the verse(s) again. Rest in silence.

7

Jeremiah 33:9

Then this city will bring me joy, glory, and honor before all the nations of the earth! The people of the world will **see all the good I do for my people**, and they will tremble with awe at the peace and prosperity I provide for them.

Beloved: Father, I don't like to think about my sin or my rebellion because then there's nothing to repent of. But by refusing that first step, I deny You the chance to cleanse me or do any of the other things listed in Scripture. Help me to be willing.

Lover: My precious treasure, you've grown up thinking you needed to be perfect even when you knew you were not. You've been living a lie, and now it is time to be honest, truthful. You are broken. You are sinful. You are rebellious and proud. We've both known it all along, so let's get it in the open so I can wash it clean. Then and only then can I truly bless you.

[9]The Lord isn't really being slow about his promise, as some people think. No, he is being patient for your sake. He does not want anyone to be destroyed, but wants everyone to repent.
(2 Peter 3:9, NLT)

[6]"But now take another look. I'm going to give this city a thorough renovation, working a true healing inside and out. I'm going to show them life whole,

life brimming with blessings. [7]I'll restore everything that was lost to Judah and Jerusalem. I'll build everything back as good as new. [8]I'll scrub them clean from the dirt they've done against me. I'll forgive everything they've done wrong, forgive all their rebellions. [9]And Jerusalem will be a center of joy and praise and glory for all the countries on earth. They'll get reports on all the good I'm doing for her. They'll be in awe of the blessings I am pouring on her.

(Jeremiah 33:6-9, *The Message*)[vi]

*   *   *   *   *   *   *   *

Read the verses above for a word or phrase that
calls to you.

Write down the word or phrase.

Why does this word call to you?

Dialogue with God. Write out your thoughts and
His response.

Read the verse(s) again. Rest in silence.

8

Matthew 6:4, 8

Give your gifts in private, and **your Father, who sees everything**, will reward you .... Don't be like them, for your Father **knows exactly what you need even before you ask him!**

Beloved: What is prayer all about?

Lover: My Child, I see everything and know everything. If that were not true, I would not be God. The point of prayer is to involve you, to let you in on a little of what I'm doing. This experience teaches you about Me and increases your faith and trust in Me. The resulting praise that you offer brings Me glory.

[26]And the Holy Spirit helps us in our weakness. For example, we don't know what God wants us to pray for. But the Holy Spirit prays for us with groanings that cannot be expressed in words. [27]And the Father who knows all hearts knows what the Spirit is saying, for the Spirit pleads for us believers in harmony with God's own will. [28]And we know that God causes everything to work together for the good of those who love God and are called according to his purpose for them.

(Romans 8:26-28, NLT)

*   *   *   *   *   *   *   *

Read the verses above for a word or phrase that calls to you.

Write down the word or phrase.

Why does this word call to you?

Dialogue with God. Write out your thoughts and His response.

Read the verse(s) again. Rest in silence.

9

Psalm 118:1
Give thanks to the LORD, for he is good! **His faithful love endures forever.**

Beloved: Here is my Psalm 118, for You.

Even in times when I've forgotten You,
      Your faithful love endured.
When I've sinned, gone my own selfish way,
      Your faithful love endured.
When I returned to You in repentance,
      Your faithful love endured.
When I went to work for You in my own strength,
      Your faithful love endured.
When I broke under the strain,
      Your faithful love endured.
When I learned to depend on You more,
      Your faithful love endured.
When I returned home to care for my mother in her frailty,
      Your faithful love endured.
When I despaired of having any further impact in the wider world,
      Your faithful love endured.
And as I seek to live out my calling each day,
      Your faithful love endures.

[11]Here is a trustworthy saying: If we died with him, we will also live with him; [12]if we endure, we will also reign with him. If we disown him, he will also

disown us; [13]if we are faithless, he remains faithful,
for he cannot disown himself.
(2 Timothy 2:11-13, NIV)[vii]

*   *   *   *   *   *   *   *

Read the verses above for a word or phrase that calls to you.

Write down the word or phrase.

Why does this word call to you?

Dialogue with God. Write out your thoughts and His response.

Read the verse(s) again. Rest in silence.

10

Matthew 7:7

Keep on asking, and you will receive what you ask for. Keep on seeking, and you will find. Keep on knocking, and the door will be opened to you.

Beloved: What are the things I really want from You? Do I believe You are interested? Are You willing to grant my requests? Am I willing to pursue You about them?

Lover: Remember what you read recently: "Bathe your soul in My Eternal Light. Deepen your soul's unseen attachments to Me in order to safeguard yourself from the world's discouragements." viii When you know Me, My desires become yours. Then you know what to ask for, and I will be pleased to give it in abundance, pressed down and running over.

5LORD, your love reaches to the heavens, your loyalty to the skies. 6Your goodness is as high as the mountains. Your justice is as deep as the great ocean. LORD, you protect both people and animals. 7God, your love is so precious! You protect people in the shadow of your wings. 8They eat the rich food in your house, and you let them drink from your river of pleasure. 9You are the giver of life. Your light lets us enjoy life.
(Psalm 36:5-9, NCV)

*   *   *   *   *   *   *   *

Read the verses above for a word or phrase that calls to you.

Write down the word or phrase.

Why does this word call to you?

Dialogue with God. Write out your thoughts and His response.

Read the verse(s) again. Rest in silence.

11

Luke 7:48

Then Jesus said to the woman, "**Your sins are forgiven**."

Beloved: Lord, I acknowledge that my sins are many and often unowned. I hope to keep them secret, pretending they don't exist and hoping no one will notice them. But You know all, and You know me inside and out. Forgive me, Lord, and as I'm blessed by that forgiveness, help me to love You well.

Lover: Dear One, I long for you to recognize and own your sins so that I can cleanse them and make you whole. I want to free you from that mask of pretense, set you free to be all that I made you to be, and enable you to show your love to Me and all who touch your life.

[1]So now, those who are in Christ Jesus are not judged guilty. [2]Through Christ Jesus the law of the Spirit that brings life made me free from the law that brings sin and death. [3]The law was without power, because the law was made weak by our sinful selves. But God did what the law could not do. He sent his own Son to earth with the same human life that others use for sin. By sending his Son to be an offering to pay for sin, God used a human life to destroy sin. [4]He did this so that we could be the kind of people the law correctly

wants us to be. Now we do not live following our sinful selves, but we live following the Spirit. [5]Those who live following their sinful selves think only about things that their sinful selves want. But those who live following the Spirit are thinking about the things the Spirit wants them to do. [6]If people's thinking is controlled by the sinful self, there is death. But if their thinking is controlled by the Spirit, there is life and peace.
(Romans 8:1-6, NCV)

*   *   *   *   *   *   *   *

Read the verses above for a word or phrase that
calls to you.

Write down the word or phrase.

Why does this word call to you?

Dialogue with God. Write out your thoughts and
His response.

Read the verse(s) again. Rest in silence.

12

Matthew 9:2

Some people brought to him a paralyzed man on a mat. Seeing their faith, Jesus said to the paralyzed man, "**Be encouraged, my child! Your sins are forgiven**."

Beloved: There are more ways to be paralyzed than being unable to use one's hands, arms, or legs. Paralysis in relationships or the inability to express emotions are just as restricting. I may "look" healthy, but inside I am withering away.

Lover: Can you accept the forgiveness I offer? I have forgiven you. Can you forgive yourself? Reach out and receive this forgiveness and be free, unchained from the bonds of guilt, fear of failure or disappointment, and expectations. Be free to be all I mean you to be. Stand up. Move ahead with your life.

9But you are not ruled by your sinful selves. You are ruled by the Spirit, if that Spirit of God really lives in you. But the person who does not have the Spirit of Christ does not belong to Christ. 10Your body will always be dead because of sin. But if Christ is in you, then the Spirit gives you life, because Christ made you right with God. 11God raised Jesus from the dead, and if God's Spirit is living in you, he will also give life to your bodies that die. God is the One who raised Christ from the dead, and he will give life through his Spirit that lives in you. [12]So, my brothers and sisters, we must not be ruled by our sinful selves or live the way our sinful selves want. [13]If you use your lives to do the wrong things your sinful selves want, you will die spiritually. But if you use the Spirit's help to stop doing the wrong things you do with your body, you will have true life. [14]The true children of God are those who let God's Spirit lead them. (Romans 8:9-14, NCV)

*   *   *   *   *   *   *   *

Read the verses above for a word or phrase that calls to you.

Write down the word or phrase.

Why does this word call to you?

Dialogue with God. Write out your thoughts and His response.

Read the verse(s) again. Rest in silence.

13

Song of Songs 2:16
[Young Woman] **My lover is mine, and I am his**.
He browses among the lilies.

Beloved: Can I really be Yours?

Lover: Yes, My love, I am wooing you just as a lover
does through all of the little moments and helpful
reminders that we share, the times we share a joke
or a enjoy sudden inspiration together, the intimate
moments of being in each other's presence—in
silence or in speech, and as we sing songs of praise
and love to each other. In those moments you learn
to be loved and to love. Let me fill that hole in your
heart. Let me teach you of unconditional love.

9You've captured my heart, dear friend. You looked
at me, and I fell in love. One look my way and I was
hopelessly in love! 10How beautiful your love, dear,
dear friend—far more pleasing than a fine, rare
wine, your fragrance more exotic than select
spices. 11The kisses of your lips are honey, my love,
every syllable you speak a delicacy to savor. Your
clothes smell like the wild outdoors, the ozone
scent of high mountains. 12Dear lover and friend,
you're a secret garden, a private and pure
fountain. (Song of Songs 4:9-12, *The Message*)

"Christ is near to you in ties of relationship. Christ is dear to you in bonds of marriage, and you are precious to Him. He grasps both of your hands with both of His, saying 'My sister, my spouse.' Remember these two firm grips that enable your Lord to get a double hold on you that He cannot and will not ever let you go. Beloved, do not be slow to return His sacred love."

—Charles Hadden Spurgeon[ix]

*   *   *   *   *   *   *   *

Read the verses above for a word or phrase that calls to you.

Write down the word or phrase.

Why does this word call to you?

Dialogue with God. Write out your thoughts and His response.

Read the verse(s) again. Rest in silence.

14

Acts 10:36

This is the message of Good News for the people of Israel—that **there is peace with God through Jesus Christ, who is Lord of all.**

Lover: Dear One, your Lover is not weak like you. No, I am Lord of all, and I have a special place in relation to God the Father. Because of My death on the cross to pay for your sins, I can bring you into God's presence in peace. You have no need to fear. I have overcome and have chosen you. The cost I paid to be in this powerful position was great. It is not to be taken lightly. Forgiveness costs.

9I pulled you in from all over the world, called you in from every dark corner of the earth, telling you, 'You're my servant, serving on my side. I've picked you. I haven't dropped you.' 10Don't panic. I'm with you. There's no need to fear for I'm your God. I'll give you strength. I'll help you. I'll hold you steady, keep a firm grip on you. 13 Because I, your God, have a firm grip on you and I'm not letting go. I'm telling you, 'Don't panic. I'm right here to help you.' (Isaiah 41:9-10, 13, *The Message*)

*   *   *   *   *   *   *   *

Read the verses above for a word or phrase that calls to you.

Write down the word or phrase.

Why does this word call to you?

Dialogue with God. Write out your thoughts and His response.

Read the verse(s) again. Rest in silence.

15

Matthew 14:31
Jesus immediately reached out and grabbed him.
"**You have so little faith. Why did you doubt
me?**"

Lover: Have I ever let you down?
Beloved: No.
Lover: Do you remember a challenge I gave you that
was fulfilled completely?
Beloved: Yes, many.
Lover: What big challenge are you wrestling with
now?
Beloved: One that seems to be overwhelming me.
Lover: Did I give you a plan?
Beloved: Yes.
Lover: Isn't that like telling Peter, "Yes, come?"
Beloved: Yes.
Lover: Indeed there are waves and strong winds,
but your focus needs to stay on Me, not on them. As
I told John, what I do with others is not your
concern. You follow Me! Take courage. I am here.

[17]"The poor and homeless are desperate for water,
their tongues parched and no water to be found.
But *I'm* there to be found, I'm there for them, and I,
God of Israel, will not leave them thirsty. [18]I'll open
up rivers for them on the barren hills, spout
fountains in the valleys. I'll turn the baked-clay
badlands into a cool pond, the waterless waste
into splashing creeks. [19]I'll plant the red cedar in
that treeless wasteland, also acacia, myrtle, and

olive. I'll place the cypress in the desert, with plenty of oaks and pines. [20]Everyone will see this. No one can miss it— unavoidable, indisputable evidence that I, God, personally did this. It's created and signed by The Holy of Israel. (Isaiah 41:17-20, *The Message*)

*   *   *   *   *   *   *   *

Read the verses above for a word or phrase that
calls to you.

Write down the word or phrase.

Why does this word call to you?

Dialogue with God. Write out your thoughts and
His response.

Read the verse(s) again. Rest in silence.

16

Colossians 1:11-12

We also pray that you will be strengthened with all his glorious power so you will have all the endurance and patience you need. **May you be filled with joy, always thanking the Father.**

Beloved: These represent the two areas I wanted to work on this year: recognizing my emotions and expressing gratitude. You are helping me with both. Thank You.

Lover: Yes, the emotional barrier is eroding away. If it disappeared too quickly, you wouldn't know how to handle it, so it is coming apart bit by bit. Keep as a goal to express your gratitude. People are blessed to hear praise and sincere thanks. And it is good for you, too, to give them. These are important signs of growth. Be encouraged. I'm still at work in you.

21All the Israelites present in Jerusalem celebrated the Passover (Feast of Unraised Bread) for seven days, celebrated exuberantly. The Levites and priests praised God day after day, filling the air with praise sounds of percussion and brass. 22Hezekiah commended the Levites for the superb way in which they had led the people in the worship of God. When the feast and festival—that glorious seven days of worship, the making of offerings, and the praising of God, the God of their ancestors—were over, the tables cleared and the floors swept, [23]they all decided to keep going for another seven days! So they just kept on celebrating, and as joyfully as they began. (2 Chronicles 30: 21-23, *The Message*)

*   *   *   *   *   *   *   *

Read the verses above for a word or phrase that
calls to you.

Write down the word or phrase.

Why does this word call to you?

Dialogue with God. Write out your thoughts and
His response.

Read the verse(s) again. Rest in silence.

17

John 5:7
"**I can't, sir**," the sick man said…

John 5:10
They said to the man who was cured, "**You can't**
work on the Sabbath! The law doesn't allow you to
carry that sleeping mat!"

Beloved: Shepherd, You are dealing with me
differently from others. You treat each person
according to individual need, and in ways that each
one can relate to. Even so, I hear myself saying,
"This can't be real. It won't last." I'm already
preparing for rejection and abandonment. Then
others imply, if not say, "You can't know God like
that!" But I do, and it is wonderful, and I yearn to
know and love You more.

Lover: I won't abandon you, for I have promised
never to forsake you. Don't abandon me either. For
I love our times together. You have much to learn of
love and trust and openness. You've seen that you
CAN. Now it is time to act on what you know.

[15]"If you love me, obey my commandments. [16]And I
will ask the Father, and he will give you another
Advocate, who will never leave you. [17]He is the Holy
Spirit, who leads into all truth. The world cannot
receive him, because it isn't looking for him and
doesn't recognize him. But you know him, because he
lives with you now and later will be in you. [18]No, I

will not abandon you as orphans—I will come to you. [19]Soon the world will no longer see me, but you will see me. Since I live, you also will live. [20]When I am raised to life again, you will know that I am in my Father, and you are in me, and I am in you. [21]Those who accept my commandments and obey them are the ones who love me. And because they love me, my Father will love them. And I will love them and reveal myself to each of them."
(John 14:15-21, NLT)

*   *   *   *   *   *   *   *

Read the verses above for a word or phrase that calls to you.

Write down the word or phrase.

Why does this word call to you?

Dialogue with God. Write out your thoughts and His response.

Read the verse(s) again. Rest in silence.

18
Psalm 133:1
How wonderful and pleasant it is when brothers live together in harmony.

Beloved: I'm feeling at odds with the community here. I want to leave them and do my own thing. Is that wrong?

Lover: If you opt out of the community in which you live, how can you be My voice? There are relatively few on earth who listen to Me, and many who seek their own paths. Yes, you will be moving on soon, but for now you are here, and you have a role to play. Harmony doesn't mean everyone agrees all the time. It means people treat each other with respect and agree not to let the disagreements destroy relationships. You may agree to disagree and still live in harmony. Respect for others is key. Just as different notes are in a chord, they can blend to make a rich, beautiful sound. To accomplish this effect requires three or more different sounds. Sometimes we fail to hear the beauty until there is a resolution of a disharmony. Then we appreciate the resulting beauty all the more.

[42]They spent their time learning the apostles' teaching, sharing, breaking bread, and praying together. [43]The apostles were doing many miracles and signs, and everyone felt great respect for God. [44]All the believers were together and shared everything. [45]They would sell their land and the

things they owned and then divide the money and give it to anyone who needed it. 46The believers met together in the Temple every day. They ate together in their homes, happy to share their food with joyful hearts. 47They praised God and were liked by all the people. Every day the Lord added those who were being saved to the group of believers.
(Acts 2:42-47, NCV)

*   *   *   *   *   *   *   *

Read the verses above for a word or phrase that calls to you.

Write down the word or phrase.

Why does this word call to you?

Dialogue with God. Write out your thoughts and His response.

Read the verse(s) again. Rest in silence.

19

Matthew 9:29

Then he touched their eyes and said, "**Because of your faith it will happen**."

Lover: Do you believe I'm going to take care of you?

Beloved: Yes. You have been faithful to me for many years. I believe, and yet sometimes I doubt. Help me not to doubt You!

Lover: I honor even a mustard seed of faith. It pleases Me that you are growing in relationship and in love. Your doubts come when you try to use your limited knowledge to figure out how I will do it. It looks impossible, like Peter on the stormy sea, so you doubt. Keep your eyes only on Me! Follow My instructions to the letter, and then you will see great and mighty things you could never have imagined.

Beloved: I'm glad my part of this is simple. Help me to be faithful to You!

[14]At the bottom of the mountain, they were met by a crowd of waiting people. As they approached, a man came out of the crowd and fell to his knees begging, [15]"Master, have mercy on my son. He goes out of his mind and suffers terribly, falling into seizures. Frequently he is pitched into the fire, other times into the river. [16]I brought him to your disciples, but they could do nothing for him."

[17]Jesus said, "What a generation! No sense of God! No focus to your lives! How many times do I have to go over these things? How much longer do I have to put up with this? Bring the boy here." [18]He ordered the afflicting demon out—and it was out, gone. From that moment on the boy was well. [19]When the disciples had Jesus off to themselves, they asked, "Why couldn't we throw it out?" [20]"Because you're not yet taking *God* seriously," said Jesus. "The simple truth is that if you had a mere kernel of faith, a poppy seed, say, you would tell this mountain, 'Move!' and it would move. There is nothing you wouldn't be able to tackle." (Matthew 17:14-20, *The Message*)

*   *   *   *   *   *   *   *

Read the verses above for a word or phrase that calls to you.

Write down the word or phrase.

Why does this word call to you?

Dialogue with God. Write out your thoughts and His response.

Read the verse(s) again. Rest in silence.

20

Luke 17:14
He looked at them and said, "Go show yourselves
to the priests." **As they went**, they were cleansed
of their leprosy.

Beloved: They weren't healed, and then told to go,
they had to start out as they were, and then the
healing came. I went to a meeting recently and felt
the disharmony and tension. It made me feel
rejected because I didn't agree with the majority. I
guess because my plans are being frustrated on
several fronts, I just feel in limbo. I hate that feeling.

Lover: Things will not always be as they are now.
You need to keep preparing for the direction I have
given you. Sometimes it is painful and emotional
and time-consuming. Be faithful and keep moving.
As you go, the rest will be revealed. You've seen Me
work like this before. You know the drill. Be
thankful and it will bring your heart to a place of
peace.

12"I still have many things to tell you, but you can't
handle them now. 13But when the Friend comes,
the Spirit of the Truth, he will take you by the hand
and guide you into all the truth there is. He won't
draw attention to himself, but will make sense out
of what is about to happen and, indeed, out of all
that I have done and said. 14He will honor me; he
will take from me and deliver it to you.

[15]Everything the Father has is also mine. That is why I've said, 'He takes from me and delivers to you.'
(John 16:12-15, *The Message*)

*   *   *   *   *   *   *   *

Read the verses above for a word or phrase that
calls to you.

Write down the word or phrase.

Why does this word call to you?

Dialogue with God. Write out your thoughts and
His response.

Read the verse(s) again. Rest in silence.

20

Psalm 32:2

What joy for those whose record the Lord has cleared of guilt, whose lives are lived in complete honesty!

Beloved: Father, I spend a lot of time trying to solve the issues of my life. I acknowledge my sin, my independent spirit, and my frustration. You have shown me that You have solutions to all my problems, however difficult, that will satisfy my needs. Help me to follow through on these plans and actions in Your time. Your forgiveness will also be part of my healing.

Lover: I take you as you are, not as you or I would want you to be. I don't leave you as I found you, but I don't overwhelm you to change faster than you can. Be patient with yourself and with others.

Beloved: I heard a song yesterday:
"Pray for what you want.
Trust Him for what you get.
Thank God for what you got.
He'll cause you to want what you need."
(Author Unknown)

[1]Brothers and sisters, in view of all we have just shared about God's compassion, I encourage you to offer your bodies as living sacrifices, dedicated to God and pleasing to him. This kind of worship is appropriate for you. [2]Don't become like the people

of this world. Instead, change the way you think. Then you will always be able to determine what God really wants—what is good, pleasing, and perfect. 3Because of the kindness that God has shown me, I ask you not to think of yourselves more highly than you should. Instead, your thoughts should lead you to use good judgment based on what God has given each of you as believers.
(Romans 12:1-3, *God's Word*)

*   *   *   *   *   *   *   *

Read the verses above for a word or phrase that
calls to you.

Write down the word or phrase.

Why does this word call to you?

Dialogue with God. Write out your thoughts and
His response.

Read the verse(s) again. Rest in silence.

22

Mark 1:15

"The time promised by God has come at last!" he announced. "The Kingdom of God is near! **Repent** of your sins and believe the Good News!"

Beloved: Father, I haven't thanked You or many others of late. I choke on the words. Open my heart and my mouth. I don't like to admit sin because that is admitting weakness and failure. But I am weak, and I have failed, and I am afraid.

Lover: Believe the good news. There is help, hope, and forgiveness. Experience it and share it. I love you as you are and see you as you will be.

1Since we have been made right with God by our faith, we have peace with God. This happened through our Lord Jesus Christ, 2who has brought us into that blessing of God's grace that we now enjoy. And we are happy because of the hope we have of sharing God's glory. 3We also have joy with our troubles, because we know that these troubles produce patience. 4And patience produces character, and character produces hope. 5And this hope will never disappoint us, because God has poured out his love to fill our hearts. He gave us his love through the Holy Spirit, whom God has given to us.
(Romans 5:1-5, NCV)

"Repentance...requires two things: humility and trust. Repentance requires the humility involved in the confession that I am a sinner, one whose life is not whole and who lacks the power both to find either the direction to wholeness or the resources for wholeness on my own. Repentance requires trust in a power that can and will ultimately sustain and establish me if I let go of myself into that power's hands. Without both trust and humility, repentance is impossible."

—Craig R. Dykstra[x]

*   *   *   *   *   *   *   *

Read the verses above for a word or phrase that calls to you.

Write down the word or phrase.

Why does this word call to you?

Dialogue with God. Write out your thoughts and His response.

Read the verse(s) again. Rest in silence.

23

Luke 5:32

"**I have come to call** not those who think they are righteous, but **those who know they are sinners and need to repent**."

Beloved: Lord, I feel such a failure. I cannot bring myself to confront those with whom I disagree, to stand up for a position, or to take a side. My mind changes like quicksilver.

Lover: Change is a slow and often painful process, but if you look back, you will see there is change. I'm patient and enduring. I will not stop the process until you are perfected in My kingdom. Let Me have My way within you, and in the end you will be free like a bird released from a cage. Hope in Me.

[15]God wants us to grow up, to know the whole truth and tell it in love—like Christ in everything. We take our lead from Christ, who is the source of everything we do. [16]He keeps us in step with each other. His very breath and blood flow through us, nourishing us so that we will grow up healthy in God, robust in love.
(Ephesians 4:14-15, *The Message*)

*   *   *   *   *   *   *   *

Read the verses above for a word or phrase that calls to you.

Write down the word or phrase.

Why does this word call to you?

Dialogue with God. Write out your thoughts and His response.

Read the verse(s) again. Rest in silence.

24

Luke 24:45

Then he opened their minds to understand the Scriptures.

Beloved: I read, but the meaning and significance of the familiar words fail to register in my mind or heart or actions. I need You to open my mind to hear. Help me understand Your heart. Break my heart over my own hardness and indifference and the brokenness of the world in which I live.

Lover: There is forgiveness of sins for all who repent. You are a witness to this. You have been forgiven much. Remember the grace shown to you and extend grace to others still on the way.

[30]Don't grieve God. Don't break his heart. His Holy Spirit, moving and breathing in you, is the most intimate part of your life, making you fit for himself. Don't take such a gift for granted. [31]Make a clean break with all cutting, backbiting, profane talk. [32]Be gentle with one another, sensitive. Forgive one another as quickly and thoroughly as God in Christ forgave you. (Ephesians 4:30-32, *The Message*)

*   *   *   *   *   *   *   *

Read the verses above for a word or phrase that
calls to you.

Write down the word or phrase.

Why does this word call to you?

Dialogue with God. Write out your thoughts and
His response.

Read the verse(s) again. Rest in silence.

25

Acts 2:38

Peter replied, "Each of you must repent of your sins and turn to God, and be baptized in the name of Jesus Christ **for the forgiveness of your sins**. Then you will receive the gift of the Holy Spirit.

Lover: I can give forgiveness, but you must receive it. It's one thing to go through baptism as a sign of this forgiveness, but then to live it out, to live as a forgiven and dearly loved child, well, that is another thing. And that is an important point essential to the freedom, joy, and relationship I am offering. Live out forgiveness. Receive it and give it. That is My way. Walk in it.

4When people work, their wages are not a gift, but something they have earned. 5But people are counted as righteous, not because of their work, but because of their faith in God who forgives sinners. 6David also spoke of this when he described the happiness of those who are declared righteous without working for it: 7"Oh, what joy for those whose disobedience is forgiven, whose sins are put out of sight. 8 Yes, what joy for those whose record the LORD has cleared of sin." (Romans 4:4-8, NLT)

*   *   *   *   *   *   *   *

Read the verses above for a word or phrase that calls to you.

Write down the word or phrase.

Why does this word call to you?

Dialogue with God. Write out your thoughts and His response.

Read the verse(s) again. Rest in silence.

26

Mark 6:34 **Jesus** saw the huge crowd as he stepped from the boat, and he **had compassion on them because they were like sheep without a shepherd**. So he began teaching them many things.

Beloved: Lord, so often I harden my heart and hold on to my resources without compassion for the needs of others. Forgive me for closing my heart. Help me have the sense to know when and how much to give.

Lover: There are many needs in the world, and you cannot possibly meet them all. But there are needs that you can meet with individuals and situations of which I make you aware. Meet those and let Me handle the rest.

[6]Remember this—a farmer who plants only a few seeds will get a small crop. But the one who plants generously will get a generous crop. [7]You must each decide in your heart how much to give. And don't give reluctantly or in response to pressure. "For God loves a person who gives cheerfully." [8]And God will generously provide all you need. Then you will always have everything you need and plenty left over to share with others. [9]As the Scriptures say, "They share freely and give generously to the poor. Their good deeds will be remembered forever."
(2 Corinthians 9:6-9, NLT)

*   *   *   *   *   *   *   *

Read the verses above for a word or phrase that calls to you.

Write down the word or phrase.

Why does this word call to you?

Dialogue with God. Write out your thoughts and His response.

Read the verse(s) again. Rest in silence.

27

Matthew 9:36
When he saw the crowds, **he had compassion on them because they were confused and helpless** like sheep without a shepherd.

Beloved: Lord, I often feel confused and helpless. Those I serve sometimes feel the same way. Friends I share with, as well as family, also seem to be floundering. Thank You that in Your mercy, You respond with compassion, not accusation or reproach.

Lover: Yes, I see the struggle and floundering in a sea of problems and indecision. I do have compassion and reach out to others and to you. Take the hand I offer; let Me lead you to the path of peace. I have a plan for you, a purpose and a clear direction. Having floundered, you will have compassion for others and can help lead them into paths of security, confidence, and the joy of living in My love.

8 The LORD is good and decent. That is why he teaches sinners the way they should live. 9 He leads humble people to do what is right, and he teaches them his way. 10 Every path of the LORD is one of mercy and truth for those who cling to his promise and written instructions.
(Psalm 25:8-10, *God's Word*)

*   *   *   *   *   *   *   *

Read the verses above for a word or phrase that calls to you.

Write down the word or phrase.

Why does this word call to you?

Dialogue with God. Write out your thoughts and His response.

Read the verse(s) again. Rest in silence.

28

Isaiah 61:3

To all who mourn in Israel, he will give a crown of beauty for ashes, a joyous blessing instead of mourning, festive praise instead of despair. In their righteousness, they will be like **great oaks that the Lord has planted for his own glory.**

Beloved: I can feel the fear and the attack of the enemy in me as I prepare for a difficult meeting today. Lord, may Your name be honored and glorified and Your purposes accomplished.

Lover: My perspective and goals are so much larger than yours, but as you open up to Me and allow Me to work in and through you, you get to share in the process and thus in the outcome. My involvement in the world's affairs brings Me glory. As you work toward fulfilling My goals, you also bring Me glory. Do not fear. Keep your eyes on Me. Together we are unbeatable.

[21]Then Moses stretched out his hand over the sea. All that night the LORD pushed back the sea with a strong east wind and turned the sea into dry ground. The water divided, [22]and the Israelites went through the middle of the sea on dry ground. The water stood like a wall on their right and on their left. [29]Meanwhile, the Israelites had gone through the sea on dry ground while the water stood like a wall on their right and on their left. [30]That day the LORD saved Israel from the Egyptians, and Israel saw the Egyptians lying dead

on the seashore. [31]When the Israelites saw the great power the LORD had used against the Egyptians, they feared the LORD and believed in him and in his servant Moses.
(Exodus 14: 21-22, 29-31, *God's Word*)

*   *   *   *   *   *   *   *

Read the verses above for a word or phrase that calls to you.

Write down the word or phrase.

Why does this word call to you?

Dialogue with God. Write out your thoughts and His response.

Read the verse(s) again. Rest in silence.

29

Isaiah 61:8, 9
I will faithfully reward my people for their
suffering and make an everlasting covenant with
them. Their descendants will be recognized and
honored among the nations. Everyone will realize
that **they are a people the Lord has blessed**.

Lover: Hard times often seem to be a punishment.
But from My perspective, these are significant
times of growth and the development of character.
Seen in this light, these are times of great blessing.
Since I have promised never to leave or forsake you,
know that even in the most difficult times, I'm there,
and you are loved.

2Remember how the LORD your God led you
through the wilderness for these forty years,
humbling you and testing you to prove your
character, and to find out whether or not you
would obey his commands. 3Yes, he humbled you
by letting you go hungry and then feeding you with
manna, a food previously unknown to you and
your ancestors. He did it to teach you that people
do not live by bread alone; rather, we live by every
word that comes from the mouth of the LORD. 4For
all these forty years your clothes didn't wear out,
and your feet didn't blister or swell. 5Think about
it: Just as a parent disciplines a child, the LORD
your God disciplines you for your own good.
(Deuteronomy 8:2-5, NLT)

"God invests time and energy in each one of us,
knowing each one of us is unique and infinitely
valuable."   —Mary Lou Redding[xi]

*   *   *   *   *   *   *   *

Read the verses above for a word or phrase that
calls to you.

Write down the word or phrase.

Why does this word call to you?

Dialogue with God. Write out your thoughts and
His response.

Read the verse(s) again. Rest in silence.

30

Luke 7:13

When the Lord saw her, his heart overflowed with compassion. "Don't cry!" he said.

Beloved: Lord, when I hear of disasters and heartbreaking situations, I feel a moment of compassion and then harden my heart. I can't help all, so I end up helping almost none.

Lover: Even when I walked the earth, I couldn't rescue everyone. I moved around to help many, but people became ill and died after I left a place or before I arrived. That's why the Holy Spirit had to come, to be in many places at once—and for the body of Christ—the church—to be My hands and feet. Listen to My promptings, and I'll show you where to act and what to do.

2Stoop down and reach out to those who are oppressed. Share their burdens, and so complete Christ's law. 3If you think you are too good for that, you are badly deceived. 4Make a careful exploration of who you are and the work you have been given, and then sink yourself into that. Don't be impressed with yourself. Don't compare yourself with others. 5Each of you must take responsibility for doing the creative best you can with your own life 8.... But the one who plants in response to God, letting God's Spirit do the growth work in him, harvests a crop of real life, eternal life.

[9]So let's not allow ourselves to get fatigued doing good. At the right time we will harvest a good crop if we don't give up, or quit. [10]Right now, therefore, every time we get the chance, let us work for the benefit of all, starting with the people closest to us in the community of faith.

(Galatians 6:2-5, 8b-10, *The Message*)

*   *   *   *   *   *   *   *

Read the verses above for a word or phrase that calls to you.

Write down the word or phrase.

Why does this word call to you?

Dialogue with God. Write out your thoughts and His response.

Read the verse(s) again. Rest in silence.

31

Matthew 14:19
Then he told the people to sit down on the grass.
Jesus took the five loaves and two fish, looked up
toward heaven, and blessed them. Then, **breaking
the bread into pieces, he gave the bread** to the
disciples, who distributed it to the people.

Lover: Sharing bread usually requires breaking. It
is in the breaking that the miracle occurs; the
boundaries are changed. The weakness and
inadequacy is clear. But at this vulnerable moment,
the power of God comes in and supplies needs
vaster and greater than any imagined.

[8]Make me hear sounds of joy and gladness; let the
bones you crushed be happy again. [9]Turn your face
from my sins and wipe out all my guilt. [10]Create in
me a pure heart, God, and make my spirit right
again. [11]Do not send me away from you or take
your Holy Spirit away from me. [12]Give me back the
joy of your salvation. Keep me strong by giving me
a willing spirit. [13]Then I will teach your ways to
those who do wrong, and sinners will turn back to
you.
(Psalm 51:8-13, NCV)

*   *   *   *   *   *   *   *

Read the verses above for a word or phrase that calls to you.

Write down the word or phrase.

Why does this word call to you?

Dialogue with God. Write out your thoughts and His response.

Read the verse(s) again. Rest in silence.

32

Mark 6:52

. . . for **they didn't understand the significance** of the miracle of the loaves. **Their hearts were too hard to take it in**.

Beloved: The disciples were where they were told to be, trying to do as instructed; but the forces of nature were against them. There's no evidence that they had cried out for Jesus to help them, so they were doing the right task in their own strength. When Jesus showed up, the disciples were more terrified – not relieved. In spite of this fear, Jesus calms the storm, amazing the disciples. They still "didn't understand the significance of the miracle of the loaves. Their hearts were too hard to take it in."

What significance? What should we understand? Jesus is Lord over ALL. Nothing is beyond his power.

Lord, soften my hard heart. Help me understand and take in what You are doing in the hard and sad times of my life.

Lover: Look for Me in the hard times. Call out to Me, for I am with you. I've promised never to leave you or forsake you. I'm faithful, and I never break My promise. Don't be afraid. Take courage. I am here!

[23]Some went off to sea in ships, plying the trade routes of the world. [24]They, too, observed the LORD's power in action, his impressive works on the deepest seas. [25]He spoke, and the winds rose, stirring up the waves. [26]Their ships were tossed to the heavens and plunged again to the depths; the sailors cringed in terror. [27]They reeled and staggered like drunkards and were at their wits' end. [28]"LORD, help!" they cried in their trouble, and he saved them from their distress. [29]He calmed the storm to a whisper and stilled the waves. [30]What a blessing was that stillness as he brought them safely into harbor! [31]Let them praise the LORD for his great love and for the wonderful things he has done for them.
(Psalm 107:23-31, NLT)

*   *   *   *   *   *   *   *

Read the verses above for a word or phrase that calls to you.

Write down the word or phrase.

Why does this word call to you?

Dialogue with God. Write out your thoughts and His response.

Read the verse(s) again. Rest in silence.

33

Acts 8:4

The believers who were scattered preached the Good News about Jesus wherever they went.

Beloved: As a result of their new faith, these peoples' lives were totally disrupted. They lost homes, possessions, and in some cases, freedom. They lost all except their message, and, as a result, many who might not have heard for a long time actually came to faith. Our inconvenience may be just the tool You need to fulfill Your greater purpose. Lord, help me to be willing to be Your faithful messenger, regardless of my situation.

Lover: I made you the way you are, so you were perfectly prepared to take on certain tasks and roles that no one else could. Some of your abilities need honing and purifying, but you are who you need to be. Enjoy getting to know yourself and discovering all that I have for you.

4But because of his great love for us, God, who is rich in mercy, 5made us alive with Christ even when we were dead in transgressions—it is by grace you have been saved. 6And God raised us up with Christ and seated us with him in the heavenly realms in Christ Jesus, 7in order that in the coming ages he might show the incomparable riches of his grace, expressed in his kindness to us in Christ Jesus. 8For it is by grace you have been saved,

through faith—and this not from yourselves, it is the gift of God— [9]not by works, so that no one can boast. [10]For we are God's workmanship, created in Christ Jesus to do good works, which God prepared in advance for us to do.
(Ephesians 2: 4-10, NIV)

*   *   *   *   *   *   *   *

Read the verses above for a word or phrase that
calls to you.

Write down the word or phrase.

Why does this word call to you?

Dialogue with God. Write out your thoughts and
His response.

Read the verse(s) again. Rest in silence.

34
Philippians 2:13
**God is working in you, giving you the desire
and power to do what pleases him!**

Lover: On this day, celebrating your birth, it is My
delight to be at work in your life, helping you to
want to please Me and giving you the power to do
what pleases Me. This is My gift to you, and
watching you use My gifts today and each day will
also add to My joy and delight.

Beloved: Thank You, Shepherd, for being my Lover
and my Friend. I'm so glad I took time to listen to
You today and each day up to now. Your words
meet the deepest needs of my soul.

And you will be given a new name by the LORD's
own mouth. 3 The LORD will hold you in his hand
for all to see— a splendid crown in the hand of
God. 4 Never again will you be called "The
Forsaken City" or "The Desolate Land." Your new
name will be "The City of God's Delight" and "The
Bride of God," for the LORD delights in you and
will claim you as his bride.
(Isaiah 62:2b-4, NLT)

"My soul dances in delight for God has visited me
with unspeakable promise, which God alone can
perform."   —N. Shawchuck and R. P. Job[xii]

*   *   *   *   *   *   *   *

Read the verses above for a word or phrase that calls to you.

Write down the word or phrase.

Why does this word call to you?

Dialogue with God. Write out your thoughts and His response.

Read the verse(s) again. Rest in silence.

35

Matthew 14:27
But Jesus spoke to them at once. "Don't be afraid,"
he said. "Take courage. I am here."

Beloved: You certainly were 'here' for me yesterday.
Upon request Your presence chased away my fears
and returned me to my more normal, calm self. The
change was dramatic; Your power and authority
were very clear. Your love for me and response to
me were precious.

Lover: You've heard of My power and love. Now you
have experienced it. Call upon Me, and I will be near
to aid and strengthen you. You are My precious one,
and I will never abandon you. When fears come, call
and don't doubt. I'm present.

[1] Then Job answered the LORD: [2]"I know that you
can do all things and that no plan of yours can be
ruined. [3]You asked, 'Who is this that made my
purpose unclear by saying things that are not
true?' Surely I spoke of things I did not
understand; I talked of things too wonderful for
me to know. [4]You said, 'Listen now, and I will
speak. I will ask you questions, and you must
answer me.' [5]My ears had heard of you before, but
now my eyes have seen you.
(Job 42:1-5, NCV)

*   *   *   *   *   *   *   *

Read the verses above for a word or phrase that calls to you.

Write down the word or phrase.

Why does this word call to you?

Dialogue with God. Write out your thoughts and His response.

Read the verse(s) again. Rest in silence.

36

Luke 24: 31

Suddenly, their eyes were opened, and **they recognized him**. And at that moment he disappeared!

Lover: Yes, My child, I'm always with you. I never leave or forsake you, but sometimes your eyes are closed to My presence, your heart hard or your fears too great. Even so, I am present, guiding, loving, and protecting you. Keep your heart open and you will see Me!

[15]Early in the morning a servant of the Holy Man got up and went out. Surprise! Horses and chariots surrounding the city! The young man exclaimed, "Oh, master! What shall we do?" [16]He said, "Don't worry about it—there are more on our side than on their side." [17]Then Elisha prayed, "O God, open his eyes and let him see." The eyes of the young man were opened and he saw. A wonder! The whole mountainside full of horses and chariots of fire surrounding Elisha!

(2 Kings 6: 13-17, *The Message*)

*   *   *   *   *   *   *   *

Read the verses above for a word or phrase that calls to you.

Write down the word or phrase.

Why does this word call to you?

Dialogue with God. Write out your thoughts and His response.

Read the verse(s) again. Rest in silence.

37

1 Thessalonians 1:3

As we pray to our God and Father about you, we think of **your faithful work, your loving deeds and the enduring hope you have because of our Lord Jesus Christ.**

Lover: "These are My gifts to you and likewise your gifts to Me. You need work to challenge you to greater things. Your faithfulness in that work honors Me. Your loving deeds bless your family, friends and colleagues. The loving attitude is a testimony of My work in you, and so honors Me. Faith in My promises brings hope, and as you cling to that hope, you endure. It is My joy to not only promise, but give you the kingdom."

3As Moses went up to meet God, God called down to him from the mountain: "Speak to the House of Jacob, tell the People of Israel: 4'You have seen what I did to Egypt and how I carried you on eagles' wings and brought you to me. 5If you will listen obediently to what I say and keep my covenant, out of all peoples you'll be my special treasure. The whole Earth is mine to choose from, 6but you're special: a kingdom of priests, a holy nation.' "This is what I want you to tell the people of Israel."

(Exodus 19: 3-6, *The Message*)

*   *   *   *   *   *   *   *

Read the verses above for a word or phrase that calls to you.

Write down the word or phrase.

Why does this word call to you?

Dialogue with God. Write out your thoughts and His response.

Read the verse(s) again. Rest in silence.

38

Philippians 3:3

For we who worship by the Spirit of God are the ones who are truly circumcised. We rely on what Christ Jesus has done for us. **We put no confidence in human effort**.

Beloved: Father, yesterday felt like a disaster. My weakness was very evident, and at the end of the day, I was tired and discouraged. Help me rely more on You today.

Lover: Sometimes you need to feel your humanness to realize how much you need and depend on Me. As you saw, not much really went wrong; just the delays and frustrations made the day seem wrong. Nothing is wasted in My economy. These lessons are valuable and help make your faith more robust. Trust Me. Press on to reach the end of the race!

11May all kings worship him. May all nations serve him. 12He will rescue the needy person who cries for help and the oppressed person who has no one's help. 13He will have pity on the poor and needy and will save the lives of the needy. 14He will rescue them from oppression and violence. Their blood will be precious in his sight.
(Psalm 72:11-14, *God's Word*)

*   *   *   *   *   *   *   *

Read the verses above for a word or phrase that calls to you.

Write down the word or phrase.

Why does this word call to you?

Dialogue with God. Write out your thoughts and His response.

Read the verse(s) again. Rest in silence.

39

Psalm 105:1

Give thanks to the Lord and proclaim his greatness. Let the whole world know what he has done.

Beloved: Shepherd, You have brought me from a depressed, fearful, disorganized person to the well-balanced, calm, hopeful, adventurous, responsible person I am today. I still have my insecurities and moments of despair, but You have been abundantly good to me. Thank You for loving me!

Lover: I work in you as you allow Me. I don't force My will upon you. However, I do put you in circumstances that cause you to cry out to Me so that you learn to do that and find I always answer, for I am never far from you. Sometimes I warn you of dangers on your way so you will avoid them in more critical circumstances later. Take heed. If you will listen to my warnings, you don't have to make serious mistakes. I love you and want only the best for you.

8Thank our God, you nations. Make the sound of his praise heard. 9He has kept us alive and has not allowed us to fall. 10You have tested us, O God. You have refined us in the same way silver is refined. 11You have trapped us in a net. You have laid burdens on our backs.
12You let people ride over our heads. We went through fire and water, but then you brought us out and refreshed us. (Psalm 66:8-12, *God's Word*)

*   *   *   *   *   *   *   *

Read the verses above for a word or phrase that calls to you.

Write down the word or phrase.

Why does this word call to you?

Dialogue with God. Write out your thoughts and His response.

Read the verse(s) again. Rest in silence.

40

Psalm 90:14

Satisfy us each morning with your unfailing love, so we may sing for joy to the end of our lives.

Beloved: Lord, if I can hear from You and be reminded that You are with me each morning, reminded of Your unfailing love, then I can have joy through that day regardless of the pain and disasters that may come. And so, throughout my life, each day needs to be blessed by your love and presence.

Lover: It delights My heart for you to stop each day and to spend time with Me. I have so much for you, but you can take in only a little at a time. So these daily doses are important to strengthen you for what I know is coming. Each day our relationship deepens, our love grows, our hearts break for another issue in the world. In these things I can show you My approval and you will find true success.

[7]We have this treasure from God, but we are like clay jars that hold the treasure. This shows that the great power is from God, not from us . . . . [16]So we do not give up. Our physical body is becoming older and weaker, but our spirit inside us is made new every day. [17]We have small troubles for a while now, but they are helping us gain an eternal glory that is much greater than the troubles. [18]We set our eyes not on what we see but on what we

cannot see. What we see will last only a short time, but what we cannot see will last forever.
(2 Corinthians 4:7, 16-18, NCV)

"In the end it is all about becoming God's picture of me."   —Northumbria Community [xiii]

*   *   *   *   *   *   *   *

Read the verses above for a word or phrase that calls to you.

Write down the word or phrase.

Why does this word call to you?

Dialogue with God. Write out your thoughts and His response.

Read the verse(s) again. Rest in silence.

41

Mark 8:18

"You have eyes—can't you see? You have ears—can't you hear? **Don't you remember anything at all?"**

Beloved: Lord, You have brought me through so many things: depression, destruction, despair, dark times, war, stress, grief. Yes, I've gone into those hard things and come out on the other side into times of joy, light, peace, rest, and love—all by Your love and grace. Help me to remember Your faithfulness and to trust You with each new life challenge.

Lover: Don't you understand yet? I'm Lord of everything! There is nothing outside of My control. I am accomplishing My purposes. You are anxious about many things. Sit at My feet. Learn of My bigger plans and let Me direct your steps. I won't overload you or give you more than you can bear. I know your frailty. Trust Me to do what is best for you and with you.

[1] "This is what the LORD says—the Holy One of Israel, and its Maker: Concerning things to come, do you question me about my children, or give me orders about the work of my hands? [12] It is I who made the earth and created mankind on it. My own hands stretched out the heavens; I marshaled their starry hosts. [13] I will raise up Cyrus in my righteousness: I will make all his ways straight.

He will rebuild my city and set my exiles free, but
not for a price or reward, says the LORD Almighty."
(Isaiah 45:11-13, NIV)

*   *   *   *   *   *   *   *

Read the verses above for a word or phrase that calls to you.

Write down the word or phrase.

Why does this word call to you?

Dialogue with God. Write out your thoughts and His response.

Read the verse(s) again. Rest in silence.

42

Psalm 127:1

Unless the LORD builds a house, the work of the builders is wasted. Unless the LORD protects a city, guarding it with sentries will do no good.

Beloved: In the past weeks I've had a lot of anxious toil as I've been trying to plan a trip and get the house ready to sell. The frustration and stress have been very high. Lord, take off my load, put Yourself in charge, and let me leave the responsibility with You! As a sheep, I am not meant to carry these burdens.

Lover: I long to give you rest. As one of My loved ones, it pains Me to see you struggling with a burden you were never meant to carry. But to put down your burden takes faith and trust. Will you trust Me? Will you believe that what I've promised, I will bring to completion? Run to Me and let Me hold you and carry all your cares.

56"Thanks be to the LORD! He has given his people Israel rest, as he had promised. None of the good promises he made through his servant Moses has failed to come true. 57May the LORD our God be with us as he was with our ancestors. May he never leave us or abandon us. 58May he bend our hearts toward him. Then we will follow him and keep his commands, laws, and rules, which he commanded our ancestors to keep. 59May these words which I have prayed to the LORD be near

the LORD our God day and night. Then he will give me and his people Israel justice every day as it is needed. [60]In this way all the people of the world will know that the LORD is God and there is no other god. [61]May your hearts be committed to the LORD our God. Then you will live by his laws and keep his commands as you have today."
(1 Kings 8:56-61, *God's Word*)

*   *   *   *   *   *   *   *

Read the verses above for a word or phrase that calls to you.

Write down the word or phrase.

Why does this word call to you?

Dialogue with God. Write out your thoughts and His response.

Read the verse(s) again. Rest in silence.

43

John 6:29
Jesus told them, "This is the only work God wants from you: **Believe in the one he has sent**."

Beloved: Shepherd, my mind is running out of control. Fear and anxiety rule me, and I know that is not from You. Deliver me, God, from this attack of the enemy. Deliver me from my fears and doubts. Give me faith and focus on what is true, right, honorable, lovely—all that is of You.

Lover: This is the cry I want to hear from you, asking Me for help. I'm present with you and I am a safe place for you to feel the loss of your home, your loneliness, your grief, your expected loss of someone dear to you. When these emotions pile up inside, anything extra just pushes your stress level over the top. It is okay to 'feel' these things with Me and to let Me hold you and comfort you, for I love you dearly, precious one.

The LORD is my rock and my fortress and my Savior, 3my God, my rock in whom I take refuge, my shield, the strength of my salvation, my stronghold, my refuge, and my Savior who saved me from violence. 4 The LORD should be praised. I called on him, and I was saved from my enemies. 7 I called on the LORD in my distress. I called to my God for help. He heard my voice from his temple, and my cry for help reached his ears.

[17] He reached down from high above and took hold of me. He pulled me out of the raging water. (2 Samuel 22: 2b-4, 7, 17, *God's Word*)

*   *   *   *   *   *   *   *

Read the verses above for a word or phrase that calls to you.

Write down the word or phrase.

Why does this word call to you?

Dialogue with God. Write out your thoughts and His response.

Read the verse(s) again. Rest in silence.

44

Philippians 4:18

At the moment **I have all I need, and more**! I am generously supplied with the gifts you sent me with Epaphroditus. They are a sweet-smelling sacrifice that is acceptable and pleasing to God.

Beloved: Thank You, Lord, for my home and all the things in it. Thank You for family and the precious times of sharing and wise counsel. I am grieving loss and putting great pressure on myself. Free me from placing myself in bondage. Let me experience Your freedom and comfort. Let me enjoy and appreciate the memories attached to the things I own. Help me to be grateful and thankful.

Lover: You need to see what and why your things are important to you. Letting go is a process and one not to be rushed. It is more important to learn about yourself than to actually divest yourself of your things. This lesson has been painful but important. Learn it and store it. Grow. Be assured of My love for you throughout this process. I never leave you or forsake you.

Cry of the Beloved

Dam bursts
Tears flow
Quiet moans of agony
Panting gasps to fill the lungs
Deprived of oxygen

Great wet drops fall
As years of pent up emotion
Are at last released.

Negative feelings must be left unsaid—
No anger, no sorrow, no pity—
UNACCEPTABLE! INTOLERABLE!
But instead ignore these,
Hold them in close, unseen.

But they will be free
Or else they'll destroy me.
Sometimes ripping their way
Out of my chest and
Landing like a rocket on
Some unsuspecting soul.

More often, in quiet unbidden moments
The tears flow, the body seizes
And squeezes out the painful ooze.
The infected pus of long-held guilt
And hurt must be expelled—
Already retained too long.
The last offending poison
Must be cleansed
Then peace and healing
At last can come
A fresh start, more balanced view.

Come, O Shepherd, my soul renew.

[12]But who can discern their own errors? Forgive
my hidden faults. [13]Keep your servant also from

willful sins; may they not rule over me. Then will I be blameless, innocent of great transgression. [14]May the words of my mouth and the meditation of my heart be pleasing in your sight, O LORD, my Rock and my Redeemer. (Psalm 19:12-14, NIV)

*   *   *   *   *   *   *   *

Read the verses above for a word or phrase that calls to you.

Write down the word or phrase.

Why does this word call to you?

Dialogue with God. Write out your thoughts and His response.

Read the verse(s) again. Rest in silence.

45

Exodus 33:17

The LORD replied to Moses, "I will indeed do what you have asked, for **I look favorably on you, and I know you by name**."

Lover: Yes, My child, I know you by name, your earthly name and the special name I've given to you. I look favorably upon you as I bring you out of darkness and into My marvelous light through the sacrifice of My Son, Jesus. As My servant, I want you to be where I am, participating in the work that I am doing. You are precious to Me, and I love you. Never doubt that.

[9]But you are the ones chosen by God, chosen for the high calling of priestly work, chosen to be a holy people, God's instruments to do his work and speak out for him, to tell others of the night-and-day difference he made for you— [10]from nothing to something, from rejected to accepted.
(1 Peter 2:9-10, *The Message*)

*   *   *   *   *   *   *   *

Read the verses above for a word or phrase that
calls to you.

Write down the word or phrase.

Why does this word call to you?

Dialogue with God. Write out your thoughts and
His response.

Read the verse(s) again. Rest in silence.

46

Psalm 99:6

Moses and Aaron were among his priests; Samuel also called on his name. **They cried to the LORD for help, and he answered them**.

Beloved: Lord, I've just been crying out to You for help, and You have brought peace to my heart and calmness to my body once more. Thank You.

Lover: You are getting very wound up in a spiral of anxiety and fear. My way for you is trust and confidence. Perfect love casts out fear. Trust in Me will push away anxiety. Regularly practicing love and trust will build confidence. Keep focused on Me.

God is love. When we take up permanent residence in a life of love, we live in God and God lives in us. [17]This way, love has the run of the house, becomes at home and mature in us, so that we're free of worry on Judgment Day—our standing in the world is identical with Christ's. [18]There is no room in love for fear. Well-formed love banishes fear. Since fear is crippling, a fearful life—fear of death, fear of judgment—is one not yet fully formed in love. [19]We, though, are going to love—love and be loved. First we were loved, now we love. He loved us first. (1 John 4:17-19, *The Message*)

*   *   *   *   *   *   *   *

Read the verses above for a word or phrase that
calls to you.

Write down the word or phrase.

Why does this word call to you?

Dialogue with God. Write out your thoughts and
His response.

Read the verse(s) again. Rest in silence.

47

John 1:38
Jesus looked around and saw them following.
"**What do you want?**" he asked them. They
replied, "Rabbi" (which means "Teacher"), "where
are you staying?"

Lover: What do you want?

Beloved: A guarantee that I can finish my goals and
that my mother will go to You before I do.

Lover: Sorry, no guarantees except one: you will
finish what My goals are for you. In that you will not
fail.

Beloved: I'm so fearful, especially in the mornings.
It is nearly incapacitating me. Why am I such a
weakling?

Lover: If things were easy and obvious, life
wouldn't require faith. You need to learn of yourself,
of Me, and to have compassion.

16I pray that out of his glorious riches he may
strengthen you with power through his Spirit in
your inner being, 17so that Christ may dwell in
your hearts through faith. And I pray that you,
being rooted and established in love, 18may have
power, together with all the Lord's holy people, to
grasp how wide and long and high and deep is the
love of Christ, 19and to know this love that

surpasses knowledge—that you may be filled to the measure of all the fullness of God. [20]Now to him who is able to do immeasurably more than all we ask or imagine, according to his power that is at work within us, [21]to him be glory in the church and in Christ Jesus throughout all generations, for ever and ever! Amen.

(Ephesians 3:16-21, NIV)

*   *   *   *   *   *   *   *

Read the verses above for a word or phrase that calls to you.

Write down the word or phrase.

Why does this word call to you?

Dialogue with God. Write out your thoughts and His response.

Read the verse(s) again. Rest in silence.

48

Isaiah 51:6

Look up to the skies above, and gaze down on the earth below. For the skies will disappear like smoke, and the earth will wear out like a piece of clothing. The people of the earth will die like flies, but my salvation lasts forever. **My righteous rule will never end**!

Beloved: Lord, in all honesty, I've been afraid of dying these past few weeks. It almost stopped me from living, and I knew that wasn't right. This body is not meant for eternity. We need new ones for that. Only Your rule and purposes remain constant.

Lover: You are part of a great plan that I have for the people of the world. Yes, your part is small, but each piece is important; so yours is also important. When your part is finished, you get to come home to Me and rejoice as the rest of the plan unfolds. Each person has his or her time and role. You are responsible for you, and you need to put your total trust in Me. It is not something to worry over or be anxious about. Each day and each night you will have all the resources that you need. I've promised and I'll deliver. Be at peace.

[20]I expect and hope that I will not fail Christ in anything but that I will have the courage now, as always, to show the greatness of Christ in my life here on earth, whether I live or die. [21]To me the only important thing about living is Christ, and

dying would be profit for me. [22]If I continue living in my body, I will be able to work for the Lord. I do not know what to choose—living or dying. [23]It is hard to choose between the two. I want to leave this life and be with Christ, which is much better, [24]but you need me here in my body. [25]Since I am sure of this, I know I will stay with you to help you grow and have joy in your faith. [26]You will be very happy in Christ Jesus when I am with you again. (Philippians 1:20-26, NCV)

*   *   *   *   *   *   *   *

Read the verses above for a word or phrase that calls to you.

Write down the word or phrase.

Why does this word call to you?

Dialogue with God. Write out your thoughts and His response.

Read the verse(s) again. Rest in silence.

49

Hebrews 11:9-10

And even when he reached the land God promised him, **he lived there by faith**—for he was like a foreigner, living in tents. And so did Isaac and Jacob, who inherited the same promise. **Abraham was confidently looking forward to a city with eternal foundations, a city designed and built by God**.

Lover: Life on earth is, by definition, imperfect and living well requires faith. It also helps to look forward as Abraham did, to the eternal city. He looked forward confidently, and that's what I want for you, to see beyond the frustrations, imperfections and sorrows of the present world, and by faith, confidently look forward to the time when sin no longer mars relationships. Today, look confidently forward."

12I do not mean that I am already as God wants me to be. I have not yet reached that goal, but I continue trying to reach it and to make it mine. Christ wants me to do that, which is the reason he made me his. 13Brothers and sisters, I know that I have not yet reached that goal, but there is one thing I always do. Forgetting the past and straining toward what is ahead, 14I keep trying to reach the goal and get the prize for which God called me through Christ to the life above.

(Philippians 3:12-14, NCV)

*   *   *   *   *   *   *   *

Read the verses above for a word or phrase that calls to you.

Write down the word or phrase.

Why does this word call to you?

Dialogue with God. Write out your thoughts and His response.

Read the verse(s) again. Rest in silence.

50

1 John 3:1

See how very much our Father loves us, for he calls us his children, and that is what we are! But the people who belong to this world don't recognize that we are God's children because they don't know him.

"And with love everlasting you besiege me; in every moment of life and death you are."
—lyrics by Bernadette Farrell[xiv]

Beloved: Shepherd, it's been a difficult week full of anxiety, fear, worry, and stress. It isn't supposed to be like this. I feel my faith has failed me. I'm more acutely aware of my great weaknesses. Maybe You are letting me see how much of me is me and how much is really You. Without You, I'm a basket case. So, when I see others falling apart, what I'm really seeing are people desperately in need of Your love and power in their lives.

Lover: You are indeed little, weak, and helpless in your own power. But you are not alone. I am with you. Whatever comes, in life or death, I'm with you every moment. Rest in My strength and know it to be Mine!

[13]As parents feel for their children, GOD feels for those who fear him. [14]He knows us inside and out, keeps in mind that we're made of mud. [15]Men and

women don't live very long; like wildflowers they spring up and blossom, [16]But a storm snuffs them out just as quickly, leaving nothing to show they were here. [17] GOD's love, though, is ever and always, eternally present to all who fear him, Making everything right for them and their children [18]as they follow his Covenant ways and remember to do whatever he said.
(Psalm 103:13-18, *The Message*)

*   *   *   *   *   *   *   *

Read the verses above for a word or phrase that calls to you.

Write down the word or phrase.

Why does this word call to you?

Dialogue with God. Write out your thoughts and His response.

Read the verse(s) again. Rest in silence.

51
Matthew 10:39
If you cling to your life, you will lose it; but **if you give up your life for me, you will find it.**

Beloved: This has certainly been true for me. When I did 'my thing' life was a disaster. My goals for me were so small. When I turned my life over to Your control, You took me further than I could have dreamed. I don't know where the journey will end, but with You, Jesus, guiding, I'm ready for anything You bring because I know You will go with me through it all.

Lover: Go into today in My peace, for I am with you.

[9]. . . I said to you, 'You are my servant. I've chosen you; I haven't rejected you.' [10] Don't be afraid, because I am with you. Don't be intimidated; I am your God. I will strengthen you. I will help you. I will support you with my victorious right hand. [13] I, the LORD your God, hold your right hand and say to you, 'Don't be afraid; I will help you.' [14] Don't be afraid, Jacob, you worm. You people of Israel, I will help you," declares the LORD, your Defender, the Holy One of Israel.
(Isaiah 41:9b-10, 13-14, *God's Word*)

*   *   *   *   *   *   *   *

Read the verses above for a word or phrase that calls to you.

Write down the word or phrase.

Why does this word call to you?

Dialogue with God. Write out your thoughts and His response.

Read the verse(s) again. Rest in silence.

52

Deuteronomy 30:20

You can make this choice by **loving the LORD your God, obeying him, and committing yourself firmly to him. This is the key to your life**. And if you love and obey the LORD, you will live long in the land the LORD swore to give your ancestors Abraham, Isaac, and Jacob.

Beloved: Life seems so fragile at the moment. My weakness is so severe I wonder how I can make it through the morning. Restore and renew me and help me to accept the good You have sent me.

Lover: Your days are in My hands, so you have nothing to fear in life or death. I have My purposes for you, and as you obey Me, you will fulfill each one. I love you, and you are precious in My sight.

[10]Though the mountains be shaken and the hills be removed, yet my unfailing love for you will not be shaken, nor my covenant of peace be removed," says the LORD, who has compassion on you. [11]"O afflicted city, lashed by storms and not comforted, I will build you with stones of turquoise, your foundations with sapphires. [12]I will make your battlements of rubies, your gates of sparkling jewels, and all your walls of precious stones. [13]All your sons will be taught by the LORD, and great will be your children's peace. (Isaiah 54: 10-13, NIV)

*   *   *   *   *   *   *   *

Read the verses above for a word or phrase that calls to you.

Write down the word or phrase.

Why does this word call to you?

Dialogue with God. Write out your thoughts and His response.

Read the verse(s) again. Rest in silence.

53
Proverbs 8:34

Joyful are those who listen to me, watching for me daily at my gates, waiting for me outside my home!

Lover: You are so small compared to Me, and yet I want you to know Me as much as possible. So, each day, we add another drop to your knowledge and love and understanding. That's why it is important not to miss even one day. I so want to bless you!

[8]"For my thoughts are not your thoughts, neither are your ways my ways," declares the LORD. [9]"As the heavens are higher than the earth, so are my ways higher than your ways and my thoughts than your thoughts. [10]As the rain and the snow come down from heaven, and do not return to it without watering the earth and making it bud and flourish, so that it yields seed for the sower and bread for the eater, [11]so is my word that goes out from my mouth: It will not return to me empty, but will accomplish what I desire and achieve the purpose for which I sent it. [12]You will go out in joy and be led forth in peace; the mountains and hills will burst into song before you, and all the trees of the field will clap their hands.
(Isaiah 55:8-12, NIV)

*   *   *   *   *   *   *   *

Read the verses above for a word or phrase that
calls to you.

Write down the word or phrase.

Why does this word call to you?

Dialogue with God. Write out your thoughts and
His response.

Read the verse(s) again. Rest in silence.

54

Romans 6:13

Do not let any part of your body become an instrument of evil to serve sin. Instead, give yourselves completely to God, for you were dead, but now you have new life. So **use your whole body as an instrument to do what is right for the glory of God.**

Beloved: Lord, I'm anxious about some health issues, symptoms I feel now and then. This anxiety threatens to hinder my plans, and I just can't discern what is of You, what is spiritual opposition, and what is just normal aging and stress. Please make this clear.

Lover: Draw close to Me in the midst of your stress and worry. Keep listening to My voice and rest in My love. If I open a door, go through it. When I close a door, accept it.

[7]"Write this letter to the angel of the church in Philadelphia. This is the message from the one who is holy and true, the one who has the key of David. What he opens, no one can close; and what he closes, no one can open. [8]"I know all the things you do, and I have opened a door for you that no one can close. You have little strength, yet you obeyed my word and did not deny me. (Revelation 3:7-8, NLT)

*   *   *   *   *   *   *   *

Read the verses above for a word or phrase that calls to you.

Write down the word or phrase.

Why does this word call to you?

Dialogue with God. Write out your thoughts and His response.

Read the verse(s) again. Rest in silence.

55

John 3:33
Anyone who accepts his testimony can affirm that
God is true.

Beloved: Father, You gave Jesus Your Spirit without
limits so that He could fully represent You on earth.
I can't contain that much in my limitations, but I ask
You to show me the truth about my current
problems. What is physical, spiritual, or mental?
How should I respond? Help me!

Lover: You were too tired and you needed rest.
Take this time to get the rest you need. It will help.
Focus on the task at hand and leave the rest for the
proper time. You've lost your joy. I want to restore
that.

10...Yet in the empty streets..., there will be heard
once more 11the sounds of joy and laughter. The
joyful voices of bridegrooms and brides will be
heard again, along with the joyous songs of people
bringing thanksgiving offerings to the LORD. They
will sing,
     'Give thanks to the LORD of Heaven's Armies,
     for the LORD is good.
     His faithful love endures forever!'
For I will restore the prosperity of this land to
what it was in the past, says the LORD.
(Jeremiah 33: 10b-11, NLT)

*   *   *   *   *   *   *   *

Read the verses above for a word or phrase that calls to you.

Write down the word or phrase.

Why does this word call to you?

Dialogue with God. Write out your thoughts and His response.

Read the verse(s) again. Rest in silence.

56

Matthew 6:33

Seek the kingdom of God above all else, and live righteously, and he will give you everything you need.

Lover: Worry and anxiety accomplish nothing. In fact, they are destructive. Bring your concerns to Me and leave them with Me. I've promised to provide all that you need. Trust Me to keep My Word.

[17] God, you have taught me since I was young. To this day I tell about the miracles you do. [18]Even though I am old and gray, do not leave me, God. I will tell the children about your power; I will tell those who live after me about your might. [19] God, your justice reaches to the skies. You have done great things; God, there is no one like you. [20] You have given me many troubles and bad times, but you will give me life again. When I am almost dead, you will keep me alive. [21] You will make me greater than ever, and you will comfort me again. (Psalm 71:17-21, NCV)

"Everywhere we go we find God waving flags, God semaphoring, God jumping up and down and waving his arms to attract our attention like a man on a desert island. Only it is we who are on the island, and God is on the rescue ship, waving to let us know that help is near, even though we are too obtuse or blind or accustomed to island life to see it."   —Rowland Croucher [xv]

*   *   *   *   *   *   *   *

Read the verses above for a word or phrase that calls to you.

Write down the word or phrase.

Why does this word call to you?

Dialogue with God. Write out your thoughts and His response.

Read the verse(s) again. Rest in silence.

57

Psalm 78:7
So each generation should **set its hope anew on God, not forgetting his glorious miracles.**
Luke 12:32
So don't be afraid, little flock. For it gives your Father great happiness to give you the kingdom.

Lover: I see your struggles and sadness. Take this opportunity to remember how far you have come and how very much I love you. Nothing is wasted. This difficult time is important for you and for others, so allow Me to do My work in you.

[1]For everything there is a season, a time for every activity under heaven. [2]A time to be born and a time to die. A time to plant and a time to harvest. [3]A time to kill and a time to heal. A time to tear down and a time to build up. [4]A time to cry and a time to laugh. A time to grieve and a time to dance. [5]A time to scatter stones and a time to gather stones. A time to embrace and a time to turn away. [6]A time to search and a time to quit searching. A time to keep and a time to throw away. [7]A time to tear and a time to mend. A time to be quiet and a time to speak. [8]A time to love and a time to hate. A time for war and a time for peace. [9]What do people really get for all their hard work? [10]I have seen the burden God has placed on us all. [11]Yet God has made everything beautiful for its own time. He has planted eternity in the human heart, but even so,

people cannot see the whole scope of God's work
from beginning to end.
(Ecclesiastes 3:1-11, NLT)

*   *   *   *   *   *   *   *

Read the verses above for a word or phrase that calls to you.

Write down the word or phrase.

Why does this word call to you?

Dialogue with God. Write out your thoughts and His response.

Read the verse(s) again. Rest in silence.

58

Ephesians 1:5

GOD decided in advance **to adopt us into his own family** by bringing us to himself **through Jesus Christ**. **This is what he wanted to do, and it gave him great pleasure.**

Beloved: It is beyond my comprehension that You could get great pleasure by having me in Your family—by being in relationship with the likes of me. While I don't comprehend how this could be, I'm very grateful to You for showing me such love.

Lover: My dearest, precious child, how I wish you could begin to know how deeply I love you—vaster, deeper than the sea. I enjoy these daily times together. I smile when you notice My little reminders to you through the day. When I sing over you in the night, your heart and mind are healed. Keep looking for Me in your day so that our relationships grows.

And the LORD himself, the King of Israel, will live among you! At last your troubles will be over, and you will never again fear disaster. 16On that day the announcement to Jerusalem will be, "Cheer up, Zion! Don't be afraid! 17For the LORD your God is living among you. He is a mighty savior. He will take delight in you with gladness. With his love, he will calm all your fears. He will rejoice over you with joyful songs."
(Zephaniah 3:15b-17, NLT)

"It seems to me then, and seems to me still, that if God speaks to us at all in the world, if God speaks anywhere, it is into our personal lives that he speaks."   —Fredrick Buechner[xvi]

*   *   *   *   *   *   *   *

Read the verses above for a word or phrase that
calls to you.

Write down the word or phrase.

Why does this word call to you?

Dialogue with God. Write out your thoughts and
His response.

Read the verse(s) again. Rest in silence.

59
1 Thessalonians 4:11
Make it your goal to live a quiet life, minding
your own business and working with your hands,
just as we instructed you before.

Isaiah 30:15
This is what the Sovereign LORD, the Holy One of
Israel, says: "Only in returning to me and resting in
me will you be saved. **In quietness and
confidence is your strength**. But you would have
none of it."

Lover: My dear, I know you are feeling very weak
and vulnerable just now. So often others see you as
strong and together, but in allowing others to see
your weak side, it encourages them to grow strong.
If you are sitting in a chair, no one will fill it. Now
you've moved so others can discover their place in
the work. When you are weak, then My strength can
come out. Rest. Be quiet. Be confident that I will
carry you.

[7]Because of the extravagance of those revelations,
and so I wouldn't get a big head, I was given the
gift of a handicap to keep me in constant touch
with my limitations. Satan's angel did his best to
get me down; what he in fact did was push me to
my knees. No danger then of walking around high
and mighty! [8]At first I didn't think of it as a gift,
and begged God to remove it. Three times I did
that, [9]and then he told me,

My grace is enough; it's all you need.
My strength comes into its own in your
weakness.

Once I heard that, I was glad to let it happen. I quit
focusing on the handicap and began appreciating
the gift. It was a case of Christ's strength moving in
on my weakness. 10Now I take limitations in stride,
and with good cheer, these limitations that cut me
down to size—abuse, accidents, opposition, bad
breaks. I just let Christ take over! And so the
weaker I get, the stronger I become.
(2 Corinthians 12: 7-10, *The Message*)

*   *   *   *   *   *   *   *

Read the verses above for a word or phrase that calls to you.

Write down the word or phrase.

Why does this word call to you?

Dialogue with God. Write out your thoughts and His response.

Read the verse(s) again. Rest in silence.

60
Luke 10:33
Then a despised Samaritan came along, and when he saw the man, **he felt compassion for him [the victim of theft and beating].**

Beloved: Why did the Samaritan feel compassion? Probably he or someone he cared about had experienced a similar trauma. It is in our suffering that we begin to feel compassion when others are suffering.

Lover: Yes, My love, I will use this difficult time in your life to teach you how to stay close to Me, to be quiet, to be patient. And later, these lessons may also help you to be more compassionate. As you let others help you, you will learn how important it is to reach out to others who are in pain.

3Praise the God and Father of our Lord Jesus Christ! He is the Father who is compassionate and the God who gives comfort. 4He comforts us whenever we suffer. That is why whenever other people suffer, we are able to comfort them by using the same comfort we have received from God. 5Because Christ suffered so much for us, we can receive so much comfort from him. 6Besides, if we suffer, it brings you comfort and salvation. If we are comforted, we can effectively comfort you when you endure the same sufferings that we endure.

[7]We have confidence in you. We know that as you share our sufferings, you also share our comfort. (2 Corinthians 1: 3-7, *God's Word*)

*   *   *   *   *   *   *   *

Read the verses above for a word or phrase that calls to you.

Write down the word or phrase.

Why does this word call to you?

Dialogue with God. Write out your thoughts and His response.

Read the verse(s) again. Rest in silence.

61
Isaiah 43:19-20

For I am about to do something new. See, I have already begun! Do you not see it? **I will make a pathway through the wilderness. I will create rivers in the dry wasteland.** The wild animals in the fields will thank me, the jackals and owls, too, for giving them water in the desert. Yes, I will make rivers in the dry wasteland **so my chosen people can be refreshed.**

Beloved: Lord, I know You've told me to take time to be with You, and I haven't done it. Now, in these days, we are doing some catching up. Time with You is always well spent. Forgive me for pushing You to the side. You are the main event!

Lover: I have made provisions for you, but sometimes you don't come to Me so I can show you what and where they are. You need to be refreshed, but the water is with Me. There is no substitute. Come, all who are thirsty, and drink.

[10]Jesus replied to her, "If you only knew what God's gift is and who is asking you for a drink, you would have asked him for a drink. He would have given you living water." [11]The woman said to him, "Sir, you don't have anything to use to get water, and the well is deep. So where are you going to get this living water? [12]You're not more important than our ancestor Jacob, are you? He gave us this well. He and his sons and his animals drank water

from it." [13]Jesus answered her, "Everyone who drinks this water will become thirsty again. [14]But those who drink the water that I will give them will never become thirsty again. In fact, the water I will give them will become in them a spring that gushes up to eternal life."
(John 4: 10-14, *God's Word*)

*   *   *   *   *   *   *   *

Read the verses above for a word or phrase that
calls to you.

Write down the word or phrase.

Why does this word call to you?

Dialogue with God. Write out your thoughts and
His response.

Read the verse(s) again. Rest in silence.

62

Revelation 21:5

And the one sitting on the throne said, "**Look, I am making everything new**!" And then he said to me, "Write this down, for what I tell you is trustworthy and true."

Beloved: As I watch the leaves falling from the maple tree outside my window, exposing the bare limbs, sadness grips me. For I miss the protection, shade, and covering from those leaves. But this is a necessary preparation for new growth to come. Lord, what are You teaching me to drop, to let go of, so that You can bring me something new?

Lover: It is all too easy to let the work become more important, more urgent than our relationship. You can always think of more things to do. But those occupations pull you away from time needed with Me. In this time of weakness, lean on Me. Let this dependency become a habit, so strong that even when your strength returns, you will keep leaning on Me.

25At that time Jesus said, "I praise you, Father, Lord of heaven and earth, because you have hidden these things from the people who are wise and smart. But you have shown them to those who are like little children. 26Yes, Father, this is what you really wanted. 28"Come to me, all of you who are tired and have heavy loads, and I will give you rest. 29Accept my teachings and learn from me, because I am gentle and humble in spirit, and you will find rest for your lives. [30]The teaching that I ask you to accept is easy; the load I give you to carry is light." (Matthew 11:25-26, 28-30, NCV)

*   *   *   *   *   *   *   *

Read the verses above for a word or phrase that calls to you.

Write down the word or phrase.

Why does this word call to you?

Dialogue with God. Write out your thoughts and His response.

Read the verse(s) again. Rest in silence.

63

2 Corinthians 3:3

Clearly, you are a letter from Christ showing the result of our ministry among you. This "letter" is written not with pen and ink, but with the Spirit of the living God. It is carved not on tablets of stone, but on human hearts.

Beloved: Lord, sometimes, actually often, I feel like an unsold or unopened book or an unread letter. It makes me feel unworthy.

Lover: Is the book unworthy because someone fails to read it? No. The reader misses the blessing because of the reader's choice. Who is the author of your book?

Beloved: You are. And You do all things well. Help me to cooperate with Your efforts.

Lover: As the Author, I'm also the publisher and distributor. You will be read and seen by those I choose. At the right time, the right portions will be seen. In the meantime, I continue to write My story in your life. Enjoy the storyline for it tells you always of My love for you.

[1] "Jerusalem, get up and shine, because your light has come, and the glory of the LORD shines on you. [2]Darkness now covers the earth; deep darkness covers her people. But the LORD shines on you, and people see his glory around you. [3]Nations will come to your

light; kings will come to the brightness of your sunrise. [4]"Look around you. People are gathering and coming to you. Your sons are coming from far away, and your daughters are coming with them. [5]When you see them, you will shine with happiness; you will be excited and full of joy, because the wealth of the nations across the seas will be given to you; the riches of the nations will come to you.
(Isaiah 60:1-5, NCV)

*   *   *   *   *   *   *   *

Read the verses above for a word or phrase that calls to you.

Write down the word or phrase.

Why does this word call to you?

Dialogue with God. Write out your thoughts and His response.

Read the verse(s) again. Rest in silence.

64

2 Corinthians 5:17,18

This means that anyone who belongs to Christ has become a new person. The old life is gone; **a new life has begun. And all of this is a gift from God**, who brought us back to himself through Christ. And God has given us this task of reconciling people to him.

Beloved: Shepherd, I spend a lot of thought and energy on future things and very little, relatively, in the present. But in these days of weakness, it's been all about now, not later, not before. You are drawing me close to Yourself and helping me learn to trust You with today and to leave tomorrow to You as well.

Lover: My dearest one, you are not alone. You are deeply and passionately loved. I want you to learn how to receive My love and to return that love. I know these waters are troubling. Past experiences have made you cautious and afraid to trust. But you need to move past these fears and find that I am faithful and true. I will never let you down. I will never desert you. You are Mine, and that brings Me such joy!

Beloved: I want to love You back. I just don't know how. Please teach me.

[1]The LORD is my shepherd; I have everything I need. [2]He lets me rest in green pastures. He leads

me to calm water. [3]He gives me new strength. He leads me on paths that are right for the good of his name. [4]Even if I walk through a very dark valley, I will not be afraid, because you are with me. Your rod and your walking stick comfort me. [5]You prepare a meal for me in front of my enemies. You pour oil on my head; you fill my cup to overflowing. [6]Surely your goodness and love will be with me all my life, and I will live in the house of the LORD forever.
(Psalm 23, NCV)

> "We read to know that we are not alone."
> —C.S. Lewis[xvii]

*   *   *   *   *   *   *   *

Read the verses above for a word or phrase that calls to you.

Write down the word or phrase.

Why does this word call to you?

Dialogue with God. Write out your thoughts and His response.

Read the verse(s) again. Rest in silence.

65

John 13:34
So now I am giving you a new commandment:
Love each other. **Just as I have loved you, you
should love each other.**

Beloved: Lord, You've loved me when I was Your
enemy, firmly running away. You've loved me when
I was broken and useless. You've loved me through
serious emotional pain and stubbornness. You've
loved me when I've ignored You. Thank You for
Your patience and perseverance. Teach me to love
as You have loved me.

Lover: Dearest One, because I know the end from
the beginning, I know you better than you know
yourself. I always see you as you will be and as you
are becoming. I also see who you are now and
rejoice in your desire to return My love. Never fear
to come to Me for I will never turn you away.

[35]What will separate us from the love Christ has for us?
Can trouble, distress, persecution, hunger, nakedness,
danger, or violent death separate us from his love?
[37]The one who loves us gives us an overwhelming
victory in all these difficulties. [38]I am convinced that
nothing can ever separate us from God's love which
Christ Jesus our Lord shows us. We can't be
separated by death or life, by angels or rulers, by
anything in the present or anything in the future, by

forces [39]or powers in the world above or in the world
below, or by anything else in creation.
(Romans 8:35, 37-39, *God's Word*)

*   *   *   *   *   *   *   *

Read the verses above for a word or phrase that
calls to you.

Write down the word or phrase.

Why does this word call to you?

Dialogue with God. Write out your thoughts and
His response.

Read the verse(s) again. Rest in silence.

66

Jeremiah 31:33

"But this is the new covenant I will make with the people of Israel on that day," says the LORD. "**I will put my instructions deep within them, and I will write them on their hearts.** I will be their God, and they will be my people."

Beloved: Lord, make my heart one with Yours. I know it is often like stone, but I long to have a responsive heart, one that is sensitive to You. For years I've felt all alone. Even though my family loved me, I couldn't receive it. I knew God loved me, but I didn't know how to receive that either. So, I've walked alone, depending only on myself.

And now You are here, seeking to win my love, my confidence, my trust. I weep as I feel all the pain of the past, some of it at least. I have to let that out so there's room for You to come in.

Lover: Dearest One, the wall of separation is coming down, and your pent up pain is spilling out. I come with healing balm to soothe and comfort. My love for you is deep and everlasting. After this, you will never be the same. I know it is painful and frightening, but I am working out My good purposes for and in you. Trust Me.

20Dear friend, listen well to my words; tune your ears to my voice. 21Keep my message in plain view at all times. Concentrate! Learn it by heart!
22Those who discover these words live, really live;

body and soul, they're bursting with health. [23]Keep vigilant watch over your heart; *that's* where life starts.
(Proverbs 4:20-23, *The Message*)

*   *   *   *   *   *   *   *

Read the verses above for a word or phrase that calls to you.

Write down the word or phrase.

Why does this word call to you?

Dialogue with God. Write out your thoughts and His response.

Read the verse(s) again. Rest in silence.

67

Ezekiel 34:16

I will search for my lost ones who strayed away, and I will bring them safely home again. I will bandage the injured and strengthen the weak. But I will destroy those who are fat and powerful. I will feed them, yes—feed them justice!

Beloved: Lord, I quote, "Come over here, where I don't want you to come. Jesus, help me to let you be yourself in my life so that I can be myself." (Malcolm Boyd)[xviii]

Lover: Precious One, I am here and though you may not yet realize it, you are safe in My care. We have more rocky ways to travel, but we will go together, you and I. Hold My hand, and, more importantly, let Me hold yours. For though your grip may fail, Mine never will.

[7]Where can I go to get away from your Spirit? Where can I run from you? [8]If I go up to the heavens, you are there. If I lie down in the grave, you are there. [9]If I rise with the sun in the east and settle in the west beyond the sea, [10]even there you would guide me. With your right hand you would hold me.
(Psalm 139: 7-10, NCV)

*   *   *   *   *   *   *   *

Read the verses above for a word or phrase that
calls to you.

Write down the word or phrase.

Why does this word call to you?

Dialogue with God. Write out your thoughts and
His response.

Read the verse(s) again. Rest in silence.

68

Psalm 100:3

Acknowledge that the Lord is God! He made us, and we are his. We are his people, the sheep of his pasture.

Beloved: I could read it and believe it, but to say it to God out loud was very hard. Why? If the Lord is God, then I am not. I am not master of my life/fate, nor am I all alone.

Lover: Acknowledging that I am God is a first step. Since I am God, you are under My care. Once you realize that in My protection and provision you are safe and cared for, you can rejoice. Rejoicing leads to praise and thanks. As you think on this progression, you will see that I am good and, as we walk together, that our relationship is eternal. This offer is for you and for all generations.

Beloved: Lord, my God, my heart is filled with praise and wonder. I could never have imagined such a wonderful prospect. Thank You for helping me see it. Make this my reality.

[47]"The LORD lives! Praise to my Rock! May God, the Rock of my salvation, be exalted! [48]He is the God who pays back those who harm me; he brings down the nations under me [49]and delivers me from my enemies. You hold me safe beyond the reach of my enemies; you save me from violent opponents. [50]For this, O LORD, I will praise you among the nations; I

will sing praises to your name. [51]You give great victories to your king; you show unfailing love to your anointed, to David and all his descendants forever."

(2 Samuel 22:47-51, NLT)

*   *   *   *   *   *   *   *

Read the verses above for a word or phrase that calls to you.

Write down the word or phrase.

Why does this word call to you?

Dialogue with God. Write out your thoughts and His response.

Read the verse(s) again. Rest in silence.

69

Ephesians 1:18, 23

I pray that your hearts will be flooded with light so that you can understand the confident hope he has given to those he called—his holy people who are his rich and glorious inheritance. And the church is his body; **it is made full and complete by Christ, who fills all things everywhere with himself**.

Beloved: A few bricks have come out of the wall that seems to separate my emotions from my rational side, and the first pressured feelings of pain have been released. Now there's room for Christ to enter with his balm and healing ointment. Not all is bleak and sad. There is joy and laughter too. As the wave of God's love begins to flow in, the pain is being diluted.

Hesitantly, fearfully, I stretch on tiptoes to peek over the wall, through the small gaps. The light is beginning to flood the dark places, to see the shriveled, undeveloped side of me: my emotions. Everywhere I look is in need of deep healing.

Can this jumble ever be well? Christ has promised to fill all things everywhere with Himself, and His presence will make even my shrunken feeling-side become full and whole.

Come, Lord Jesus, do Your work.

Lover: Dearest, your invitation pleases Me, and I gladly accept. Let's begin with gratitude.

[16]Lord, your discipline is good, for it leads to life and health. You restore my health and allow me to live! [17]Yes, this anguish was good for me, for you have rescued me from death and forgiven all my sins. [18]For the dead cannot praise you; they cannot raise their voices in praise. Those who go down to the grave can no longer hope in your faithfulness. [19]Only the living can praise you as I do today. Each generation tells of your faithfulness to the next. [20]Think of it—the LORD is ready to heal me! I will sing his praises with instruments every day of my life in the Temple of the LORD.

(Isaiah 38:16-20, NLT)

*   *   *   *   *   *   *   *

Read the verses above for a word or phrase that
calls to you.

Write down the word or phrase.

Why does this word call to you?

Dialogue with God. Write out your thoughts and
His response.

Read the verse(s) again. Rest in silence.

70

Hebrews 9:28

. . . so also Christ died once for all time as a sacrifice to take away the sins of many people. He will come again, not to deal with our sins, but to bring salvation to all who are eagerly waiting for him.

Beloved: Thank You, Jesus, for coming to show us what God is like, to live among us without sin, to die such a horrible death for me, to suffer shame and mocking, to rise victorious over death, to intercede for me before the very throne of God. It is beyond my understanding why You would do this, how You could love that much. Take my life and make it Yours. You bought me, and I rejoice to be Your child forever.

Lover: How deep the Father's love for you, how vast beyond all measure. We love you so much, and We are delighted that you are returning that love. As We have shown you our love for you, seek to show love to those around you, reaching out, listening, loving.

35Then Jesus said, "I am the bread that gives life. Whoever comes to me will never be hungry, and whoever believes in me will never be thirsty. 36But as I told you before, you have seen me and still don't believe. 37The Father gives me my people. Every one of them will come to me, and I will always accept them. 38I came down from heaven to

do what God wants me to do, not what I want to do. [39]Here is what the One who sent me wants me to do: I must not lose even one whom God gave me, but I must raise them all on the last day. [40]Those who see the Son and believe in him have eternal life, and I will raise them on the last day. This is what my Father wants."
(John 6:35-40, NCV)

*   *   *   *   *   *   *   *

Read the verses above for a word or phrase that calls to you.

Write down the word or phrase.

Why does this word call to you?

Dialogue with God. Write out your thoughts and His response.

Read the verse(s) again. Rest in silence.

71

John 12:28
"**Father, bring glory to your name**." Then a voice spoke from heaven, saying, "I have already brought glory to my name, and I will do so again."

Beloved: If this statement was Jesus' desire, then as his disciple, it is also mine. Lord, bring glory to Your name in my life, by my life, through my life.

Lover: Precious One, in your weakness others will see My strength. Just as the changes in your life, the improvements and developments have always been the result of your deepening your relationship with Me. Stay close to Me, and I will work all things out for your good and My glory."

[14]The LORD upholds all those who fall and lifts up all who are bowed down. [15]The eyes of all look to you, and you give them their food at the proper time. [16]You open your hand and satisfy the desires of every living thing. [17]The LORD is righteous in all his ways and loving toward all he has made. [18]The LORD is near to all who call on him, to all who call on him in truth. [19]He fulfills the desires of those who fear him; he hears their cry and saves them. [20]The LORD watches over all who love him, but all the wicked he will destroy. [21]My mouth will speak in praise of the LORD. Let every creature praise his holy name for ever and ever.
(Psalm 145:14-21, NIV)

*   *   *   *   *   *   *   *

Read the verses above for a word or phrase that calls to you.

Write down the word or phrase.

Why does this word call to you?

Dialogue with God. Write out your thoughts and His response.

Read the verse(s) again. Rest in silence.

72

2 Thessalonians 1:11

So we keep on praying for you, asking our God to enable you to live a life worthy of his call. **May he give you the power to accomplish all the good things your faith prompts you to do**.

Beloved: So, do I gather from this that what I was doing was okay, but that it was not okay how I was relying on my own strength to do it?

Lover: I gave you the work you have and the ability to do it well; however, the essence of life is learning to receive My power and strength. Also, you need to share the work with others. This time of weakness will help you do both of these things because you have no other choice. When you are stronger, you need to keep making the right choice to trust Me, lean on Me, and watch My power at work to make our vision a reality.

12Wealth and honor come from you alone, for you rule over everything. Power and might are in your hand, and at your discretion people are made great and given strength. 13"O our God, we thank you and praise your glorious name! 14But who am I, and who are my people, that we could give anything to you? Everything we have has come from you, and we give you only what you first gave us! 15We are here for only a moment, visitors and strangers in the land as our ancestors were before

us. Our days on earth are like a passing shadow, gone so soon without a trace.
(I Chronicles 29:12-15, NLT)

*   *   *   *   *   *   *   *

Read the verses above for a word or phrase that
calls to you.

Write down the word or phrase.

Why does this word call to you?

Dialogue with God. Write out your thoughts and
His response.

Read the verse(s) again. Rest in silence.

73

Isaiah 2:5
Come, descendants of Jacob, **let us walk in the light of the LORD**.

Beloved: To walk in the light is to stay out of the shadows and dark places. It is to walk in purity and holiness and in fellowship with my Shepherd. 1 John 1:7 says, "If you walk in the light as He is in the light, you have fellowship one with another." (NIV)

Lover: As you learn to walk in the light with Me, learn to trust, to be loved and thus to love. It will open your heart to love others also in new and wonderful ways. I long to show you the height and length and breadth of My love for you."

[1]See how very much our Father loves us, for he calls us his children, and that is what we are! But the people who belong to this world don't recognize that we are God's children because they don't know him. [2]Dear friends, we are already God's children, but he has not yet shown us what we will be like when Christ appears. But we do know that we will be like him, for we will see him as he really is. [3]And all who have this eager expectation will keep themselves pure, just as he is pure... [18]Dear children, let's not merely say that we love each other; let us show the truth by our actions. [19]Our actions will show that we belong to the truth, so we will be confident when we stand

before God. [20]Even if we feel guilty, God is greater
than our feelings, and he knows everything.
(1 John 3:1-3, 18-20, NLT)

*   *   *   *   *   *   *   *

Read the verses above for a word or phrase that calls to you.

Write down the word or phrase.

Why does this word call to you?

Dialogue with God. Write out your thoughts and His response.

Read the verse(s) again. Rest in silence.

74

Psalm 131:3
O Israel, **put your hope in the Lord -- now and always**.

Beloved: I think of hope as the expectation of a good outcome. This verse challenges me to trust in the Lord for that good outcome in the present and forever. It also means I can't take on expectations for myself—things too great and awesome for me to grasp—but instead content myself with those things that I can do, those everyday tasks that You give me to work on. I thought I was doing that, but somehow it went wrong.

Lover: Put your hope in Me. It is all too easy to begin to trust in your own ability to fulfill your expectations. Instead you need to focus on Me to know what My expectations are and to see how I will work in and through you to accomplish them. Remember the mouse who rode across the swinging bridge on the elephant and cried out, "We really made that bridge move!" Remember who is really swinging the bridge!

6Praise be to the LORD, for he has heard my cry for mercy. 7The LORD is my strength and my shield; my heart trusts in him, and I am helped. My heart leaps for joy and I will give thanks to him in song. 8The LORD is the strength of his people, a fortress of salvation for his anointed one. 9Save your

people and bless your inheritance; be their
shepherd and carry them forever.
(Psalm 28:6-9, NIV)

*   *   *   *   *   *   *   *

Read the verses above for a word or phrase that calls to you.

Write down the word or phrase.

Why does this word call to you?

Dialogue with God. Write out your thoughts and His response.

Read the verse(s) again. Rest in silence.

75
Isaiah 40:2

"Speak tenderly to Jerusalem. Tell her that **her sad days are gone and her sins are pardoned**. Yes, the LORD has punished her twice over for all her sins."

Lover: Now we start afresh. Using what you've learned in this time of weakness, you and I can begin to grow in love and trust. Notice I didn't say, "DO." The doing will come, but it is not the primary objective. Our relationship is the highest priority.

[5]God is keeping careful watch over us and the future. The Day is coming when you'll have it all— life healed and whole. [6]I know how great this makes you feel, even though you have to put up with every kind of aggravation in the meantime. [7]Pure gold put in the fire comes out of it *proved* pure; genuine faith put through this suffering comes out *proved* genuine. When Jesus wraps this all up, it's your faith, not your gold, that God will have on display as evidence of his victory. [8]You never saw him, yet you love him. You still don't see him, yet you trust him—with laughter and singing. [9]Because you kept on believing, you'll get what you're looking forward to: total salvation. (1 Peter 1:5-9, *The Message*)

*   *   *   *   *   *   *   *

Read the verses above for a word or phrase that calls to you.

Write down the word or phrase.

Why does this word call to you?

Dialogue with God. Write out your thoughts and His response.

Read the verse(s) again. Rest in silence.

76
Isaiah 40:11
He will feed his flock like a shepherd. **He will carry the lambs in his arms, holding them close to his heart**. He will gently lead the mother sheep with their young.

Beloved: Shepherd, You are holding me, carrying me, and I am near Your heart. I am content and comfortable, glad to be in Your arms. I don't want to lose this connection; that scares me. Please protect me from myself and my wandering ways.

Lover: My precious lamb, I will never leave you or forsake you. My answer is always "yes" and "amen, so be it" to your desire to be close to Me. Nothing could bring Me greater joy than being in relationship with you. With Me it is safe to be the real you. After all, I already know you completely.

20Whatever God has promised gets stamped with the Yes of Jesus. In him, this is what we preach and pray, the great Amen, God's Yes and our Yes together, gloriously evident. 21God affirms us, making us a sure thing in Christ, putting his Yes within us. 22By his Spirit he has stamped us with his eternal pledge—a sure beginning of what he is destined to complete.
(2 Corinthians 1:20-22, *The Message*)

*   *   *   *   *   *   *   *

Read the verses above for a word or phrase that calls to you.

Write down the word or phrase.

Why does this word call to you?

Dialogue with God. Write out your thoughts and His response.

Read the verse(s) again. Rest in silence.

77
Luke 12:38
He may come in the middle of the night or just
before dawn. But **whenever he comes, he will
reward the servants who are ready**.

Beloved: To be ready is to be doing my job, being
alert to signs of Your coming. I watch for the
Shepherd!

Lover: In these days you have been forced to be still.
And in the silence, you have heard Me and
experienced Me. We have drawn closer, and you've
begun to learn of My deep love for you. You are also
beginning to acknowledge and learn about your
feelings, and this is an area that needs much more
development. Go deep into the stillness.

[33]So keep a sharp lookout, for you don't know the
timetable. [34]It's like a man who takes a trip, leaving
home and putting his servants in charge, each
assigned a task, and commanding the gatekeeper to
stand watch. [35]So, stay at your post, watching. You
have no idea when the homeowner is returning,
whether evening, midnight, cockcrow, or morning.
[36]You don't want him showing up unannounced, with
you asleep on the job. [37]I say it to you, and I'm saying
it to all: Stay at your post. Keep watch."
(Mark 13: 33-37, *The Message*)

*   *   *   *   *   *   *   *

Read the verses above for a word or phrase that calls to you.

Write down the word or phrase.

Why does this word call to you?

Dialogue with God. Write out your thoughts and His response.

Read the verse(s) again. Rest in silence.

78

Luke 1:18

Zechariah said to the angel, "**How can I be sure this will happen?** I'm an old man now, and my wife is also well along in years."

Beloved: I fear my feelings. It's easier to be busy and ignore them. But You won't let me do that. I'm angry that I'm in pain, angry that I'm not able to do what I want to do, afraid all this won't get fixed, and ashamed of my weakness.

Lover: I see your impatience. You want to take what you know and run back into the fray, where your relationship with Me will slip away into the background. No, you need to stay in the weakness a bit longer to really learn the lesson of trust and love. Endure.

[26]Brothers and sisters, look at what you were when God called you. Not many of you were wise in the way the world judges wisdom. Not many of you had great influence. Not many of you came from important families. [27]But God chose the foolish things of the world to shame the wise, and he chose the weak things of the world to shame the strong. [28]He chose what the world thinks is unimportant and what the world looks down on and thinks is nothing in order to destroy what the world thinks is important. [29]God did this so that no one can brag in his presence. [30]Because of God you are in Christ Jesus, who has become for us wisdom

from God. In Christ we are put right with God, and have been made holy, and have been set free from sin. [31]So, as the Scripture says, "If someone wants to brag, he should brag only about the Lord." (1 Corinthians 1: 26-31, NCV)

"Many voices ask for our attention. There is a voice that says, 'Prove that you are a good person.' Another voice says, 'You'd better be ashamed of yourself.' There also is a voice that says, 'Nobody really cares about you,' and one that says, 'Be sure to become successful, popular, and powerful.' But underneath all these often very noisy voices is a still, small voice that says, 'You are my Beloved, my favor rests on you.' That's the voice we need most of all to hear. To hear that voice, however, requires special effort; it requires solitude, silence, and a strong determination to listen. That's what prayer is. It is listening to the voice that calls us 'my Beloved'."   —Henri Nouwen[xix]

*   *   *   *   *   *   *   *

Read the verses above for a word or phrase that calls to you.

Write down the word or phrase.

Why does this word call to you?

Dialogue with God. Write out your thoughts and His response.

Read the verse(s) again. Rest in silence.

79

Isaiah 40:29

He gives power to the weak and strength to the powerless.

Beloved: I'm feeling particularly weak and powerless as my illness continues. The anxiety seems to be gone for the most part. I still need to deal with this 'emotion' thing. I see emotions as dangerous; letting them show makes one vulnerable. It can be lonely shut up in the fortress alone; safe, but lonely.

Lover: I can reach you even in your fortress. My love reaches you wherever you are. But love needs to be shared. You and I share it, and you need to share with others. So, eventually, you must open the gate, lower the drawbridge, and let others in as you venture forth, yourself. You will need My strength to do this, and it won't be easy or without pain. But it is possible, and it is right.

[35]"I tell you, love your enemies. Help and give without expecting a return. You'll never—I promise—regret it. Live out this God-created identity the way our Father lives toward us, generously and graciously, even when we're at our worst. [36]Our Father is kind; you be kind.

[38]Give away your life; you'll find life given back, but not merely given back—given back with bonus and

blessing. Giving, not getting, is the way. Generosity begets generosity." (Luke 6:35-36, 38, *The Message*)

*   *   *   *   *   *   *   *

Read the verses above for a word or phrase that calls to you.

Write down the word or phrase.

Why does this word call to you?

Dialogue with God. Write out your thoughts and His response.

Read the verse(s) again. Rest in silence.

80

Psalm 85:8

I listen carefully to what GOD the LORD is saying, for he speaks peace to his faithful people. But let them not return to their foolish ways.

Beloved: This warning frightens me, for I know how foolish and headstrong I am. I want to be angry with You for allowing me to do horrible things, but it is really my fault.

Lover: Precious One, you are cleansed and forgiven, made whole as you asked. The soothing balm of My peace is flowing into you, through you. Now that you've let Me in, rest and let My healing bring you to wholeness.

[12]I write to you, dear children, because your sins have been forgiven on account of his name. Do not love the world or anything in the world. If anyone loves the world, the love of the Father is not in him. [16]For everything in the world—the cravings of the sinful man, the lust of his eyes and the boasting of what he has and does—comes not from the Father but from the world. [17]The world and its desires pass away, but the man who does the will of GOD lives forever. (1 John 1:12, 15-17, NIV)

*   *   *   *   *   *   *   *

Read the verses above for a word or phrase that calls to you.

Write down the word or phrase.

Why does this word call to you?

Dialogue with God. Write out your thoughts and His response.

Read the verse(s) again. Rest in silence.

81

Romans 8:23

And we believers also groan, even though we have the Holy Spirit within us as a foretaste of future glory, for we long for our bodies to be released from sin and suffering. **We, too, wait with eager hope for the day when God will give us our full rights as his adopted children** including the new bodies he has promised us.

Beloved: As I get to know You better, I trust my longing for 'home' will also increase. I just can't imagine what it will be like!

Lover: Dear One, the world you see as being so very real is only a passing shadow. It is only after you pass through this shadow that you come to the true reality. Trust Me. You will be thrilled with it. You catch glimpses of it now and then, in a sunrise, the color of a bird against the somber winter grays, the love you feel from Me. Dance, sing, laugh with Me. Let the healing balm flow and know joy as well as pain. You asked for wholeness, and I am granting that request. And no, you will never be the same.

[1]Then I saw a new heaven and a new earth. The first heaven and the first earth had disappeared, and there was no sea anymore. [2]And I saw the holy city, the new Jerusalem, coming down out of heaven from God. It was prepared like a bride dressed for her husband. [3]And I heard a loud voice from the throne, saying, "Now God's presence is with people, and he will live

with them, and they will be his people. God himself will be with them and will be their God. [4]He will wipe away every tear from their eyes, and there will be no more death, sadness, crying, or pain, because all the old ways are gone." [5]The One who was sitting on the throne said, "Look! I am making everything new!" Then he said, "Write this, because these words are true and can be trusted."

(Rev 21:1-5, NCV)

*   *   *   *   *   *   *   *

Read the verses above for a word or phrase that calls to you.

Write down the word or phrase.

Why does this word call to you?

Dialogue with God. Write out your thoughts and His response.

Read the verse(s) again. Rest in silence.

82

Galatians 5:6
For when we place our faith in Christ Jesus, there is no benefit in being circumcised or being uncircumcised. **What is important is faith expressing itself in love.**

Beloved: I've always thought of faith finding expression in actions and attitudes, not in emotions! Love is action and attitude, but the motivation is an emotion. I love many people, some more than others. I've loved pets and grieved and still grieve for them. I'm almost afraid to cry for fear I'll never stop. With the tears come healing and more of my wall of separation comes down.

Lover: Dear One, you've experienced confessing, accepting responsibility for your actions, and now grieving. These are big steps in the healing process. Practice letting your rational and emotional sides get to know and inform each other. This is an important part of the healing process.

[5]This is the message we heard from Christ and are reporting to you: God is light, and there isn't any darkness in him. [6]If we say, "We have a relationship with God" and yet live in the dark, we're lying. We aren't being truthful. [7]But if we live in the light in the same way that God is in the light, we have a relationship with each other. And the blood of his Son Jesus cleanses us from every sin. [8]If we say, "We aren't sinful" we are deceiving ourselves, and the truth is not

in us. [9]God is faithful and reliable. If we confess our sins, he forgives them and cleanses us from everything we've done wrong. [10]If we say, "We have never sinned," we turn God into a liar and his Word is not in us.

(1 John 1:5-10, *God's Word*)

*   *   *   *   *   *   *   *

Read the verses above for a word or phrase that
calls to you.

Write down the word or phrase.

Why does this word call to you?

Dialogue with God. Write out your thoughts and
His response.

Read the verse(s) again. Rest in silence.

83

Zephaniah 3:17

For the LORD your God is living among you. He is a mighty savior. **He will take delight in you with gladness. With his love, he will calm all your fears. He will rejoice over you with joyful songs**.

Beloved: These words make me happy, loved, and special. Lord, I delight in Your presence, in our relationship. Keep me responsive to You always.

Lover: Precious One, all relationships take constant attention. I will do My part, but you must also do yours. As we meet each day in times of quiet and as you learn to listen and watch for Me through the day, our relationship will deepen and grow. There will be times when you draw away but know that I will always welcome you back.

[35]Then Jesus declared, "I am the bread of life. He who comes to me will never go hungry, and he who believes in me will never be thirsty. [37]All that the Father gives me will come to me, and whoever comes to me I will never drive away. [38]For I have come down from heaven not to do my will but to do the will of him who sent me. [39]And this is the will of him who sent me, that I shall lose none of all that he has given me, but raise them up at the last day. [40]For my Father's will is that everyone who looks to the Son and believes in him shall have eternal life, and I will raise him up at the last day." (John 6:35, 37-40, NIV)

*   *   *   *   *   *   *   *

Read the verses above for a word or phrase that calls to you.

Write down the word or phrase.

Why does this word call to you?

Dialogue with God. Write out your thoughts and His response.

Read the verse(s) again. Rest in silence.

84
Isaiah 12:3
With joy you will drink deeply from the fountain of salvation!

Beloved: It's all too easy to be lured by the activities and resources around me and to think they or others can somehow meet my deep longings for love, acceptance, and forgiveness. I want someone who is always there, someone who always cares. No human can meet that standard; only my Shepherd can. So let me drink deeply of Your mercy, grace, and love and in that fountain of blessing find satisfaction, security, and joy.

Lover: Yes, My dear, in Me you will find all your heart truly desires, for I deny My beloved no good thing. I long for you to know Me so well that you run to Me, call to Me, lean on Me. I'm always with you and all that you think, speak, and do is important to Me. My love for you is faithful and true, deep and passionate. For you, I'm always there and I always care. Learn to trust that and you will also find joy.

5You keep me going when times are tough—
my bedrock, GOD, since my childhood. 6I've hung
on you from the day of my birth, the day you took
me from the cradle; I'll never run out of praise.
7Many gasp in alarm when they see me, but you
take me in stride. 8Just as each day brims with
your beauty, my mouth brims with praise.
(Psalm 71:5-8, *The Message*)

*   *   *   *   *   *   *   *

Read the verses above for a word or phrase that calls to you.

Write down the word or phrase.

Why does this word call to you?

Dialogue with God. Write out your thoughts and His response.

Read the verse(s) again. Rest in silence.

85

1 Samuel 3:10
And the LORD came and called as before, "Samuel! Samuel!" And Samuel replied, "**Speak, your servant is listening**."

Beloved: That's my breath prayer: Loving Shepherd, I'm listening. Lord, it seems You are entrusting me with health and energy again. That must mean You are trusting that I will be more intentional and determined to keep our relationship a close one. Thank You for this time. May I never be the same. I know that in my own strength, I will not be able to keep that commitment any more than the Israelites could. So, loving Shepherd, hold on to me and keep me close.

Lover: Never fear, My precious one. You've begun to grasp once more that I am the only one, the only thing that really matters. With that perspective you can be fearless and face whatever comes. You've learned to hear My voice in the quiet. Now you must practice hearing Me in the midst of noise, others, and life. I'm still there. Watch for Me, and I will surprise you with joy.

[3]. . . The sheep listen to the voice of the shepherd. He calls his own sheep by name and leads them out. [4]When he brings all his sheep out, he goes ahead of them, and they follow him because they know his voice. [5]But they will never follow a stranger. [27]My sheep listen to my voice; I know

them, and they follow me. [28]I give them eternal life, and they will never die, and no one can steal them out of my hand. [29]My Father gave my sheep to me. He is greater than all, and no person can steal my sheep out of my Father's hand. [30]The Father and I are one."

(John 10: 3-5, 27-30, NCV)

*   *   *   *   *   *   *   *

Read the verses above for a word or phrase that calls to you.

Write down the word or phrase.

Why does this word call to you?

Dialogue with God. Write out your thoughts and His response.

Read the verse(s) again. Rest in silence.

86

Mark 9:7

Then a cloud overshadowed them, and a voice from the cloud said, "**This is my dearly loved Son. Listen to him**."

Beloved: Calm my mind and body that I may hear Your voice.

Lover: I am with you in every moment and all situations, in each choice you make whether good or bad. It is My work to redeem time, actions, and events to glorify My Father. You cannot stray from My love or thwart My purposes, for I am the sovereign God. But as you listen to Me and follow My direction, you will be working in harmony with Me.

[1]Help, GOD—the bottom has fallen out of my life! Master, hear my cry for help! [2]Listen hard! Open your ears! Listen to my cries for mercy. [3]If you, GOD, kept records on wrongdoings, who would stand a chance? [4]As it turns out, forgiveness is your habit, and that's why you're worshiped. [5]I pray to GOD—my life a prayer—and wait for what he'll say and do. [6]My life's on the line before God, my Lord, waiting and watching till morning, waiting and watching till morning. [7]O Israel, wait and watch for GOD—with GOD's arrival comes love, with GOD's arrival comes generous redemption. (Psalm 130: 1-7, *The Message*)

*   *   *   *   *   *   *   *

Read the verses above for a word or phrase that
calls to you.

Write down the word or phrase.

Why does this word call to you?

Dialogue with God. Write out your thoughts and
His response.

Read the verse(s) again. Rest in silence.

87

John 10:3-4

The gatekeeper opens the gate for him, and the sheep recognize his voice and come to him. **He calls his own sheep by name and leads them out**. After he has gathered his own flock, he walks ahead of them, and **they follow him because they know his voice**.

Beloved: It is in the quiet of the meadows and pools in the streams that the sheep learn to hear the voice of the Shepherd. Then in the noise of a town, they can pick out his voice from among all the others. Lord, sometimes I still confuse my voice and Your voice. You want to give me a rich and satisfying life. I want to expend all my energy to please those around me and be seen as a good person. But Your opinion is the only one that truly matters. Help me to keep that perspective and to listen to You!

Lover: Precious One, how much I long to bless you. You are deeply loved and important to Me. Our relationship is a delight and a joy. When you recognize and listen to My voice, when we share the special intimacies of very close friends, lovers, it brings us both joy. It should also bring you a sense of security, for My job is to protect you from harm. So when you feel afraid or insecure, look for Me. I'm nearby. Listen for My voice, the voice of love that drives away fear.

[8]And you will make a new start, listening obediently to GOD, keeping all his commandments that I'm commanding you today. [9]GOD, your God, will outdo himself in making things go well for you: you'll have babies, get calves, grow crops, and enjoy an all-around good life. Yes, God will start enjoying you again, making things go well for you just as he enjoyed doing it for your ancestors. [10]But only if you listen obediently to GOD, your God, and keep the commandments and regulations written in this Book of Revelation. Nothing halfhearted here; you must return to GOD, your God, totally, heart and soul, holding nothing back. [16]And I command you today: Love God, your God. Walk in his ways. Keep his commandments, regulations, and rules so that you will live, really live, live exuberantly, blessed by GOD, your God… Choose life so that you and your children will live. [20]And love GOD, your God, listening obediently to him, firmly embracing him. (Deuteronomy 30: 8-10, 16-20a, *The Message*)

*   *   *   *   *   *   *   *

Read the verses above for a word or phrase that calls to you.

Write down the word or phrase.

Why does this word call to you?

Dialogue with God. Write out your thoughts and His response.

Read the verse(s) again. Rest in silence.

88

Luke 1:38

Mary responded, "**I am the Lord's servant. May everything you have said about me come true.**" And then the angel left her.

Beloved: Lord, I am Yours. No if's, and's, or but's. I long to do Your will and faithfully do whatever You ask. Help me to hear You well.

Lover: I have given you many gifts. You have the chance to bless many with the talents I've given you, but to do that and your job without wearing yourself down will require care. Don't just add something new to everything else. Remember, My yoke is easy and My burden is light. Don't push yourself beyond the boundaries I have set for you. I know how I made you and what your limits are.

[2]I'm an open book to you; even from a distance, you know what I'm thinking. [3]You know when I leave and when I get back; I'm never out of your sight. [4]You know everything I'm going to say before I start the first sentence. [5]I look behind me and you're there, then up ahead and you're there, too—your reassuring presence, coming and going. [6]This is too much, too wonderful—I can't take it all in! [14]I thank you, High God—you're breathtaking! Body and soul, I am marvelously made! I worship in adoration—what a creation!

(Psalm 139:2-6, 14, *The Message*)

*   *   *   *   *   *   *   *

Read the verses above for a word or phrase that calls to you.

Write down the word or phrase.

Why does this word call to you?

Dialogue with God. Write out your thoughts and His response.

Read the verse(s) again. Rest in silence.

89

Psalm 80:3

Turn us again to yourself, O God. Make your face shine down upon us. Only then will we be saved.

Beloved: I'm dependent on You to keep me pointed in the right direction: toward You. My tendency is to wander off into a multitude of distractions, forgetting yet again that You are my Center and my Treasure. Turn me again to Yourself as often as I turn away. Keep me focused on You alone.

Lover: My Beloved One, what joy it brings Me when you pray this prayer of longing to remain in relationship with Me. When I am your Center, your choices and limits become more clear. You know what to say no to as well as when to say yes. Life becomes more simple, less cluttered. Worry can be put aside, for it has no place in My presence. With Me as your Center, your heart can be at peace even in the midst of the storm."

[6]Don't worry about anything; instead, pray about everything. Tell God what you need, and thank him for all he has done. [7]Then you will experience God's peace, which exceeds anything we can understand. His peace will guard your hearts and minds as you live in Christ Jesus. [8]And now, dear brothers and sisters, one final thing. Fix your thoughts on what is true, and honorable, and right, and pure, and lovely, and admirable. Think about things that are excellent and worthy of praise. (Philippians 4: 6-8, NLT)

*   *   *   *   *   *   *   *

Read the verses above for a word or phrase that calls to you.

Write down the word or phrase.

Why does this word call to you?

Dialogue with God. Write out your thoughts and His response.

Read the verse(s) again. Rest in silence.

90

Hebrews 10:5

That is why, when Christ came into the world, he **(Jesus) said to God**, "You did not want animal sacrifices or sin offerings. But **you have given me a body to offer."**

Beloved: Father, You gave Jesus a body to offer back to You, and by fulfilling Your law perfectly, his sacrifice brought my salvation. I, too, have a body to offer. You paid the price for me and have given me a new life as part of Your family, the hope of eternal life with You. Lord, in gratitude to You, help me to offer You my body, mind, strength, and resources to accomplish Your purposes.

Lover: Thank you. I accept your offer. It pleases Me that you offer yourself not out of fear or obligation, but out of gratitude and trust. Releasing control is scary, and your willingness to give Me control shows that you are confident in My love for you and that My purposes for your life are ultimately for your good.

Those who trust God's action in them find that God's Spirit is in them—living and breathing God! Obsession with self in these matters is a dead end; attention to God leads us out into the open, into a spacious, free life. [10]But for you who welcome him, in whom he dwells—even though you still experience all the limitations of sin—you yourself experience life on God's terms.
(Romans 8: 5b-6, 10, *The Message*)

*   *   *   *   *   *   *   *

Read the verses above for a word or phrase that
calls to you.

Write down the word or phrase.

Why does this word call to you?

Dialogue with God. Write out your thoughts and
His response.

Read the verse(s) again. Rest in silence.

91
Luke 1:45
You are blessed because you believed that the Lord would do what he said.

Beloved: Lord, I find such peace and joy just sitting in Your presence. Sometimes my eyes fill with tears that are soon followed by a smile. I begin to feel Your tender love flowing into my hard heart and bringing feeling, softness, and responsiveness that have not been there for a very long time. I begin to sense that the emptiness of my soul is being filled by Your presence, and in that hope, I have joy.

Lover: My beloved, it is My deepest desire to flood your being with My great love for you, to meet those deepest needs that I placed in you, made a part of your being so that you would seek Me. And at last you are finding Me and beginning to understand how I want things to be between us. And I, too, am filled with joy.

[9]"...learn to know the God of your ancestors intimately. Worship and serve him with your whole heart and a willing mind. For the LORD sees every heart and knows every plan and thought. If you seek him, you will find him. But if you forsake him, he will reject you forever. [10]So take this seriously.
(1 Chronicles 28: 9-10a, NLT)

*   *   *   *   *   *   *   *

Read the verses above for a word or phrase that
calls to you.

Write down the word or phrase.

Why does this word call to you?

Dialogue with God. Write out your thoughts and
His response.

Read the verse(s) again. Rest in silence.

92
Luke 18:19
"**Why do you call me good?**" Jesus asked him.
"Only God is truly good."

Beloved: Lord, during this Christmas season so many have mocked You, ignored You, dismissed You, that I want to scream out in response, "You've missed the whole point!" I've felt anxiety during the last three days from the stress of being with many who deny You. Missing my time with You was painful. Lack of sleep and concern for a sick friend have been stressful. You are good because I can give You these cares, and You not only handle them, but also lift the burdens from me. You love me when I ignore You or fail to find time with You. Hold me close and never let me go.

Lover: Dearest, you can see the problems in the world and in those close to you, but it is not your job to fix them. That is My role. As you draw closer to Me, it will be harder to see and be with those who deny Me, but you are My witness to them. The love and care you show others is an example to them that they can't deny or dismiss. Your goodness reflects well on Me.

145 I pray with all my heart; answer me, LORD! I will obey your decrees. 146I cry out to you; rescue me, that I may obey your laws. 147I rise early, before the sun is up; I cry out for help and put my hope in your words. 148I stay awake through the

night, thinking about your promise. [149]In your faithful love, O LORD, hear my cry; let me be revived by following your regulations. [150]Lawless people are coming to attack me; they live far from your instructions. [151]But you are near, O LORD, and all your commands are true. [152]I have known from my earliest days that your laws will last forever.
(Psalm 119:145-152, NLT)

*   *   *   *   *   *   *   *

Read the verses above for a word or phrase that calls to you.

Write down the word or phrase.

Why does this word call to you?

Dialogue with God. Write out your thoughts and His response.

Read the verse(s) again. Rest in silence.

93

Isaiah 9:7

His government and its peace will never end. He will rule with fairness and justice from the throne of his ancestor David for all eternity. **The passionate commitment (zeal) of the LORD of Heaven's Armies will make this happen!**

Beloved: Lord, for thousands of years You have maintained that passionate commitment. We have just celebrated the birth of Jesus that was the beginning of the fulfillment of Your goal. And in Your loving pursuit of me, I also see Your passionate commitment. I don't hold firmly to too many things. Help me to respond to Your love and to become passionately committed to You.

Lover: My precious and beloved, My love for you is beyond your understanding, but it is nonetheless real. My love is healing. I bring wholeness. Mine is not a manipulative love, but a love that desires only the best for you. And unlike any earthly love, Mine is forever. Come away with Me, My love, there is so much I have to give you, show you, share with you. Come.

10My lover spoke and said to me, "Get up, my darling; let's go away, my beautiful one. 11Look, the winter is past; the rains are over and gone. 12Blossoms appear through all the land. The time has come to sing; the cooing of doves is heard in our land. 13There are young figs on the fig trees,

and the blossoms on the vines smell sweet.
Get up, my darling; let's go away, my beautiful
one."
(Song of Songs 2: 10-13, NCV)

"Action is charity looking outward to other men,
and contemplation is charity drawn inward to its
divine source. Action is the stream and
contemplation is the spring. The spring remains
more important than the stream, for the only thing
that really matters is for love to spring
inexhaustibly from the infinite abyss of Christ and
of God."   —Thomas Merton, *No Man is an Island*[xx]

*   *   *   *   *   *   *   *

Read the verses above for a word or phrase that calls to you.

Write down the word or phrase.

Why does this word call to you?

Dialogue with God. Write out your thoughts and His response.

Read the verse(s) again. Rest in silence.

94
Isaiah 42:4
He will not falter or lose heart until justice prevails throughout the earth. **Even distant lands beyond the sea will wait for his instruction**.

Beloved: Lord, thank You for this reminder that time is under Your control. All the nations, peoples, and events are ultimately controlled by You. So, my small goals and timeframes are also in Your hands. Help me not to strive for more than You allot me each day, to rest in Your timetable, and to enjoy those times of stillness that You bring me.

Lover: It is important to listen to Me each day, to understand what your part in it will be. I know the end from the beginning, and I also control time and seasons. So, who is the better judge of what should be on your 'list' each day? I know what is coming and if you listen and respond without being distracted by your own list, you will find all is in order when it needs to be. Trust Me, and you will find that I am faithful to My word.

9Remember the things I have done in the past. For I alone am God! I am God, and there is none like me. 10Only I can tell you the future before it even happens. Everything I plan will come to pass, for I do whatever I wish. 11I will call a swift bird of prey from the east—a leader from a distant land to come and do my bidding. I have said what I would do, and I will do it.
(Isaiah 46:9-11, NLT)

*   *   *   *   *   *   *   *

Read the verses above for a word or phrase that calls to you.

Write down the word or phrase.

Why does this word call to you?

Dialogue with God. Write out your thoughts and His response.

Read the verse(s) again. Rest in silence.

95

Hebrews 1:9

You love justice and hate evil. **Therefore, O God, your God has anointed you, pouring out the oil of joy on you more than on anyone else.**

Beloved: Shepherd, it is wonderful to think that You and Father God are so in tune with each other. He honors what You do, pouring out the oil of joy. So, that means Your love for me is not something done in secret but with Father God's full approval. I don't have to worry about any uncomfortable introductions or disapproving looks, for He will and does welcome me with joy. I can't imagine why, but I won't say no.

Lover: Yes, Beloved, My Father loves you as I love you, and He welcomes you as My bride. You still see yourself as you are, with your sinful nature still hanging on. We see you as you really are; pure, forgiven, holy, perfect. And together, pouring into you that oil of joy, We long to bring you healing and wholeness. When you receive My gift, it brings Me great pleasure. I love to give you wonderful things.

23In that day you will not ask me for anything. I tell you the truth, my Father will give you anything you ask for in my name. 24Until now you have not asked for anything in my name. Ask and you will receive, so that your joy will be the fullest possible joy. 25"I have told you these things, using stories that hide the meaning. But the time will come when I will not use stories like that to tell you things; I will speak to you in plain words about the Father. [26]In that day you will ask the Father for things in my name. I mean, I will not need to ask the Father for you. [27]The Father himself loves you. He loves you because you loved me and believed that I came from God. (John 16: 23-27, NCV)

"God's acceptance of Christ is your acceptance. The love the Father set on a perfect Christ, He now sets on you."   —Charles Hadden Spurgeon[xxi]

*   *   *   *   *   *   *   *

Read the verses above for a word or phrase that calls to you.

Write down the word or phrase.

Why does this word call to you?

Dialogue with God. Write out your thoughts and His response.

Read the verse(s) again. Rest in silence.

96

John 1:14
So the Word became human and made his home among us. **He was full of unfailing love and faithfulness**. And we have seen his glory, the glory of the Father's one and only Son.

Beloved: Shepherd, it has been a very eventful year, and as it comes to a close, I look forward to growing more in love with You, becoming more adept at seeing You throughout the day, and hearing all the wonderful things You want to share with me.

Lover: Yes, I too, have enjoyed our developing closeness and look forward to walking with you in the new year. You will find out what unfailing love is all about. You will also grow in your understanding of My faithfulness. In short, I want you to be secure in My unfailing love.

4 "Fear not; you will no longer live in shame. Don't be afraid; there is no more disgrace for you. You will no longer remember the shame of your youth and the sorrows of widowhood. 5For your Creator will be your husband; the LORD of Heaven's Armies is his name! He is your Redeemer, the Holy One of Israel, the God of all the earth. 6For the LORD has called you back from your grief—as though you were a young wife abandoned by her husband," says your God. 7"For a brief moment I abandoned you, but with great compassion I will take you back. 8In a burst of anger I turned my face

away for a little while. But with everlasting love I
will have compassion on you," says the LORD, your
Redeemer. 9"Just as I swore in the time of Noah
that I would never again let a flood cover the earth,
so now I swear that I will never again be angry and
punish you. 10For the mountains may move and
the hills disappear, but even then my faithful love
for you will remain. My covenant of blessing will
never be broken," says the LORD, who has mercy
on you. 11 "O storm-battered city, troubled and
desolate! I will rebuild you with precious
jewels and make your foundations from lapis
lazuli. 12I will make your towers of sparkling
rubies, your gates of shining gems, and your walls
of precious stones. 13I will teach all your children,
and they will enjoy great peace.
(Isaiah 54: 4-13, NLT)

"Then one day I'll see Him as He sees me
Face to face the Lover and the loved
No more words the longing will be over
There with my precious Jesus."
                                —Stuart Townend from
            "O My Soul, Arise and Bless Your Maker"xxii

*   *   *   *   *   *   *   *

Read the verses above for a word or phrase that calls to you.

Write down the word or phrase.

Why does this word call to you?

Dialogue with God. Write out your thoughts and His response.

Read the verse(s) again. Rest in silence.

ENDNOTES
_____

[i] All initial verses come from the New Living Translation. Also throughout this book, I have made use of the program Quick Verse. Electronic Edition STEP Files Copyright © 2005, QuickVerse. All rights reserved. Another source for the New Living Translation came from http://www.blueletterbible.org/.

[ii] The Holy Bible, New Living Translation **Edition:** Second **Copyright:** Holy Bible, New Living Translation, copyright © 1996 by Tyndale Charitable Trust. All rights reserved. **Publisher:** Tyndale House Publishers **Publisher Location:** Wheaton, Illinois 60189

[iii] Scripture taken from the New Century Version. Copyright © 2005 by Thomas Nelson, Inc. Used by permission. All rights reserved.

[iv] Scripture is taken from *GOD'S WORD®*. Copyright 1995 God's Word to the Nations. Used by permission of Baker Publishing Group. All rights reserved.

[v] http://www.spurgeon.org/sermons/1024.htm (1871)

[vi] Scripture taken from *The Message*. Copyright © 1993, 1994, 1995, 1996, 2000, 2001, 2002. Used by permission of NavPress Publishing Group

[vii] THE HOLY BIBLE, NEW INTERNATIONAL VERSION®, NIV® Copyright © 1973, 1978, 1984, 2010 by Biblica, Inc.™ Used by permission. All rights reserved worldwide.

[viii] Evelyn Underhill (1926) *Concerning the Inner Life.* E.P. Dutton & Co.

[ix] Spurgeon, Charles H. 1994 *Morning and Evening*, An updated Edition of the Classic Devotional in Today's Language, Ed by Roy H. Clarke. Jan 7. Evening.

[x] Dykstra, Craig R. *Vision and Character* p 320 in *A Guide to prayer for all who seek God*, Shawchuck and Job (eds).

[xi] Mary Lou Redding (2006) While We Wait, p 33 in *A Guide to prayer for all who seek God*, Shawchuck and Job (eds) Upper Room, Nashville.

[xii] Shawchuck, N. and R. P. Job, (2006) *A Guide for Prayer for all who seek God.* p 23. Upper Room, Nashville.

[xiii] Northumbria Community (2002) *Celtic Daily Prayer*, Harper Collins, San Francisco. p 573.

[xiv] Farrell, Bernadette (Taken from "O God, You Search Me" Used with permission)

[xv] Croucher, Rowland (ed) 1987, *Still Waters, Deep Waters* Meditations and Prayers for Busy People. Week 52, p 307. Lion Publishing, Tring, England.

[xvi] Buechner, Fredrick *The Sacred Journey* as quoted by Ken Gire in The Divine Embrace 2003 Published by Tyndale in association with the literary agency of Alive Communications, Inc., Colorado Springs, CO. p 105.

[xvii] Lewis, C.S. as quoted by Ken Gire in *The Divine Embrace* 2003 Published by Tyndale in association with the literary agency of Alive Communications, Inc., Colorado Springs, CO. p 106

[xviii] Malcolm Boyd Are you running with Me, Jesus? From *Still Waters, Deep Waters*. 284.

[xix] Nouwen, Henri J.M., 1997. *Bread for the Journey*, Harper, San Francisco

xx Taken from *Still Waters Deep Waters*, Ed by
Rowland Croucher. 1987. Albatross Books Pty Ltd
and Lions Publishing, Tring England. Reprinted in
1992. Page 21.
xxi Spurgeon, Charles H. 1994 *Morning and Evening*,
An updated Edition of the Classic Devotional in
Today's Language, Ed by Roy H. Clarke. Jan 3.
Morning.
xxii

http://www.higherpraise.com/lyrics/awesome/a
wesome1705.html

REFERENCES
Buechner, Fredrick *The Sacred Journey* as quoted
by Ken Gire in The Divine Embrace (2003)
Published by Tyndale in association with the
literary agency of Alive Communications, Inc.,
Colorado Springs, CO

Boyd, Malcolm, Are you running with Me, Jesus?
From *Still Waters, Deep Waters*. 284. Croucher,
Rowland (ed) (1987), *Still Waters, Deep Waters*
Meditations and Prayers for Busy People. Week
52, p 307. Lion Publishing, Tring, England.

Dykstra, Craig R. *Vision and Character* p 320 in *A
Guide to prayer for all who seek God*, Shawchuck
and Job (eds). Upper Room. Nashville.

GOD'S WORD®. Copyright 1995 God's Word to the
Nations. Used by permission of Baker Publishing
Group. All rights reserved.

Lewis, C.S. as quoted by Ken Gire in *The Divine Embrace* 2003 Published by Tyndale in association with the literary agency of Alive Communications, Inc., Colorado Springs, CO.

Scripture taken from the New Century Version. Copyright © 2005 by Thomas Nelson, Inc. Used by permission. All rights reserved.

New Living Translation came from http://www.blueletterbible.org/

Northumbria Community (2002) *Celtic Daily Prayer*, Harper Collins, San Francisco

Nouwen, Henri J.M., 1997. *Bread for the Journey*, Harper, San Francisco

QuickVerse Electronic Edition STEP Files Copyright © 2005, QuickVerse. All rights reserved.

Redding, Mary Lou (2006) While We Wait, p 33 in *A Guide to prayer for all who seek God*, Shawchuck and Job (eds) Upper Room, Nashville

Shawchuck, N. and R. P. Job (eds), (2006) *A Guide for Prayer for all who seek God.* p 23. Upper Room, Nashville

Spurgeon, Charles H. (1994) *Morning and Evening*, An updated Edition of the Classic Devotional in Today's Language, Ed by Roy H. Clarke. Jan 7. Evening.

THE HOLY BIBLE, NEW INTERNATIONAL VERSION®, NIV® Copyright © 1973, 1978, 1984, 2010 by Biblica, Inc.™ Used by permission. All rights reserved worldwide.

The Holy Bible, New Living Translation **Edition:** Second **Copyright:** Holy Bible, New Living Translation, copyright © 1996 by Tyndale Charitable Trust. All rights reserved. **Publisher:** Tyndale House Publishers **Publisher Location:** Wheaton, Illinois 60189

The Message. Copyright © 1993, 1994, 1995, 1996, 2000, 2001, 2002. Used by permission of NavPress Publishing Group

Underhill, Evelyn (1926) *Concerning the Inner Life.* E.P. Dutton & Co.

Young, Sarah (2008) *Nearer to Jesus* Thomas Nelson, Nashville.